Chasing Northern Lights

Arun Chandran

First Edition

August 2024

Copyright © 2024 Arun Chandran

All rights reserved.

ChasingNorthernLights.com

Cover photo taken by Arun Chandran in Longyearbyen, Svalbard

No part of this book may be reproduced, stored in a retrieval system, or transmitted in any form or by any means, electronic, mechanical, photocopying, recording, or otherwise, without the prior written permission of the author, except in the case of brief quotations embodied in critical reviews and certain other non-commercial uses permitted by copyright law.

For permission requests, please write to the author at:

chasingnorthernlights@outlook.com

ISBN: 978-1-7636266-2-1

Dedicated to all Aurora Chasers!

CONTENTS

1	The Science Behind Aurora Borealis	1
2	Myths And Legends About Northern Lights	6
3	The Best Time To See The Northern Lights	15
4	Understanding The Aurora Oval / Aurora Zone	22
5	Understanding Aurora Forecast Parameters	38
6	Aurora Apps, Websites & Facebook Groups	46
7	Mastering The Skies With Cloud Cover Forecasts	69
8	Lights, Camera, Action!	74
9	The Epic Geomagnetic Storm Of May 2024	85
10	The Patience And Thrill Of Aurora Hunting	87
11	Prime Aurora Locations - Alaska	91
12	Prime Aurora Locations - Canada	97
13	Prime Aurora Locations - Contiguous United States	112
14	Prime Aurora Locations - Greenland	116
15	Prime Aurora Locations - Iceland	120
16	Prime Aurora Locations - Faroe Islands	127

17	Prime Aurora Locations - Ireland	131
18	Prime Aurora Locations - UK	135
19	Prime Aurora Locations - Svalbard	147
20	Prime Aurora Locations - Norway	150
21	Prime Aurora Locations - Sweden	163
22	Prime Aurora Locations - Finland	168
23	Prime Aurora Locations - Russia	174
24	FAQs On Northern Lights	180
25	Space Weather Glossary	238

1
THE SCIENCE BEHIND AURORA BOREALIS

The captivating story of the Northern Lights, or Aurora Borealis, begins a staggering 93 million miles (150 million kilometres) away with our celestial powerhouse, the Sun. Visualize the Sun as a colossal sphere of fiery gas, simmering and bubbling like an overactive pot of soup. Periodically, it unleashes a monumental burst of energy and charged particles into space. This fiery outburst, known as a solar wind, is the key ingredient behind the Northern Lights. At times, the Sun adds an extra dose of drama with solar flares or coronal mass ejections (CMEs), enhancing the cosmic light show.

Alright, let's dive into the scoop on sunspots! These dark splotches on the Sun's surface, cooler than the blazing areas around them, signal that the Sun is getting ready to unleash its thrilling drama. Sunspots are like the Sun's magnetic hotspots, a precursor to some major action, like solar flares and those spectacular CMEs. Get ready, because things are about to get wild!

Solar flares are akin to the Sun's impromptu fireworks show—sudden, intense bursts of energy and radiation that erupt from its surface. Our reliable space paparazzi, such as the Solar Dynamics Observatory (SDO), keep a close watch on these fiery spectacles. They capture images in X-ray and UV light, providing us with information about the flare's intensity and size. The brightness in these images indicates the power of the flare. Scientists use a scale from A, B, C, M, and X, with A being the smallest and X being the largest flares, to measure their intensity.

Imagine CMEs as the Sun's version of spring cleaning, flinging out massive bursts of solar stuff—plasma and charged particles—zipping through the solar system.

Tracking CMEs is like playing cosmic detective with some super cool gadgets! Scientists use spacecraft like the Solar and Heliospheric Observatory (SOHO) and the Solar Dynamics Observatory (SDO) to keep tabs on these solar sneezes.

Here's how they pull it off:

Eyes on the Sun: Imagine having super-special sunglasses that let you see way beyond what our regular eyes can! These spacecrafts have instruments that snap pictures of the Sun in all sorts of wavelengths, like ultraviolet and X-ray light. This helps scientists catch a CME in the act as it blasts out from the Sun.

Speedometer for Solar Stuff: Once scientists spot a CME, they need to figure out how fast solar material is zooming through space. They use data from these spacecrafts to clock the speed of solar material heading our way. It's like timing a cosmic cannonball!

Size Matters: Just like measuring the height of a giant wave, scientists also check out the size of a CME. They look at how much solar stuff is being hurled into space. Some CMEs are just baby waves, while others are monstrous space tsunamis!

By combining all this data, scientists can better understand these solar eruptions and predict how they might affect our planet. It's like solving a cosmic puzzle, one solar storm at a time!

Meet DSCOVR (Deep Space Climate Observatory), Earth's cosmic scout and a superstar in the aurora game! This spacecraft isn't just floating around aimlessly—it's on a mission to uncover the secrets of those dazzling light shows in the sky:

Aurora Forecaster: Picture DSCOVR as our spacey weather reporter, chilling a million miles (1.6 million kilometres) away between Earth and the Sun. It focuses on solar storms and CMEs (Coronal Mass Ejections) that can light the night sky with auroras. By catching these cosmic fireworks early, DSCOVR helps scientists predict when and where the auroras will dance.

Solar Wind Whisperer: DSCOVR is like the Sun's gossip buddy, listening to the solar wind—a never-ending stream of charged particles flowing from the Sun. When the solar wind's speed and density change, it can supercharge the auroras. DSCOVR gives us a heads-up on how spectacular the auroras will be by tracking these solar breezes.

Guardian of Space Weather: Beyond admiring the auroras,

DSCOVR is a crucial player in understanding space weather. It studies how solar activity messes with Earth's magnetic field, affecting everything from satellites to power grids. By decoding these cosmic interactions, DSCOVR helps protect our technology from space storms.

But don't worry; our planet's superhero is the magnetic field. Picture Earth as a giant cosmic dynamo, with swirling molten metal in its core generating this magnetic field. This invisible shield protects us from most of the Sun's charged particles.

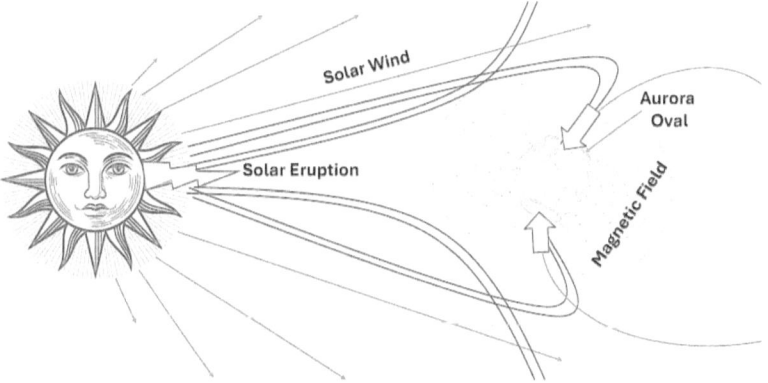

Here's how this magnetic force field works its magic:

Deflecting Solar Particles: Imagine tiny charged particles racing towards Earth from the Sun. Earth's magnetic field acts like a giant force field as it approaches, deflecting most of these particles away from our atmosphere. It's like having a magnetic umbrella that redirects the solar wind around us, keeping life on the surface nice and safe.

Creating the Magnetosphere: Earth's magnetic field forms a region around our planet called the magnetosphere. This invisible shield extends far into space, protecting us from the Sun's harmful radiation and energetic particles. Think of it as Earth's protective bubble in the vast cosmic ocean.

Triggering Auroras: Sometimes, a few solar wind particles sneak through Earth's magnetic field near the poles. When these charged particles collide with gases in our atmosphere, they create stunning auroras—those shimmering light curtains in the polar skies. It's like

Earth turning cosmic energy into a breathtaking light show to enjoy.

Now, here's where the magic happens. Those charged particles collide with gases in the atmosphere, like oxygen and nitrogen. But party-goers can't stay excited forever. When the gases chill out and return to normal, they release that extra energy as light. The specific colours depend on the type of gas and the collision's altitude.

The stunning colours of auroras are like a cosmic light show caused by the interaction between solar particles and Earth's atmosphere. Here's a fun breakdown of the colours and what causes them:

Green Auroras

Cause: The most common auroral colour, green, happens when solar particles smack into oxygen atoms high in Earth's atmosphere (around 100-250 kilometres or 62-155 miles up).

Mechanism: When these energetic particles hit oxygen atoms, the atoms get all excited. As they calm down, they release a green light. This magic happens at lower altitudes in the atmosphere.

Red Auroras

Cause: Red auroras appear when solar particles bump into oxygen atoms at even higher altitudes (above 250 kilometres or 155 miles).

Mechanism: The collisions at these heights excite the atoms differently, making them release red light as they chill out. Red auroras are rarer but stunning.

Blue and Purple Auroras

Cause: These colours come from interactions between solar particles and nitrogen molecules in the upper atmosphere (above 100 kilometres or 62 miles).

Mechanism: When solar particles collide with nitrogen molecules, the molecules get excited. As they relax, they emit blue and purple light. Blue auroras are less common but can be seen at higher altitudes with higher nitrogen levels.

Yellow and Pink Auroras

Cause: These rare colours typically occur during intense geomagnetic storms.

Mechanism: They result from a mix of oxygen and nitrogen emissions at different altitudes. Pink auroras, for example, appear when red and blue emissions blend in the upper atmosphere.

White Auroras

Cause: White auroras are less common and usually appear as diffused faint light.

Mechanism: They result from a broad mix of emissions across various altitudes or when the auroral activity is less intense.

The lights usually appear as shimmering curtains, swirling arcs, or even spirals, dancing across the sky like they're auditioning for a cosmic ballet. Earth's magnetic field and the intensity of the solar wind direct the shape and movement of these auroras.

Astronauts aboard the International Space Station (ISS) get the ultimate front-row seats to this spectacular light show. From their spacey perch, they see the auroras as glowing, colourful curtains of light swaying across Earth's atmosphere. The view from space is a unique perspective, giving them a celestial VIP pass to a light show we can only dream of from down here!

2
MYTHS AND LEGENDS ABOUT NORTHERN LIGHTS

Today, we know the science behind the Northern Lights. These stunning light displays are created by interacting charged particles from the sun with the Earth's atmosphere. This scientific understanding, however, still retains the awe and wonder that the Northern Lights inspire. Imagine looking up at the sky and seeing green, red, and purple lights dancing around, not knowing what they are. Unsurprisingly, the aurora borealis has inspired so much folklore and legends over the years!

Alaska

These myths and legends have been passed down through generations, shaping the cultural identity of the Alaskan people.

The Celestial Ball Game: Inuit folklore, a significant part of the cultural heritage of the indigenous people of the Arctic, has a playful twist on the Northern Lights. They believed the lights were spirits playing a game like soccer with a walrus skull. The sky became their field, and every flicker and flash were a goal scored by these spirited players. Imagine looking up and thinking the Northern Lights were the ultimate cosmic sports match, a sight that fills you with wonder and intrigue!

The Dancing Spirits: The Yupik people of Alaska believed that the Northern Lights were not just random lights in the sky but the joyous spirits of animals like deer, seals, and whales dancing in a celestial celebration. These animal spirits would light up the heavens with their joyous movements, creating a celestial dance party with all your favourite Arctic animals showing off their best moves! It's a joyous and entertaining sight that uplifts the spirit.

The Whistling Lights: There's a legend among the Native Alaskan tribes that if you whistle at the Northern Lights, they will come closer to you. But this closeness can be dangerous, as they might take you away. So, while it might be tempting to call them down, it's best to enjoy the view from a safe distance, respecting the power and mystery of the lights.

The Spirits of the Dead: In some Alaskan cultures, the Northern Lights were thought to be the spirits of the deceased, especially those who had met a violent end. These spirits were believed to be attempting to communicate with the living. The dancing lights were their way of reaching out, bridging the gap between the earthly realm and the afterlife.

The Fire Fox: Like Finnish folklore, some Alaskan legends tell of a magical fox that runs so fast across the snow that its tail causes sparks, creating the Northern Lights. Imagine a speedy fox zipping around, setting the sky ablaze with its fiery tail!

The Sky Dwellers: Some legends speak of mysterious sky dwellers who live in a land far beyond the reach of humans. These beings create the Northern Lights to communicate with people on Earth. They are said to send guidance, warning, or celebration messages through the shimmering colours.

Canada

Let's dive into some fun and fascinating myths and legends about the Northern Lights from Canada.

The Sky Spirits' Dance Party: In many First Nations legends, the Northern Lights are believed to be the spirits of ancestors dancing in the sky. Imagine looking up and seeing your great-great-grandparents having a celestial dance-off, their joyous movements lighting up the night. It's the ultimate family reunion, with a light show included, a tradition that makes you feel connected to your roots.

The Whistling Lights: Some Canadian Indigenous tribes say they will come closer to you if you whistle at the Northern Lights. But watch out! If they get too close, they might whisk you away. So, while it might be tempting to call them down for a better look, enjoying the view from afar is safer.

The Animal Spirits: In certain Inuit tales, the Northern Lights are the spirits of animals, like deer and seals, frolicking in the sky. These animal spirits play and dance, turning the night into a vibrant celebration. Picture a celestial zoo where all your favourite animals are putting on a spectacular show just for you!

The Celestial Fire: Some Cree legends describe the Northern Lights as the spirits of warriors who died in battle. They light fires in the sky to guide the souls of the deceased to the afterlife. Imagine a giant bonfire party in the sky, with brave warriors lighting the way and sharing stories around the celestial campfire.

The Torches of the Spirits: According to some Algonquin legends, the Northern Lights are torches held by spirits to light the way for those travelling to the afterlife. These spirits are like cosmic tour guides, making sure no soul gets lost on their journey. It's like having a group of friendly ghosts lighting up the night with their magical torches.

The Great Fisher: In one Ojibwe legend, the Northern Lights are linked to the story of the Great Fisher, a brave hero who climbed into the sky to free the birds trapped by the ice. His journey created a bridge of light, which we now see as the auroras. Imagine a heroic fisher lighting up the sky with his daring rescue mission!

Greenland

Let's explore some fascinating and fun myths and legends about the Northern Lights from Greenland.

The Sky Kickball Game: In Greenlandic Inuit folklore, the Northern Lights are believed to be the spirits of children who passed away too soon. These playful spirits kick around a walrus skull, turning the sky into their playground. Imagine looking up and seeing a cosmic kickball game, with the kids having a blast lighting up the night!

The Whistling Lights: Like in other Arctic cultures, Greenlandic legends warn against whistling at the Northern Lights. If you do, the lights will come closer and could even take you away. So, while it might be tempting to whistle and get a better view, it's safer to enjoy the show from a distance.

The Dancing Spirits: Greenlandic Inuit also believed the Northern Lights were spirits of the dead dancing in the sky. These spirits celebrated and showed off their moves, lighting up the heavens with joy. Picture a celestial dance party where the ancestors are having a great time and putting on a light show for everyone below!

The Animal Spirits: In some Greenlandic tales, the Northern Lights are the spirits of animals like seals and whales playing in the sky. These animal spirits are frolicking and having fun, creating beautiful lights as they move. Imagine a cosmic playground where all your favourite Arctic animals put on a dazzling show just for you!

The Guiding Spirits: Greenlandic myths also describe the Northern Lights as guides for souls travelling to the afterlife. The spirits use the lights to help lost souls find their way. It's like having a team of friendly ghosts holding glowing lanterns, ensuring everyone reaches their destination safely.

The Celestial Torches: Some legends describe the Northern Lights as torches held by spirits to light the way for hunters and travellers at night. These spirits are like cosmic guardians, ensuring everyone finds their path. Imagine a team of helpful spirits lighting up the night with their torches, ensuring you always keep your way.

Iceland

Let's dive into some fun and fascinating myths and legends about the Northern Lights from Iceland.

The Celestial Vikings: In Icelandic folklore, the Aurora Borealis were believed to be reflections of the Valkyries' armour as they rode into battle. These fierce warrior women were escorting fallen warriors to Valhalla, lighting up the sky with their shining gear. Imagine looking up and thinking the Northern Lights are the ultimate Viking disco, with

Valkyries partying and showing off their bling!

The Elfin Laundry: Another charming Icelandic tale suggests that the Northern Lights result from elves doing their laundry. The colourful lights reflect their bright clothes being hung out to dry. Picture a sky-high laundry line with elves cheerfully hanging up their glowing garments, turning the heavens into a magical clothesline!

The Whale Dance: Some Icelandic legends describe the Northern Lights as the spirits of whales playing and dancing in the sky. These majestic creatures light up the night with their graceful movements. Imagine a celestial ocean where whales swim through the stars, creating a spectacular light show with every move.

The Guiding Lights: Icelandic seafarers believed the Northern Lights were there to guide them on their voyages. The lights were seen as friendly spirits lighting the way, ensuring safe travels. Think of the auroras as cosmic GPS, helping sailors navigate through the dark, icy waters with their glowing paths.

The Midwives' Magic: One Icelandic tale tells of midwives who used the light from the auroras to safely deliver babies during long, dark winter nights. The Northern Lights were thought to bring good luck and protection to the newborns. Imagine the sky lighting up to celebrate each new arrival, with the auroras acting as nature's nightlight for the little ones.

The Aurora Creatures: Some Icelandic myths speak of mythical creatures with magical powers that create the Northern Lights. These beings, often mischievous but benevolent, frolic in the sky, painting it with vibrant colours. Picture playful sky-dwellers waving their magic wands, transforming the night into a spectacular light show.

Norway & Svalbard

Let's explore some fun and fascinating myths and legends about the Northern Lights from Norway and Svalbard.

The Valkyrie Lights: In Norway, many believed that the Northern Lights were reflections of the Valkyries' armour as they rode to Valhalla. These warrior maidens were guiding fallen heroes to their eternal resting place. Imagine the sky turning into a sparkling battlefield, with Valkyries showing off their shiny armour and throwing the ultimate celestial party!

The Heavenly Bridge: Some Norwegian legends suggest that the Northern Lights are the Bifrost, the rainbow bridge connecting the world of the gods (Asgard) to Earth (Midgard). It's like a magical highway for gods to visit us, mere mortals. Picture the gods commuting across the sky on a dazzling rainbow bridge, maybe even getting stuck in cosmic traffic!

The Sky Fireworks: In Svalbard, the Sami people believed the Northern Lights were the souls of the dead playing in the sky. These spirits would gather to celebrate and have fun, creating a spectacular light show. Imagine a celestial playground where spirits are having the time of their afterlife, lighting up the night with their joyous antics.

The Whale Dance: Some Norwegian fishermen believed that the Northern Lights were caused by whales swimming in the sky, their movements creating beautiful lights. These majestic creatures were thought to be guiding the fishermen home. Picture a pod of whales gracefully dancing through the stars, turning the sky into their own personal aquarium.

The Aurora Dragons: In some Norwegian tales, the Northern Lights were seen as the fire breath of dragons battling in the sky. These epic dragon duels lit up the night with their fiery breath. Imagine looking up and seeing dragons duking it out in a grand light show, each fiery blast painting the sky with vibrant colours.

The Lanterns of the Dead: In Svalbard, another belief was that the Northern Lights were lanterns carried by the spirits of the dead. These spirits used the lights to guide lost souls to the afterlife. Picture a parade of friendly ghosts holding glowing lanterns, lighting up the sky to ensure everyone finds their way home.

Sweden

Let's explore some fun and fascinating myths and legends about the Northern Lights from Sweden.

The Sky Fox: In Swedish folklore, the Northern Lights are called

"Revontulet," which means "fox fires." The story is about a magical fox racing across the snowy landscape, its tail sweeping snowflakes into the sky. These snowflakes catch the moonlight and burst into colourful lights. Imagine a speedy fox zipping around, setting the sky ablaze with its fiery tail. It's like a cosmic game of tag with the stars!

The Celestial Herring: Fishermen in Sweden used to believe that the Northern Lights were caused by giant shoals of herring reflecting the moonlight. This belief was so strong that they'd head to sea whenever the lights appeared, hoping for a bountiful catch. Picture the night sky as a giant aquarium, with shimmering fish lighting up the heavens and leading fishermen to their prize.

The Wedding Lights: In some parts of Sweden, the Northern Lights were believed to be a sign of good fortune and a happy marriage. Seeing the auroras on your wedding night was considered an auspicious omen. Imagine tying the knot under a sky filled with dancing lights, as if the universe is celebrating your love story.

The Spirits' Revelry: Many Swedes believed that the Aurora Borealis were the spirits of their ancestors cavorting in the sky. These spirits would gather to dance, play, and celebrate, creating a spectacular light show. Picture a celestial family reunion with your great-great-grandparents showing off their best moves and lighting up the night with joyful antics.

The Flaming Sword: Another legend describes the Northern Lights as a flaming sword wielded by the gods to protect the heavens from evil. This fiery weapon would light up the sky during battles, warding off dark forces. Imagine a divine guardian swishing a giant sword across the sky, each swipe creating brilliant arcs of light to keep the universe safe.

The Cosmic Fertility Boost: In some Swedish traditions, the Northern Lights were believed to increase fertility. Couples would go out under the auroras, hoping the magical lights would bless them with children. Imagine looking up at the sky, thinking it's not just a beautiful display but also nature's way of lending a helping hand to hopeful parents.

Finland

Let's explore some fun and fascinating myths and legends about the Northern Lights from Finland.

The Magical Fox Fires: In Finnish folklore, the Northern Lights are called "Revontulet," meaning "fox fires." The story is about a magical Arctic fox running so fast across the snowy landscape that its tail sweeps snowflakes into the sky. These snowflakes catch the moonlight and burst into colourful lights. Imagine a speedy fox zipping around, painting the sky with its fiery tail. It's like a cosmic light show by a very energetic fox!

The Sky Dancers: Some Finnish legends describe the Northern Lights as the spirits of brave warriors dancing in the sky. These warriors celebrate their heroic deeds by putting on a spectacular light show. Picture a celestial dance party with warriors busting their best moves, lighting up the night with their energetic celebration.

The Spirits' Path: Another Finnish belief is that the Northern Lights are the pathway for souls travelling to the afterlife. The lights guide these spirits safely on their journey. Imagine a glowing road in the sky, lined with twinkling lights, helping souls find their way to the great beyond. It's like the ultimate cosmic GPS!

The Celestial Salmon: In some Finnish tales, the Northern Lights are thought to be caused by giant salmon swimming in the sky. These celestial fish swim through the stars, their movements creating beautiful auroras. Picture a massive school of salmon gracefully gliding through the night sky, turning it into a giant, sparkling aquarium.

The Fertility Blessing: Finns also believed the Northern Lights could boost fertility. Couples hoping to have children would go out under the auroras, believing the magical lights would bless them. Imagine a romantic night out under the glowing sky, thinking that the shimmering lights above are nature's way of lending a helping hand.

The Aurora Giants: Some Finnish legends speak of giants who live in the far north and create the Northern Lights with their bonfires. These giants gather around their massive fires, lighting the sky with glowing embers. Picture enormous, friendly giants sitting around a campfire, tossing sparks into the air that turn into the breathtaking auroras we see.

Russia

Let's dive into some fun and fascinating myths and legends about the Northern Lights from Russia.

The Heavenly Battle: In Russian folklore, the Northern Lights are often seen as the reflection of grand battles in the sky. Warriors clash with swords that create sparks, lighting up the heavens. Imagine looking up and seeing a celestial fight club, where each clash of swords sets the sky on fire with brilliant colours!

The Spirits' Dance: Some Russian tales describe the Northern Lights as the spirits of the dead dancing joyfully in the sky. These spirits celebrate and show off their best moves, creating a stunning light show. Picture a ghostly dance party in the clouds, with spirits twirling and leaping, turning the night into their dance floor.

The Aurora Bears: In Siberian legends, the Northern Lights are believed to be caused by bears playing in the sky. These cosmic bears run and jump, their fur sparkling with light. Imagine a bunch of playful bears having the time of their lives in the sky, creating a dazzling display with their every move. It's like the ultimate bear playground!

The Enchanted Lights: The Northern Lights are seen as a magical force in some Russian stories. People believed these lights could protect them from evil spirits and bad luck. Imagine the auroras as a glowing shield in the sky, warding off all the bad vibes and keeping everyone safe and sound.

The Cosmic Fireworks: Some Russian fishermen thought the Northern Lights were the spirits of fish swimming in the sky, their scales catching the light and creating a sparkling display. Picture a sky filled with shimmering fish, turning the night into a giant, glowing aquarium. It's like nature's fireworks show, courtesy of some flashy fish!

The Aurora Wedding: There's a charming belief that seeing the Northern Lights on your wedding day brings good luck and a happy marriage. Imagine tying the knot under a sky with colourful lights, as if the universe is celebrating your special day with a cosmic light show.

3
THE BEST TIME TO SEE THE NORTHERN LIGHTS

Catching a glimpse of the Northern Lights is like chasing a cosmic disco! Your odds of seeing these dazzling light shows can change depending on where you are and the time of year.

At least 4 hours of true darkness

To boost your chances, aim for at least 4 hours of true darkness in the location you are going. The skies are dark outside: Civil Twilight, Nautical Twilight, and Astronomical Twilight.

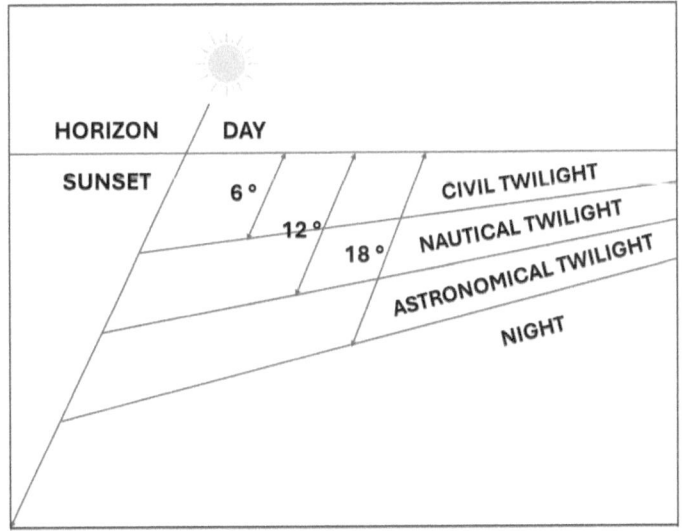

Let's dive into these twilight zones and see what they're all about!

Civil Twilight

Civil twilight starts in the morning when the Sun is 6 degrees below the horizon and wraps up at sunrise. Civil twilight starts at sunset in the evening and ends when the Sun dips 6 degrees below the horizon.

Civil twilight is the brightest part of the three twilight phases.

There's so much natural sunlight that you might not need to flick on a flashlight for outdoor activities. Only the brightest celestial objects can be seen with the naked eye during this time. So, if you're into stargazing, you might have to wait longer for the darker skies.

Nautical Twilight

Nautical twilight happens when the Sun is 6 to 12 degrees below the horizon. Most stars become visible during nautical twilight, making it ideal for stargazers. However, it is still early for Aurora to be visible to the naked eye. If the aurora is bright, you might glimpse it at the end of Nautical Twilight. However, waiting for it to get even darker will give you an even better view.

Astronomical Twilight

Welcome to astronomical twilight, when the Sun is between 12 and 18 degrees below the horizon. This is when the sky truly becomes a playground for stargazers.

During astronomical twilight, most celestial objects are ready for their close-up. The stars are out, the planets are shining, and the Moon might be showing off a bit. However, there's a tiny catch. The atmosphere still likes to scatter and bend a bit of sunlight. It's like having a very faint spotlight, making it tricky for astronomers to see the faintest stars and galaxies. Once Astronomical Twilight ends, the Sun's light won't affect the sky anymore.

The more hours of darkness you have, the better your chances of seeing the aurora. For example, if you plan to visit Fairbanks, the best time to experience the Northern Lights is between September 15th and March 31st. During this period, Fairbanks has at least 4 hours of total darkness each night, providing ideal conditions for viewing the aurora.

To determine the total hours of darkness at your destination, you will need the Sunrise/Sunset time, as well as the start and end time of Astronomical Twilight.

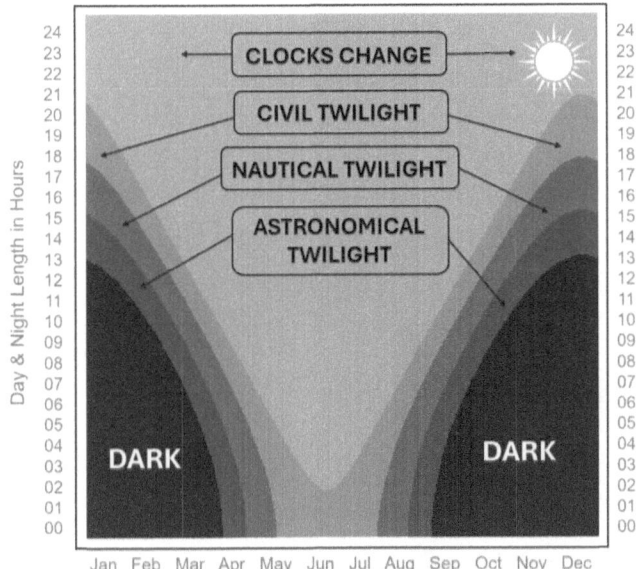

Solar Maximum: Between 2024 - 2026

Solar Cycle 25 is heating up, folks! The Sun's getting ready to throw a spectacular party, and the National Oceanic and Atmospheric Administration's (NOAA) Space Weather Prediction Center (SWPC) says the peak of the bash will be between late 2024 and early 2026. Get ready for a solar maximum that's set to dazzle!

Let's dive into this sunny shindig and explore the wild ride between solar maximum and solar minimum and how they whip up those fantastic auroras in the night sky.

First up, solar maximum. This is when the Sun cranks the volume to eleven every 11 years. During this peak, the Sun is like a firework factory—shooting out solar flares and solar wind (streams of charged particles) like there's no tomorrow. When these particles crash into Earth's magnetic field, it's like a cosmic light show, creating those stunning auroras. So, during a solar maximum, grab your popcorn and keep your eyes peeled for some seriously epic sky bling.

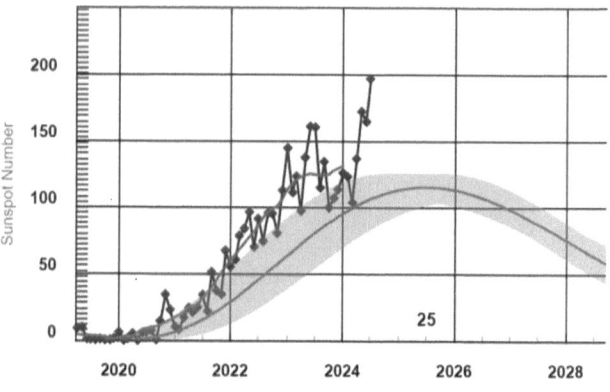

swpc.noaa.gov

Now, let's flip the script to solar minimum. This is when the Sun takes a chill pill and quiets down. There are fewer solar flares and less solar wind, which means auroras are less frequent and not as flashy. Don't pack away your stargazing gear just yet! Even during a solar minimum, you can still catch some auroras. They might be more like a soft glow than a full-on disco, but they're still magical. So, whether the Sun is throwing a wild solar max party or having a mellow solar min moment, there's always a chance to glimpse those mesmerizing auroras.

Why Winter is the Best Season to See the Magical Aurora

Winter is prime time for aurora hunting, and here's why it's magical:

First, winter nights are like extra-long movies – perfect for aurora viewing. The Sun sets early and takes its sweet time returning, giving you many nighttime hours to catch the celestial light show. Plus, with the Sun snoozing, there's less daylight to mess up your aurora-spotting with pesky light pollution. Then, there's the weather. Winter might be chilly, but those cold, crisp nights often bring clear skies – ideal for aurora watching. The air is fresher and more precise, making the stars and auroras pop like neon signs. So, bundle up, brave the cold, and enjoy the dazzling display!

Equinoxes: March and September

(Only applicable to locations that have 4 hours of true darkness)

Twice a year, around March 21 and September 21, we get these magical moments called equinoxes. These days, day and night are nearly equal in length, making them unique. But there's an extra twist that makes them excellent for aurora-watching!

During the equinoxes, Earth's magnetic field and the solar wind do this fantastic dance and align perfectly. It's like finding a secret key to unlock an epic light show. This alignment lets solar particles stream into our atmosphere more efficiently, creating those breathtaking auroras. So, if you want to catch nature's ultimate sky party, the equinoxes are your golden ticket!

New Moon Phases or the Moon Below Horizon

When it's the new moon phase, the Moon plays hide-and-seek—except it's good at hiding. No moonlight means the sky is as dark as a ninja's pyjamas, and this deep darkness makes those shimmering auroras pop like never before. It's like turning off the lights before a movie—everything looks way cooler!

With the Moon out of the picture, auroras stand out more, and the stars come out to play. A new moon night is like getting a double feature in the great outdoors, with a sky full of twinkling stars creating a magical backdrop. It's like a cosmic playground up there!

Moonlight is pretty and all, but when you're hunting for auroras, it can be a bit of a party pooper. During a new moon, there's no moon glare to wash out the vibrant colours of the auroras. You see those greens, pinks, and purples in full, unfiltered glory. Without the bright moonlight, your eyes can adjust to the darkness better.

Magical Time: 10 PM to 2 AM
(Only applicable when the skies are dark)

Between 10 PM and 2 AM, this magical ring-shaped zone aligns perfectly with your viewing spot. This cosmic timing makes the lights more intense and way easier to see.

Darkness is your BFF when you're on an aurora hunt. The night is darkest and most mysterious between 10 PM and 2 AM. This deep darkness makes those vibrant aurora colours pop against the night sky, giving you a front-row seat to nature's most spectacular show. Late night to early morning usually means clearer skies. The hustle and bustle of daytime winds down, reducing atmospheric disturbances. Fewer clouds mean better conditions to enjoy the light show.

High Kp Index Nights

The Kp index is like the aurora's hype meter, measuring geomagnetic activity and telling us how wild the light show might get. The scale goes from 0 (total snooze-fest) to 9 (Aurora Party of the Century!). When the Kp index is high, the Sun gives Earth's magnetic field a severe energy boost. This results in more intense, colourful, and widespread auroras that light up the sky like a cosmic disco.

One of the most incredible things about high Kp index nights is that you can see auroras in places you'd never expect. With a high Kp index, the aurora oval expands, bringing the dazzling lights closer to your doorstep. It's like the aurora is hitting the road for a world tour, and your backyard might just be one of its stops!

During Geomagnetic Storms

A geomagnetic storm is like a cosmic showdown when the solar wind—a stream of charged particles from the Sun—smashes into Earth's magnetic field. This space drama stirs the magnetosphere and lights the sky with vibrant auroras. During one of these storms, the aurora gets a major power-up. The storm cranks up the intensity and frequency of the lights, making them brighter and more colourful. It's like nature turning up the volume on its best playlist just for you!

Geomagnetic storms also expand the aurora oval—the ring-shaped zone where auroras are visible. This means you might see the lights even far from the poles. It's like scoring VIP access to a front-row seat at Earth's most incredible light show! These storms make the aurora dance across the night sky, creating stunning shapes and patterns. You might see swirls, waves, and bursts of light. It's like watching a celestial ballet unfold right above you. The bright, intense auroras are perfect for amazing pictures. You'll capture those greens, pinks, and purples in all their glory.

Clear, Cloudless Nights

If you're itching to catch the dazzling auroras, there's one golden rule: clear, cloudless nights are your best friend. Imagine stepping outside on a chilly night, looking up, and seeing the sky filled with vibrant colours dancing above you. That's the aurora at its best. But if the sky is full of clouds, you might miss out on this spectacular show. So, why do clear nights matter so much?

Low-Level Clouds: The Party Poopers

Low-level clouds, like stratus and cumulus, hang close to the ground (up to 6,500 feet). These thick clouds often cover the entire sky, blocking your view entirely.

Middle-Level Clouds: The Sneaky Spoilers

Middle-level clouds, such as altostratus and altocumulus, float between 6,500 and 20,000 feet. These clouds can be patchy but still dense enough to obscure the aurora. It's like trying to watch a movie through frosted glass—blurry and frustrating!

High-Level Clouds: The Veil of Disappointment

High-level clouds, like cirrus and cirrostratus, drift above 20,000 feet. They're thin and wispy, but don't be fooled! Even these delicate clouds can scatter the light and dull the aurora's brilliance. It's like viewing the aurora through a hazy filter—pretty, but not the whole experience.

A cloudless sky means nothing stands between you and the aurora. The lights appear brighter and more vivid, making their movements easier to follow. You get to see the aurora in all its glory, with no clouds to spoil the view.

4
UNDERSTANDING THE AURORA OVAL / AURORA ZONE

The Aurora Oval, a unique and magical area near the Earth's magnetic poles, is where the Northern Lights love to perform. It's not just a static shape but a dynamic entity that changes in size and form over time, always ready to dazzle—planning a trip to see the Northern Lights? Take the chance to step inside this one-of-a-kind oval-shaped spotlight for the best views.

The Aurora Borealis throws a dazzling dance party in the sky, right above the Earth's Geomagnetic North Pole, forming a giant glowing ring known as the Auroral Oval. You'd think this sky show would be visible from the same spot all around the world, but nope! Since it's centred on the true North and not the geographical North Pole, it plays by its own quirky rules.

A Tale of Three Norths: The Geomagnetic, Geographic, and Magnetic Poles

Geographic North Pole

First up, we have the Geographic North Pole. This is the big cheese of the North, the top of the world, the grand finale of the Earth's axis. Sitting pretty at 90°N latitude, it's the spot where all lines of longitude meet. Picture Santa's workshop - this is where all the magic happens. The Geographic North Pole is as fixed as it gets, but don't expect to find any land there. It's just a whole lot of ice floating on the Arctic Ocean. While it doesn't directly affect the Northern Lights, it's an excellent place to start your polar adventure!

North Geomagnetic Pole

Next, let's meet the North Geomagnetic Pole. This one's a bit of a rebel, always on the move! It's the point where the Earth's magnetic field points directly down into the planet. Imagine it as the cool, slightly unpredictable cousin who's always jet-setting around the Arctic. Currently, it's hanging out north of Canada. This pole is crucial for the

Northern Lights because it influences where those shimmering curtains of light appear. When solar particles hit the Earth's atmosphere, they're guided by the magnetic field towards this pole, creating the spectacular auroras we all love.

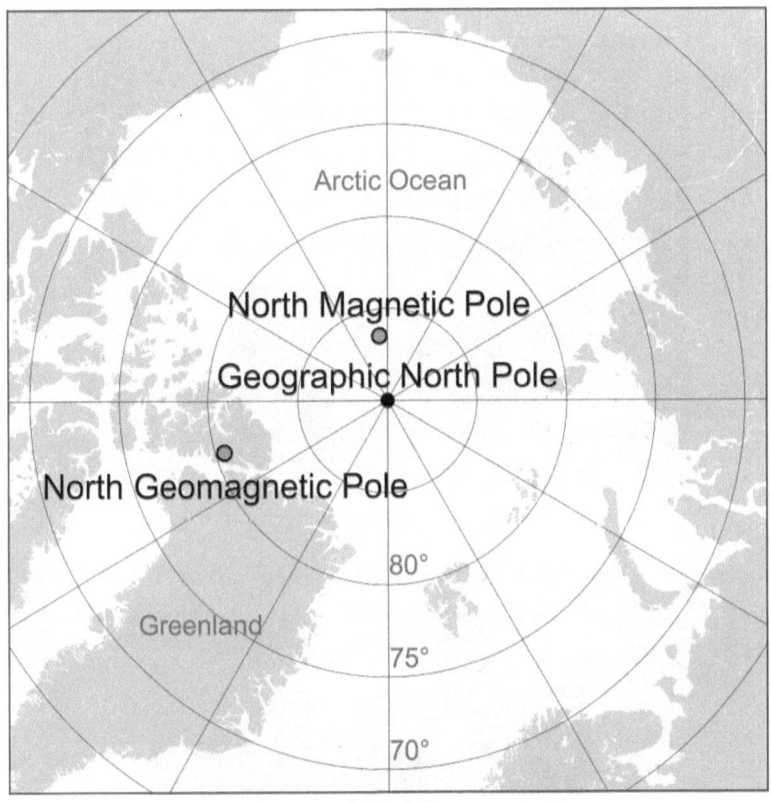

NOAA

North Magnetic Pole

Finally, we have the North Magnetic Pole. This guy is the life of the party regarding navigation and the Northern Lights. It's where your compass needle points. But like the Geomagnetic Pole, it's not a fan of staying in one place. It drifts around due to changes in the Earth's molten core. It's in the Arctic right now, and its position affects where the Northern Lights are most often seen. As it moves, so do the best spots to catch the aurora borealis. Understanding the role of the North Magnetic Pole can give you a head start in your aurora hunting adventure.

How do changes in Kp Affect the Aurora?

Europe & Asia

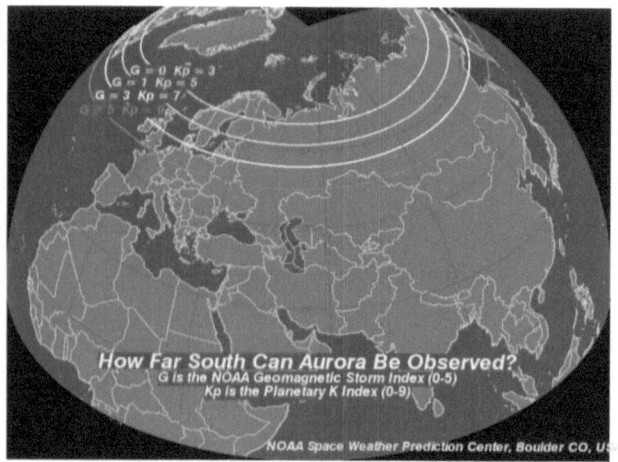

NOAA

North America

Kp = 3 (Quiet Aurora)

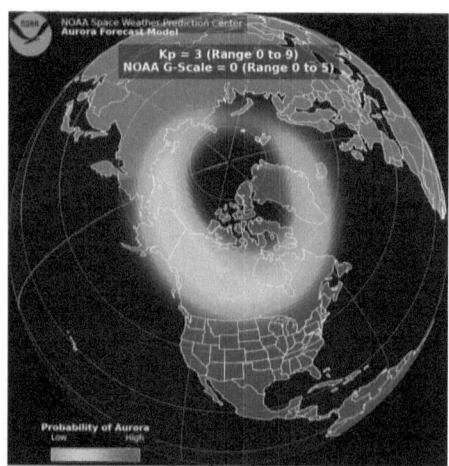

NOAA

Kp = 5 (Moderate Aurora)

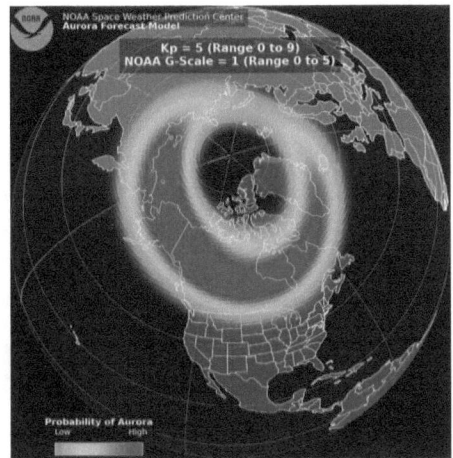

NOAA

Kp = 7 (Active Aurora)

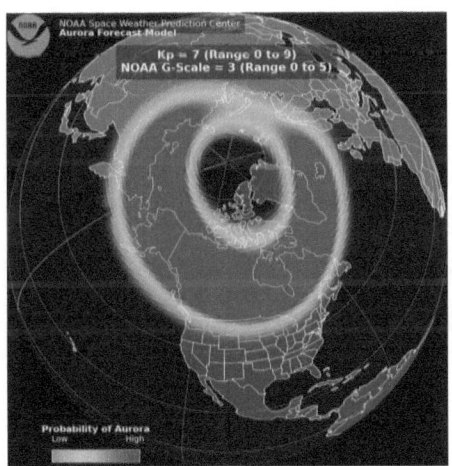

NOAA

Kp = 9 (Very Active Aurora)

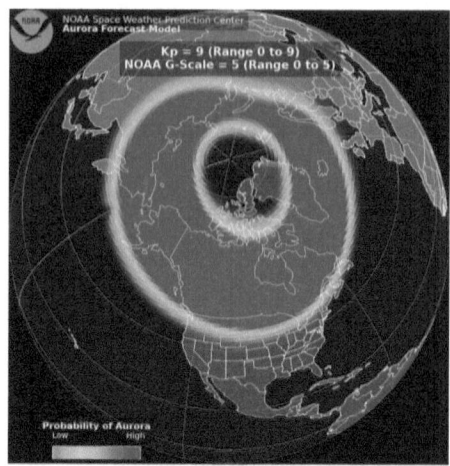

NOAA

Hot spots under the Aurora Oval

Alaska

Alaska has some prime locations under the auroral oval where the magic happens.

Fairbanks

Fairbanks is the superstar of Aurora viewing. Located almost smack dab under the auroral oval, this city offers a fantastic vantage point for Northern Lights enthusiasts. With its long, dark winters and clear skies, Fairbanks is your best bet. All you need is a Kp index of 4.

Coldfoot

Coldfoot might sound chilly, and it is! But it's also a hotspot for aurora viewing. Situated north of the Arctic Circle, Coldfoot is remote and dark—perfect for an uninterrupted view of the Northern Lights. A Kp index of 4 is your golden ticket to the light show.

Utqiaġvik (Barrow)

The aurora is a regular guest way up north in Utqiaġvik, formerly known as Barrow. This town is about as far north as you can get in the United States, offering excellent chances to see the lights, especially during the long polar nights. To catch the lights in Utqiaġvik, aim for a Kp index of 3.

Nome

Nome is another excellent spot on the western edge of Alaska. This coastal town provides a unique backdrop for the aurora; you can say you've watched the lights dance over the Bering Sea. For Nome, aim for a Kp index of 5 to catch the lights.

Bettles

Bettles is a small village near the Koyukuk River, deep in the heart of Alaska. It's known for its clear skies and minimal light pollution, making it a prime location for aurora hunters. A Kp index of 4 should be enough to see the aurora here.

Canada

Canada has some top spots under the auroral oval where the sky is spectacular.

Yellowknife, Northwest Territories

Yellowknife is the rock star of Aurora viewing in Canada. With clear skies and long winter nights, you need a Kp index of around 4 to see the Northern Lights. Plus, there are plenty of tours and cozy lodges for aurora hunters.

Whitehorse, Yukon

Next up, Whitehorse in the Yukon. This charming city offers stunning landscapes and great views of the lights. A Kp index of 4 will do the trick here. It's less crowded than some other spots, giving you a more intimate encounter with the aurora.

Churchill, Manitoba

Churchill is famous for polar bears but also a fantastic spot for the Northern Lights. Located on the shores of Hudson Bay, Churchill's remote location means dark skies and incredible aurora displays. A Kp index of 5 is enough to catch the lights here.

CHASING NORTHERN LIGHTS

Fort McMurray, Alberta

Fort McMurray might be known for its oil sands, but it's also a hidden gem for aurora watchers. This city is an excellent base for exploring the lights in northern Alberta. Just head outside the city to escape light pollution. A Kp index of 4-5 is your golden ticket here.

Yellowhead County, Alberta

Yellowhead County is another excellent spot for aurora viewing. Areas like Edson and Hinton offer clear skies and minimal light interference, perfect for a night of aurora chasing. To catch the lights in this area, aim for a Kp index of 5.

Northern Quebec (Nunavik)

Nunavik, the northernmost part of Quebec, offers some of the best aurora viewing in eastern Canada. The remote villages and wide-open spaces provide an unspoiled backdrop for the Northern Lights. A Kp index of 4 is enough to see the aurora here.

Iqaluit, Nunavut

Iqaluit, the capital of Nunavut, is another fantastic location for aurora enthusiasts. Situated on Baffin Island, Iqaluit's northern position and clear, dark skies make it ideal for watching the aurora dance. A Kp index of 4 will light up the sky for you here.

Contiguous United States

There are some fantastic spots where the aurora oval dips south enough for a spectacular show. Let's dive into these prime locations and the Kp index you'll need for a light show!

Northern Minnesota

First up, Northern Minnesota. Think of it as the Land of 10,000 Lakes and one amazing light show! Head to places like Ely or the Boundary Waters Canoe Area for a great view. You'll need a Kp index of around 5 to catch the aurora here.

Northern Wisconsin

Next, we have Northern Wisconsin. Head to areas like Bayfield or Apostle Islands National Lakeshore for a front-row seat to the Northern Lights. Aim for a Kp index of 5-6.

Michigan's Upper Peninsula

Michigan's Upper Peninsula, or the "U.P." as the locals call it, is another fantastic spot. Check out places like Marquette or Pictured Rocks National Lakeshore. Here, a Kp index 5 is your ticket to the light show.

Northern Maine

Maine isn't just for lobster! Northern Maine offers some stunning views of the Northern Lights. Head to places like Baxter State Park or Aroostook County. You'll need a Kp index of 5-6 to see the lights dance.

Northern Washington

Northern Washington State is another hidden gem, especially around Mount Baker or the North Cascades. Aim for a Kp index of 5-6 to catch the aurora.

Greenland

Greenland has some top spots under the auroral oval where the sky is spectacular.

Nuuk

First up is Nuuk, the capital of Greenland. This city offers a fantastic mix of culture and stunning aurora views. All you need is a Kp index of around 4 to see the Northern Lights dance above the city.

Kangerlussuaq

Next, we have Kangerlussuaq. This small town is known for its clear skies and fantastic aurora displays. A Kp index of 4 will do the trick here.

Ilulissat

Ilulissat, famous for its icebergs, also offers a front-row seat to the Northern Lights. Head to the Ilulissat Icefjord for a breathtaking backdrop. Aim for a Kp index of 4 to catch the lights.

Tasiilaq

Tasiilaq, located on the east coast, is another fantastic spot. This town's remote location ensures dark skies and incredible aurora displays. A Kp index of 4 is your golden ticket here.

Qaanaaq

Qaanaaq, one of the northernmost towns in Greenland, offers some of the best aurora views. This place is so far north that you might feel like you're on top of the world! A Kp index of 3 is enough to see the lights here.

Iceland

Ready to see the Northern Lights in the land of fire and ice? Iceland is one of the best places to catch the aurora borealis, with fantastic spots under the auroral oval.

Reykjavik

First up, Reykjavik is the capital city. While it's a bit bright due to city lights, you can still catch the aurora if you head to the outskirts. A Kp index of around 5 should light up the sky here.

Thingvellir National Park

Next, we have Thingvellir National Park. This spot is steeped in history and offers amazing views of the Northern Lights. With a Kp index of 4, you're set for a dazzling display.

Vik

Vik, located on the southern coast, is famous for its black sand beaches and stunning aurora views. A Kp index of 4 will do the trick here.

Akureyri

Head north to Akureyri, the charming town known as the "Capital of North Iceland." Here, a Kp index of 4 is enough to see the lights.

Jokulsarlon Glacier Lagoon

Jokulsarlon Glacier Lagoon offers a surreal backdrop for the Northern Lights. Imagine the lights dancing over icebergs! To catch the show, aim for a Kp index of 4.

Snaefellsnes Peninsula

The Snaefellsnes Peninsula, often called "Iceland in Miniature," provides a diverse landscape for aurora viewing. A Kp index of 4 is your golden ticket here.

Faroe Islands

You'll generally need a Kp Index of 4 or higher to see the aurora in the Faroe Islands. That's right—the aurora is more likely to appear in these northern skies than in more southern locations. If the Kp Index climbs to 5 or 6, your chances get even better, so don't forget to check those aurora forecasts!

Here are some top spots to set up for your aurora-watching adventure:

Saksun

This picturesque village is surrounded by mountains, offering a beautiful and remote spot for aurora viewing. With a Kp Index of 4 or higher, you could see the lights reflecting off the tranquil waters of the fjord.

Gjógv

Located on the island of Eysturoy, Gjógv is known for its dramatic cliffs and dark skies. It's far from city lights, making it a perfect place to catch the aurora with a Kp Index of 4 or higher.

Tjørnuvík

As one of the northernmost villages in the Faroes, Tjørnuvík offers incredible views of the night sky. With the iconic sea stacks Risin and Kellingin in the background, this spot is perfect for aurora spotting when the Kp Index hits 4 or above.

Kirkjubøur

This historic village on Streymoy Island blends cultural history and natural beauty. Head here when the Kp Index is at 4 or higher, and you might see the aurora dancing above the ancient ruins.

Ireland

For Ireland, you're looking at a Kp Index of 6 or higher to have a decent chance of seeing the aurora. If the Kp Index hits 7 or above, the chances of spotting those swirling lights get even better, especially if you're in a spot with little to no light pollution.

Here are some of the best spots in Ireland to set up camp when the Kp Index is just right:

Donegal (Malin Head)

As Ireland's northernmost point, Malin Head is your top bet. A Kp Index of **6 or higher** should make for a good show. The remote and dark area boasts a fantastic view of the horizon.

County Mayo (Achill Island & Ballycroy National Park)

These locations are perfect for aurora spotting, as they are far away from city lights. You'll need a Kp Index of **6 or higher** to catch the lights overhead.

Sperrin Mountains

Tucked between County Tyrone and County Londonderry, this spot offers dark skies and stunning mountain views. A Kp Index **6 or higher** will give you a good shot at seeing the aurora.

Connemara (Clifden & Sky Road)

Connemara is another excellent option with its wild landscapes and dark skies. You'll want a Kp Index of **6 or higher** for the best chances of seeing those dancing lights.

United Kingdom

Did you know you can see the Northern Lights in the U.K.? That's right, there's no need for a trip to the Arctic! There are some fantastic spots where the auroral oval dips south enough for a spectacular show.

Shetland Islands

First up, the Shetland Islands. These far-northern islands are prime territory for catching the Northern Lights. With a Kp index of around 4, you'll have a good chance of seeing the sky light up.

Orkney Islands

Next, we have the Orkney Islands. These islands are a bit further south than Shetland but offer fantastic aurora views. A Kp index of 5 should do the trick.

Caithness

Caithness, located on the northern tip of mainland Scotland, offers stunning landscapes and a great view of the Northern Lights. Aim for a Kp index of 5 here.

Outer Hebrides

The Outer Hebrides, especially places like Lewis and Harris, are perfect for aurora hunting. The remote, dark skies are ideal for viewing the lights. It would help if you had a Kp index of 5.

Northern Ireland

Yes, you can even catch the aurora in Northern Ireland! Head to places like the Antrim coast to see the lights. You'll need a Kp index of around 6 to see the aurora here.

Norway & Svalbard

If you're ready to see the Northern Lights in Norway, you're in for a treat. This Scandinavian wonderland has some of the best spots under the auroral oval. Let's check out these prime locations and the Kp index you'll need to catch the lights!

Tromsø

First up, Tromsø! Known as the "Gateway to the Arctic," this city is a top spot for aurora viewing. With a Kp index of around 2-3, you're almost guaranteed a light show.

Alta

Next, we have Alta, the "City of the Northern Lights." A Kp index of 3 will have you seeing the sky dance in no time.

Lofoten Islands

The Lofoten Islands offer a stunning backdrop for the Northern Lights. With rugged landscapes and clear skies, a Kp index of 3 is all you need.

Kirkenes

Kirkenes, located in the far northeast, is another fantastic spot. Aim for a Kp index of 3 here.

Svalbard

Suppose you're up for an adventure, head to Svalbard. This remote archipelago is about as far north as you can go without joining Santa's workshop. A Kp index of 2 is enough to catch the lights here.

Narvik

Narvik is another excellent location, with its beautiful fjords providing a dramatic backdrop for the aurora. A Kp index of 3 will do the trick.

Sweden

Sweden has some fantastic spots under the auroral oval where the sky is spectacular.

Abisko

First up, Abisko! This place is a dream come true for aurora hunters. With its clear skies and stunning landscapes, Abisko is among the best spots to see the Northern Lights. A Kp index of around 2-3 should light up your night.

Kiruna

Next, we have Kiruna, the northernmost town in Sweden. Known for its ice hotel and winter wonderland vibes, Kiruna is also a fantastic spot for aurora viewing. A Kp index of 3 will do the trick.

Jokkmokk

Jokkmokk, famous for its winter market, offers excellent chances to see the Northern Lights. This charming town combines cultural richness with natural beauty. Aim for a Kp index of 4 here.

Luleå

Luleå, on the northern coast, offers a beautiful mix of city life and aurora viewing. Head to the outskirts of the archipelago for the best views. A Kp index of 4 should suffice.

Piteå

Piteå, also located on the coast, is another excellent spot to catch the Northern Lights. With its stunning winter scenery, a Kp index of 4 will light up the sky.

Arjeplog

Arjeplog, surrounded by lakes and mountains, offers a remote and serene setting for aurora viewing. A Kp index of 3 is enough to see the lights here.

Finland

Finland is a fantastic spot for aurora viewing, with plenty of places under the auroral oval.

Rovaniemi

First up, Rovaniemi! Known as the official hometown of Santa Claus, this place offers more than just holiday cheer. With a Kp index of around 4, you can see the Northern Lights dance over Santa's village.

Kakslauttanen

Next, we have Kakslauttanen. Famous for its glass igloos, you can watch the aurora from the comfort of your cozy bed. A Kp index of 4 will light up the sky.

Saariselkä

Saariselkä is a winter wonderland perfect for catching the Northern Lights. With activities like skiing and husky sledding, the aurora is just the icing on the cake. Aim for a Kp index of 4 here.

Levi

Levi, a popular ski resort, also offers stunning aurora views. Hit the slopes during the day and enjoy the lights at night. A Kp index of 4 should do the trick.

Inari

Inari, located in the far North, is known for its clear skies and frequent auroras. A Kp index of 3 is enough to catch the lights here.

Kilpisjärvi

Kilpisjärvi, near the Finnish-Norwegian border, is another fantastic spot for aurora hunting. With its remote location and minimal light pollution, a Kp index of 3 will light up your night.

Russia

Russia has some top spots under the auroral oval where the sky lights up like a cosmic dance party.

Murmansk

First up, Murmansk! This port city is one of the best places in Russia to catch the Northern Lights. With a Kp index of around 3-4, you're almost guaranteed a show.

Teriberka

Next, we have Teriberka, a small village on the Kola Peninsula. This remote spot offers stunning views of the aurora over the Arctic Ocean. Aim for a Kp index of 4 here.

Arkhangelsk

Arkhangelsk, located on the northern coast, offers a beautiful mix of historical charm and aurora viewing. A Kp index of 4 will do the trick.

Naryan-Mar

Naryan-Mar, the capital of the Nenets Autonomous Okrug, is another fantastic spot. This town's remote location ensures dark skies and incredible aurora displays. It would help if you had a Kp index of 3-4.

Yakutsk

Head to Yakutsk for a unique aurora viewing experience. Known as one of the coldest cities on Earth, it offers a frosty yet fantastic backdrop for the Northern Lights. A Kp index of 4 is enough to see the lights here.

Norilsk

Norilsk, one of Russia's northernmost cities, is another prime location for aurora hunting. With its industrial backdrop, the Northern Lights create a surreal and stunning contrast. Aim for a Kp index of 3-4.

5
UNDERSTANDING AURORA FORECAST PARAMETERS

Embarking on an aurora-hunting adventure is an exhilarating experience, especially when you know the key parameters that guide your journey. Let's delve into these important factors and ignite your excitement for the hunt.

Auroral Oval Location

What it is: The Auroral Oval Location is your trusty guide, leading you to the enchanting spectacle of auroras. It's like having a treasure map that ensures you're always on the right path in your aurora-hunting journey, giving you a sense of preparedness and excitement!

The higher the Kp, the further the northern lights stretch their dazzling glow toward the equator like they're on a world tour. At a chill Kp of 0, the aurora is content to hang out around the 66° geomagnetic latitude. But for every level the Kp cranks up, those lights get 2° closer to the equator—like moving the party two steps down the dance floor. So, when the Kp hits 4, you can expect the aurora to grove around the 58° mark.

When we say the aurora "reaches" a particular spot, we mean you're in prime position for an overhead light show. But don't worry, if the Kp is a couple of notches lower, you'll still catch the aurora shining on the horizon. It's like getting a front-row seat or a balcony view—either way, you're in for a treat!

Kp 0 - 66.5°N and above

Aurora is typically only visible within the Arctic Circle, close to the geomagnetic poles (e.g., Northern Alaska and Northern Scandinavia).

Kp 1 - 64.5°N to 66.5°N

Slightly south of the Arctic Circle (e.g., Fairbanks, Alaska;

Rovaniemi, Finland).

Kp 2 - 62.4°N to 64.5°N

Further south in high-latitude areas (e.g., Tromsø, Norway; Reykjavik, Iceland).

Kp 3 - 60.4°N to 62.4°N

Northern regions of Canada and Scandinavia (e.g., Anchorage, Alaska; Oulu, Finland).

Kp 4 - 58.3°N to 60.4°N

Extends to lower latitudes, including central Scandinavia and parts of Canada (e.g., Edmonton, Canada; Stockholm, Sweden).

Kp 5 (G1 - Minor Geomagnetic Storm) - 56.3°N to 58.3°N

Aurora is visible in southern locations such as Scotland and Northern Germany (e.g., Glasgow, Scotland; Hamburg, Germany).

Kp 6 (G2 - Moderate Geomagnetic Storm) - 54.2°N to 56.3°N

Aurora is visible in parts of the UK and Northern Europe (e.g., London, UK; Berlin, Germany).

Kp 7 (G3 - Strong Geomagnetic Storm) - 52.2°N to 54.2°N

Aurora is visible in central Europe and the northern United States (e.g., Amsterdam, Netherlands; Calgary, Canada).

Kp 8 (G4 - Severe Geomagnetic Storm) - 50.1°N to 52.2°N

Aurora is visible further south, including parts of central Europe and the northern US (e.g., Dublin, Ireland; New York, USA).

Kp 9 (G5 - Extreme Geomagnetic Storm) - 48.0°N to 50.1°N

Aurora is visible in much lower latitudes, including the southern parts of the UK, central US, and northern France (e.g., Paris, France; Seattle, USA).

Why it matters: Understanding the location helps you to figure out where to look or travel to catch the best light show in the sky.

The Kp Index

What it is: Understanding the Kp index is like having a cosmic party meter for predicting auroras. The index ranges from 0 to 9, with higher numbers indicating a greater likelihood of witnessing a vibrant aurora display. This knowledge enables you to make informed decisions about your aurora-hunting prospects.

Solar winds collide with Earth's magnetic shield and generate magnetic activity. The Kp index serves as a scoreboard, indicating the level of intensity in our magnetic shield.

Here's the breakdown:

0-2: Calm conditions with no magnetic storms.
3-4: Mild magnetic activity, indicating things are heating up.
5-6: Auroras may start appearing in the sky. It's time to look up!
7-9: Severe magnetic storms. Expect dazzling auroras and potential disruptions for satellites and power grids.

Why it matters: A higher Kp index increases the likelihood of witnessing a spectacular aurora. The higher the number, the more intense the space weather.

Solar Wind Speed

What it is: The speed at which particles from the Sun travel towards Earth determines the solar wind's impact on the formation of auroras. The solar wind can be categorized into three speeds: slow (200-400 km/s), moderate (400-600 km/s), and fast (600+ km/s). Each speed has different effects on auroras.

Why it matters: Slow solar wind produces faint auroras near the poles, while moderate solar wind creates brighter auroras in more places. Fast solar wind leads to powerful auroras that can be seen far from the poles. It's important to note that faster solar wind speeds can produce more intense auroras.

IMF Bt

What it is: The Interplanetary Magnetic Field (IMF) Bt measures the total strength of the magnetic field originating from the Sun.

Low IMF Bt (0-5 nT): Gentle beats, faint auroras.

Moderate IMF Bt (6-10 nT): Livelier music, more noticeable auroras.

High IMF Bt (11-20 nT): Strong beats, dynamic auroras.

Very High IMF Bt (21+ nT): Maximum volume, spectacular auroras.

Why it matters: IMF Bt values are a volume control for the Sun's energy. Higher values result in brighter auroras.

IMF Bz

What it is: The IMF Bz component of the solar wind's magnetic field can point either north or south.

North (Bz Positive): The solar wind bounces off Earth's magnetic shield, calm auroras.

South (Bz Negative): The solar wind connects with Earth's magnetic field, creating stunning auroras.

Why it matters: A southward Bz (negative value) interacts more effectively with Earth's magnetic field, enhancing aurora activity.

Density of Solar Wind

What it is: This measures how many solar particles are packed into a cubic centimetre of space.

Low Density (1-5 particles): Imagine a gentle drizzle. This gives you faint auroras, just a subtle glow.

Medium Density (6-10 particles): Think steady rain. Auroras get brighter, like a light show in the sky.

High Density (11-20 particles): Picture a heavy downpour. Auroras become spectacular, lighting up the night.

Very High Density (21+ particles): It's a torrential rainstorm. Get ready for a stunning aurora extravaganza!

Why it matters: Higher Density means more particles, which leads to brighter and more impressive auroras. So, the more particles, the better the light shows!

Local Weather Conditions

What it is: Remember that clear skies are crucial for observing auroras. Different types of clouds can interfere with your view in various ways:

Low-Level Clouds: These thick blankets completely block auroras from sight.

Medium-Level Clouds: This type of cloud acts like a sheer curtain, partially obscuring the light show.

High-Level Clouds: A thin veil of these clouds slightly dims the spectacle.

Why it matters: Even the most fantastic aurora display can be concealed by clouds, so clear skies are necessary!

Hemispheric Power

What it is: This measures how much energy from the Sun hits Earth's upper atmosphere.

Low (10-20 gigawatts): Gentle and subtle auroras create a soft glow in the sky.

Medium (20-50 gigawatts): Brighter and more colourful auroras that add extra sparkle.

High (50-100 gigawatts): Vibrant auroras that can be seen further from the poles, making the night sky come alive.

Very High (100+ gigawatts): Spectacular auroras that light up the entire sky, creating a breathtaking show.

Why it matters: Higher hemispheric power increases the likelihood of witnessing a spectacular aurora display. More energy results in a more impressive light show!

The Moon Phase

What it is: The Moon can affect how well you see auroras.

New Moon: Dark sky, perfect for spotting auroras.

Crescent Moon: Dim light, still great for aurora watching.

Quarter Moon: Some moonlight auroras are visible but could be more brightly.

Full Moon: Bright sky, making it harder to see auroras.

Why it matters: Less moonlight means better visibility for auroras.

% Negative IMF

What it is: It shows how much of the IMF is pointing southward.

0-20%: Slim chance of impressive auroras.

20-50%: Some nice auroras to enjoy.

50-80%: Bright and lively auroras.

80-100%: A spectacular light show!

Why it matters: Higher percentages mean better chances for vivid auroras. The more southward, the better the display!

Solar Wind Pressure

What it is: This is the force with which the solar wind hits Earth's magnetic field.

Low Pressure (< 1 nanoPascal): Faint auroras, barely visible.

Moderate Pressure (1-5 nanoPascals): Nice auroras, worth watching.

High Pressure (5-10 nanoPascals): Bright and active auroras, quite a show!

Very High Pressure (> 10 nanoPascals): Spectacular auroras, an unforgettable display.

Why it matters: Higher Pressure means better visibility and more impressive auroras.

IMF Clock Angle

What it is: Understanding the Interplanetary Magnetic Field (IMF) clock angle can be tricky. Let's break it down. Please think of the IMF clock angle as the hands of a cosmic clock in space that helps us understand how the solar wind's magnetic field aligns with Earth's. The angle indicates the relationship between Earth's magnetic field and the solar wind's magnetic field.

Perfect Alignment (Southward IMF): When the IMF is southward, it's like the clock hand pointing straight down (6 o'clock). This means the solar wind's magnetic field aligns perfectly with Earth's, allowing charged particles to flow into our atmosphere and create stunning auroras.

Not So Perfect Alignment (Northward IMF): When the IMF is northward, it's like the clock hand pointing straight up (noon). This position indicates that the solar wind's magnetic field opposes Earth's, resulting in fewer or weaker auroras.

In Between (East or West IMF): If the clock hand points to the sides (3 or 9 o'clock), the alignment could be better, but it's not entirely opposed either. Some particles can still enter the atmosphere, leading to moderate aurora activity.

Why it matters: When planning your aurora hunt, check the IMF clock angle to gauge your chances of seeing auroras:

Southward (-180°): Best chance for auroras! Get your camera and hot cocoa ready.

Northward (0°): Low chance for auroras. Maybe plan a cozy night in.

East or West (90° or 270°): Mixed chances. Keep an eye on the sky and prepare to head out if conditions change.

Putting It All Together

Kp Index of 5+: Good chance of seeing auroras.

Solar Wind Speed > 400 km/s: Increased auroral activity.

Negative Bz: Higher likelihood of intense auroras.

High Solar Wind Density: Expect brighter auroras.

Auroral Oval over your location: You're in the aurora zone.

Clear Skies: Essential for viewing, find a dark, clear spot.

Hemispheric Power > 50 gigawatts: Auroras may be visible.

Moon Phase: New and crescent moons are best; full moons are least favourable.

Substorm Strength > -1000 nT: Auroras may be visible.

% Negative IMF 80-100% for 2-3 hours: Higher chance of auroras.

Solar Wind Pressure > 5 nanoPascals: Auroras are intensifying.

IMF clock angle Southward (-180°): Favourable for auroras.

Auroras are unpredictable, so some luck is involved, making every night under the stars potentially magical. Happy Aurora Hunting!

6
AURORA APPS, WEBSITES & FACEBOOK GROUPS

Modern technology makes chasing the Northern Lights easier. The Aurora app, forecast websites, and Facebook groups can help make your dream a reality. The Aurora apps provide real-time alerts and predictions for Aurora activity, offering instant notifications when there's a good chance of seeing the lights.

Aurora Apps

1. Glendale App

Andy Stables created the Glendale Aurora App to help people worldwide see and capture stunning auroras. The app uses live data from 31 magnetometers in various countries and taps into satellite data for real-time Sun, moon, and twilight information. It also offers community-driven live sighting reports for real-time aurora sightings. Check out the Glendale Aurora App for real-time tracking of geomagnetic substorms and alerts about auroras and Interplanetary Magnetic Field conditions.

Android Setup

Step 1: Open the Download Link: Fire your Chrome app and head to aurora-alerts.uk. For the best experience, make sure Chrome is set as your default browser. Let's get this aurora party started!

Step 2: Allow Location Access: When the app asks, give it permission to use your location 'always'. This way, you'll get spot-on Aurora alerts based on where you are—no more guessing games!

Step 3: Add to Home Screen

1. Scroll to the address bar at the top right.
2. Tap the icon with three vertical dots.

3. In the popup menu, select 'Add to Home Screen'. Now you've got Aurora magic at your fingertips!

Step 4: Enable Alerts

1. Open the app and click 'Enable Manual Alerts'. Let the app make updates so you stay in the loop.
2. Finally, click 'Enable Automatic Alerts' to ensure you get real-time notifications.

Apple / iOS Setup

Step 1: Open the Download Link

Launch Safari and head over to aurora-alerts.uk. Let's get this aurora party started!

Step 2: Allow Location Access

When prompted, allow the app to use your location 'always'. This ensures precise aurora tracking so you won't miss a thing.

Step 3: Add to Home Screen

1. Turn your device to landscape mode (longways) for easier navigation.
2. Scroll to the address bar at the top right.
3. Tap the square icon with an arrow pointing out of it.
4. In the popup menu, select 'Add to Home Screen'. Now you're all set!

Key Features:

Current Geomagnetic Substorm Summary: Get the latest buzz on geomagnetic substorms, moon phase details, and when it's expected to get dark in your neck of the woods.

Current Substorm: Stay updated on the latest substorm activity.

Be the first to know when things get exciting!

Coronal Holes: Identify coronal holes and their impact. Spot the solar troublemakers!

Coronal Mass Ejections (CMEs) and ETA: Track CMEs and their estimated arrival time at Earth. Watch out for these solar spitballs!

IMF (at Earth): Check out the current interplanetary magnetic field at Earth to see what's happening in our cosmic neighbourhood.

IMF Bt/Bz (24 hours): Track the interplanetary magnetic field's behaviour for the past day. It's geeky but oh-so-cool.

IMF Clock/Theta (24 hours): See the IMF clock and theta angles for the last 24 hours—more data = more fun.

Latest Alerts: Stay in the loop with real-time alerts for solar flares and aurora sightings. Never miss a beat!

Live Aurora Reports: Check out live reports from fellow sky watchers. It's like having a global Aurora fan club.

Long-Range Forecast: Plan with long-range space weather forecasts. Be prepared for future aurora adventures!

Magnetic Field (6 hours): View magnetic field data for the past 6 hours. Keep an eye on the Earth's protective shield.
Solar Flares and ETA: Follow solar flares and when they'll hit Earth. Catch the solar fireworks.

Solar Wind: Keep tabs on current solar wind conditions. Be informed about the solar breeze.

Solar Wind (2 hours, 6 hours): Get solar wind updates for the last 2 and 6 hours. Stay current with solar conditions.

Speed & Density (24 Hours): Follow the solar Wind's speed and Density throughout the day to keep up with the cosmic breeze.

Substorm Strength (24 hours): Monitor the strength of

geomagnetic substorms over the past 24 hours to see how wild the space weather has been!

TGO Stackplot (24 Hours): Access detailed TGO stack plots for the past 24 hours. Perfect for the data-hungry.

Twilight and Moon Times: Know precisely when twilight and moonrise will occur so you can plan your viewing party.

2. SpaceWeatherLive app

SpaceWeatherLive is the go-to app for anyone eager to catch the northern lights or monitor solar activity. The app offers a popup with more details to answer your questions and help you become an aurora expert. You can easily switch between auroral and solar activity modes with just one click. Best of all, SpaceWeatherLive is entirely free! While there are ads, you can remove them by purchasing a subscription, which helps keep the app running smoothly. So, get ready to dive into the dazzling world of auroras and solar fun with SpaceWeatherLive!

Android Download Link

iOS Download Link

Key Features:

Aurora Oval: A handy aurora oval map shows where the aurora will likely be visible. Find the sweet spots for the best views.

Coronal Holes: Identify current coronal holes and their effects. Find out where the solar Wind is sneaking out.

Coronal Mass Ejections: Track CMEs and their expected arrival times at Earth. Brace yourself for these solar spitballs!

Disturbance Storm Time Index: Use the Dst index to track geomagnetic storm activity and know when the space weather is getting stormy!

Far Side: Get information on solar activity on the Sun's far side. Because even the Sun has a mysterious dark side!

Hemispheric Power: Keep tabs on the power levels in the Northern and Southern Hemispheres.

Kp-index: Check the Kp-index to see how wild the auroras are right now. Is it a light show or a snooze fest?

Magnetometers: View real-time readings from magnetometers and get the inside scoop on Earth's magnetic vibes.

Moon Phase: Know the current moon phase to plan your night sky viewing. Moonlit night or dark as a ninja's hideout?

Real-Time Solar Wind: Get the latest scoop on solar Wind, Density, and the interplanetary magnetic field (Bt, Bz). It's like having a weather forecast for space!

Solar Activity (Past Two Hours): Check out solar activity over the last two hours to see what the Sun has been doing recently.

Solar Flares: Stay updated on recent solar flares and their potential impact.

Solar Protons: Monitor proton flux and EPAM data to see solar proton activity. Proton party in space!

Sunspot Regions: Discover the latest sunspot regions on the Sun. Spot those sunspots like a pro!

3. Aurora Alerts App

Aurora Alerts is your go-to buddy for catching those magical northern lights! Whether you're cozy at home or out on an adventure, this app keeps tabs on real-time aurora activity and gives you a heads-up if there's a chance you'll see the aurora tonight. One of its most remarkable features is a short-term forecast for the next hour, complete with weather conditions and moon illumination. So, get ready to light up your night with Aurora Alerts!

Android Download Link

iOS Download Link

Key Features:

ACE Parameters: Monitor key space weather parameters from the ACE satellite.

Aurora Forecast %: Check the chances of seeing the aurora both overhead and on the horizon. Get ready for some sky magic!

Aurora Oval: See where the aurora will likely appear with our aurora oval map.

Kp Index: See the current Kp index and what it will be like in one hour. Perfect for planning your aurora viewing.

Long Forecast: Get long-range forecasts to see what's coming up in the sky. Be ahead of the game!

Magnetogram: View real-time magnetograms to understand the Sun's magnetic field activity.

Solar Wind Data from DSCOVR: Stay updated with real-time solar wind speed, Bz, Density, and Bt. It's like having a solar weather station in your pocket.

Weather and Moon Details: Know the weather and moon phase to plan the best night for aurora watching.

Weekly K Index: Track the K index over the past week to see trends and patterns.

4. My Aurora Forecasts & Alerts

My Aurora Forecast is the ultimate app for anyone enchanted by the northern lights! Its sleek, dark design is perfect for tourists and serious aurora enthusiasts. Want to know your chances of seeing the aurora borealis or get details about solar winds and high-res sun imagery? This app has got you covered.

Android Download Link

iOS Download Link

Key Features:

Aurora Map: Find the best spots to view the aurora right now with our handy map.

Cloud Coverage: Know the cloud coverage in your area tonight to plan the perfect aurora viewing.

Current KP Index: Check the current KP index to see your chances of catching the Northern Lights.

Global Aurora Strength: Explore a global map showing aurora strength based on the SWPC ovation auroral forecast.

KP Index Forecast: Get the KP index for the next hour and upcoming hours and days.

Live Aurora Webcams: Watch live aurora action from webcams around the world.

Push Notifications: Receive free push notifications when auroral activity spikes, so you never miss a moment of the action.

Solar Wind Data: Stay updated with solar wind speeds, Density, Bz, and Bt.

Sun Images: Marvel at breathtaking images of the Sun.

User-Shared Aurora Photos: Enjoy stunning aurora photos shared by other users.

Viewing Probability: See the likelihood of aurora sightings in your location.

Aurora Websites

While the Aurora apps are fantastic for quick, on-the-go updates, Aurora forecast websites are perfect for in-depth planning. Sites like SpaceWeatherLive and NOAA offer comprehensive forecasts and valuable data for the dedicated aurora chaser. For all you data enthusiasts, these websites present live data and graphs showing current aurora activity. You can get real-time updates on solar winds and magnetic fields, helping you pinpoint the best times to catch the lights. Dive deep and get ready for some serious aurora action!

Glendale - Aurora-Alerts.uk

The Glendale website provides all the features you get on the app, plus more! Check it out at aurora-alerts.uk

Coronal Holes: Identify coronal holes and their impact.

Coronal Mass Ejections (CMEs) and ETA: Track CMEs and their estimated arrival time at Earth.

Current Geomagnetic Substorm Summary: Get the latest scoop on geomagnetic substorms, moon phase details, and when it's expected to get dark at your location.

Current Substorm: Stay updated on the latest substorm activity.

IMF (at Earth): Check out the current interplanetary magnetic field at Earth.

IMF Bt/Bz (24 hours): Track the interplanetary magnetic field's behaviour for the past day.

IMF Clock/Theta (24 hours): This chart shows the IMF clock and theta angles for the last 24 hours.

Latest Alerts: Stay informed with real-time alerts for solar flares and aurora sightings.

Live Aurora Reports: Check out live reports of aurora sightings from fellow sky watchers.

Long-Range Forecast: Plan ahead with long-range space weather forecasts.

Magnetic Field (6 hours): View the magnetic field data for the past 6 hours.

Solar Flares and ETA: Follow solar flares and when they'll hit Earth.

Solar Wind: Keep tabs on current solar wind conditions.

Solar Wind (2 hours, 6 hours): Get solar wind updates for the last 2 and 6 hours.

Speed & Density (24 hours): Follow solar wind speed and Density throughout the day.

Substorm Strength (24 hours): Monitor the strength of geomagnetic substorms over the past 24 hours.

TGO Stackplot (24 hours): Access detailed TGO stack plots for the past 24 hours.

Twilight and Moon Times: Know precisely when twilight and moonrise will occur so you can plan your viewing.

Space weather live - SpaceWeatherLive.com

Space Weather Live website offers all the features and additional functionality available on the app.

SpaceWeatherLive.com

Key Features:

3-Day Forecast: Plan ahead with a 3-day space weather forecast.

Aurora Oval: Discover where the aurora will likely be visible with our aurora oval map.

Coronal Holes: Identify current coronal holes and their effects.
Coronal Mass Ejections: Track CMEs and their expected arrival times at Earth.

Disturbance Storm Time Index: Keep track of geomagnetic storm activity with the Dst index.

Far Side: Get information on solar activity happening on the far side of the Sun.

Hemispheric Power: Monitor the power levels in both the Northern and Southern Hemispheres.

Kp-index: Check the Kp-index to see how active the auroras are right now.

Latest News Updates: Stay in the loop with updates on upcoming CMEs and solar flares.

Magnetometers: View real-time readings from magnetometers.

Moon Phase: Know the current moon phase to plan your perfect night sky viewing.

NOAA SWPC Alerts, Watches, and Warnings: Receive alerts, watches, and warnings from NOAA SWPC.

Radio Blackout: Be informed about potential radio blackouts.

Real-Time Solar Wind: Get up-to-the-minute data on solar wind speed, Density, and the interplanetary magnetic field (Bt, Bz).

Solar Activity (Past Two Hours): Check out solar activity over the last two hours.

Solar Activity Reports: Access detailed reports on solar activity.

Solar Cycle Progression: Track the progression of the solar cycle.

Solar Flares: Stay updated on recent solar flares and their potential impact.

Solar Protons: Monitor proton flux and EPAM data to see solar proton activity.

Sunspot Regions: Discover the latest sunspot regions on the Sun.

Webcams: Watch live aurora action from webcams around the world.

WSA-Enlil Solar Wind Prediction: Get predictions on solar Wind from the WSA-Enlil model.

NOAA Aurora Page

The Space Weather Prediction Center (SWPC) is a part of the National Oceanic and Atmospheric Administration. It maintains a dedicated Aurora Page with numerous forecasts utilized by websites worldwide.

swpc.noaa.gov

Key Features:

24-Hour Observed Space Weather Conditions: Stay in the loop with a full day's space weather updates.

27-Day Forecast: Plan with nearly a month's space weather predictions.

3-Day Forecast: A sneak peek at the next three days of space weather.

Aurora - 30-Minute Forecast: Get a short-term forecast for Aurora activity.

Aurora Oval: See where auroras are most likely to appear.

Coronal Mass Ejections: Big solar eruptions that can light up the skies!

Estimated K Index: Check out the estimated K index to gauge geomagnetic activity.

Estimated Planetary K Index (3 hours data): Get a quick update on global geomagnetic activity.

Geospace Geomagnetic Activity Plot: Visualize geomagnetic activity in real-time.

GOES Proton Flux: Monitor solar proton levels.

GOES X-Ray Flux: Track solar X-ray activity.

Latest Observed Space Weather Conditions: Get the freshest space weather reports.

Predicted Space Weather Conditions: See what's coming up in the space weather forecast.

Predicted Sunspot Number and Radio Flux: Find out about upcoming sunspots and radioactivity.

Solar Cycle Progression: Follow the long-term trends in solar activity.

WSA-Enlil Solar Wind Prediction: See predictions for solar wind conditions.

Facebook Groups

One of the most excellent parts of chasing the Northern Lights is the community of fellow aurora enthusiasts. These vibrant spaces let you connect, share experiences, and get tips from seasoned aurora hunters. Just remember to read the group rules and featured posts before diving in. Group members often post real-time reports of aurora sightings, complete with photos and location details. These reports are super helpful for finding the best viewing spots and knowing when to head out. Plus, those gorgeous photos will crank up your excitement to sky-high levels!

The community has valuable tips and tricks, from the best camera settings to the coziest viewing spots. Whether you're a seasoned chaser or a newbie, you'll find plenty of advice to help make your Aurora adventure successful. There's something magical about sharing your aurora experiences with others who get the thrill. Swap stories, celebrate sightings, and share photos in these groups. It turns the solitary act of sky-watching into a shared adventure. Here are some of the valuable groups:

Northern Lights/ Aurora Borealis - All Countries

Northern Lights

facebook.com/groups/auroranorthernlights

Northern Lights Alert

facebook.com/groups/northernlightsalert

Northern lights (nolights)

facebook.com/groups/nolights

Aurora Borealis Notifications Group

facebook.com/groups/auroraborealisnotificationsgroup

Northern Lights Watch

facebook.com/groups/212075792194227

Aurora Borealis

facebook.com/groups/worldaurora

Alaska

Northern Lights Alaska

facebook.com/groups/northernlightsalaska/

Northern Lights Search Alaska

facebook.com/groups/1494563237521209/

Juneau, Alaska Aurora Borealis

facebook.com/groups/352852175934262/

Canada

Northern Lights Canada

facebook.com/groups/northernlightsincanada/

Saskatchewan Aurora Hunters

facebook.com/groups/skaurorahunters/

Alberta Aurora Chasers

facebook.com/groups/AlbertaAuroraChasers/

Calgary Northern Lights Chaser And Area

facebook.com/groups/173397844408429/

Alberta Northern Lights Chasing

facebook.com/groups/729756505263413/

Ontario Aurora Chasers

facebook.com/groups/ontarioaurorachasers/

USA

Northern Lights USA

facebook.com/groups/northernlightsusa

Aurora Borealis Washington State

facebook.com/groups/AuroraBorealisWA/

Aurora Borealis Montana

facebook.com/groups/auroraborealismontana/

North Dakota Northern Lights Network

facebook.com/groups/516072035234847/

Twin Cities Aurora Chasers

facebook.com/groups/3733102993580854/

Northern Lights of Wisconsin

facebook.com/groups/858173715166253/

Michigan Aurora Chasers

facebook.com/groups/michiganaurorachasers/

Vermont Aurora Borealis Sightings

facebook.com/groups/179940748405645/

Greenland

Northern Lights Greenland

facebook.com/groups/northernlightsgreenland

Iceland

Northern Lights Iceland

facebook.com/groups/northernlightsiceland/

Aurora Hunters Iceland

facebook.com/groups/607880159324957/

Aurora Hunters UK & Iceland

facebook.com/groups/492548942452002/

Aurora alerts - Iceland

facebook.com/groups/auroraalerts/

Northern lights Iceland

facebook.com/groups/565170257602035/

Aurora Reykjavik, Northern Lights Hunters

facebook.com/groups/NorthernLightsHunters/

Faroe Islands

Northern Lights Faroe Islands

facebook.com/groups/northernlightsfaroeislands

Ireland

Northern Lights Ireland

facebook.com/groups/northernlightsireland

Aurora Alerts & Updates Ireland

facebook.com/groups/397535722464291

UK

Northern Lights UK

facebook.com/groups/northernlightsuk/

UK Aurora Updates

facebook.com/groups/533466928773909/

Northern Lights Hunters North East England

facebook.com/groups/1644954579271783/

Scotland Northern Lights

facebook.com/groups/447678496089112/

Scotland's Aurora Watch Help & Advice

facebook.com/groups/1386947995250510/

Aurora-Hunters UK

facebook.com/groups/aurora.hunters.uk/

Norway

Northern Lights Tromsø

facebook.com/groups/northernlightstromso

Aurora Norway

facebook.com/groups/auroranorway/

Tromsø Northern Lights Q&A

facebook.com/groups/tromsoalert/

Aurora Borealis Observatory - Visit Senja

facebook.com/groups/1792618197423232/

Svalbard

Northern Lights Svalbard

facebook.com/groups/northernlightssvalbard

Nordlys i Longyearbyen.... Aurora Boreal

facebook.com/groups/1662320487357628/

Svalbard Aurora Chasers

facebook.com/groups/759412309213935/

Sweden

Northern Lights Sweden

facebook.com/groups/northernlightssweden

Aurora Info, Luleå, Sweden

facebook.com/groups/aurora.in.lulea/

Umeå Aurora Hunters (Observation & Photography)

facebook.com/groups/umeaaurorahunters/

Finland

Northern Lights Finland

facebook.com/groups/1940767603022698

Aurora alerts in Finland

facebook.com/groups/AurorasInFinland/

Oulu Aurora Spotters

facebook.com/groups/Ouluauroraspotters/

Lapland - Rovaniemi Travel Forum

facebook.com/groups/laplandrovaniemitravelforum/

Northern Lights of Finland

facebook.com/groups/NorthernLightsofFinland/

Aurora Borealis Saariselkä-Inari Lapland

facebook.com/groups/821773168946103/

Russia

Northern Lights Russia

facebook.com/groups/northernlightsrussia

7
MASTERING THE SKIES WITH CLOUD COVER FORECASTS

Cloud cover is like the bouncer at the Northern Lights party—you need to know when to sneak past and when to move along. Understanding how these skyward gatekeepers can enhance or hinder your Aurora adventure is crucial. Let's break down their impact on your viewing experience!

Low Clouds: The Party Crashers

These clouds are the ultimate uninvited guests. Hanging below 2 kilometres (about 1.2 miles), they're like thick, cottony blankets draping over the sky and blocking everything. Think stratus clouds. If you see these guys, your chances of spotting the elusive Aurora are as slim as finding a needle in a haystack. If the sky is swarming with low clouds, grab a hot chocolate and call it a night.

Medium Clouds: The Moody Middle

Medium clouds, floating between 2 and 6 kilometres (about 1.2 to 3.7 miles), are like the moody teens of the cloud world—sometimes cooperative, sometimes not. Altostratus and altocumulus clouds fall into this category. They can still block your view but often have gaps, giving you occasional peeks of the Northern Lights. It's like waiting for a shy performer to finally enter the spotlight.

High Clouds: The Spectator-Friendly Seats

High clouds are your VIP tickets to the Aurora show. Hanging above 6 kilometres (about 3.7 miles), these wispy cirrus and cirrostratus clouds are like delicate veils that add drama to a stage performance. They're thin enough that they won't block your view and can even reflect the magical green and pink hues of the Aurora, making your photos look like they belong on a postcard.

Maximize your chances of witnessing Aurora by closely monitoring cloud cover predictions. Clear skies are your golden ticket but remember, the Aurora is a diva and might appear unexpectedly. If you're serious about capturing this natural wonder, be ready to hop to a new location where the sky is clearer. This level of preparedness will make you feel informed and ready for your Aurora adventure.

1. Ventusky

ventusky.com

Ready to become a weather wizard? "Ventusky" is your magic portal, brought to you by the clever folks at the Czech meteorological firm InMeteo. This web app is like a treasure map for cloud cover, offering interactive visuals that let you dive into various weather stats, including Total Cloud Cover, Fog, Low Clouds, Middle Clouds, and High Clouds. Its user-friendly features will make you feel empowered and in control of your Aurora viewing plans.

At the bottom of the page, you'll find a timeline that puts you in control of the data. Select the forecast period for your Aurora hunting escapade and review the cloud cover for your chosen location. The best part? The time adjusts to your computer's time zone, making it easy to plan your adventure.

2. Yr.no

yr.no/en

Meet Yr, your go-to weather buddy from the Norwegian Meteorological Institute (met.no) and the Norwegian Broadcasting Corporation (NRK). These two Norwegian powerhouses have been teaming up since 1923 to bring top-notch weather forecasts to Norway and beyond. Whether you're planning a picnic or chasing the Northern Lights, Yr's got your back with accurate weather updates.

Their detailed stats are like a weather nerd's dream! You get hourly updates on Temperature, Dew Point, Wind Speed, Total Cloud Cover percentage, Fog, Low Cloud percentage, Middle Cloud percentage, and High Cloud percentage for any location. It's like having a personal weather station at your fingertips, ready to spill the tea on every cloud in the sky!

3. AccuWeather

accuweather.com

AccuWeather is your ultimate weather sidekick! Packed with global real-time and historical data, stellar forecast models, and thorough validation results, it's one of the most accurate weather companies.

Want to know the hourly cloud cover at your destination? Just download the AccuWeather app or visit their website. It's like having a weather wizard in your pocket, ready to help you chase the perfect skies!

4. The Weather Channel

weather.com

Check out the hourly weather and cloud cover percentages on The Weather Channel website and app.

5a. Cananda Clouds Forecast For Astronomical Purposes

weather.gc.ca/astro/clds_vis_e.html

5b. Graphical Forecasts for Alaska & USA - Sky Cover %

digital.weather.gov

5c. UK Cloud Cover Map

metoffice.gov.uk/weather/maps-and-charts/cloud-cover-map

5d. Greenland Cloud Cover Forecast

mountain-forecast.com/maps/Greenland/cloud/6

5e. Icelandic Meteorological office

https://en.vedur.is/weather/forecasts/cloudcover

5f. Norway, Sweden & Finland Cloud Cover

snow-forecast.com/maps/static/scand/6/cloud

5g. Clouds in Finland

foreca.fi/Finland/inari/map/visirsat

5h. Cloud forecasts in Scandinavia

windy.com/-Clouds-clouds?clouds,64.435,29.575,4

5i Russian Weather Forecast

meteoinfo.ru/en/forecasts-eng

5j. Faroe Islands Cloud Cover

weather-forecast.com/maps/Faroe-Islands?hr=3&over=arrows&symbols=none&type=cloud

5k. Ireland Cloud Cover

met.ie/latest-reports/satellites/europe-infrared

Now that you're a cloud cover expert, it's time to put those forecasts to good use and become an Aurora hunting pro! Use these tools to plan your Aurora viewing trips and prepare for exciting adventures.

8
LIGHTS, CAMERA, ACTION!

Get ready for an exhilarating journey into the world of Aurora photography! Whether using a camera or a smartphone, these tips and tricks will help you snap those dazzling Northern Lights like a pro.

Face North and Find the Perfect Spot

First things first—look north! You'll want to find a spot with minimal light pollution, a clear horizon view, and maybe even a reflective surface like a pond for that extra wow factor. Check it out during the day to ensure it's safe for your nighttime adventure. The reflection can create a stunning mirror effect when the Aurora dances across the sky, making those colours pop even more!

Bundle Up for the Winter Wonderland

The Aurora loves to appear in winter, so it's time to bundle up! Warm boots, a cozy hat, and gloves that let you handle your camera without freezing your fingers are a must. Keep in mind that while the Aurora may look like a swirling, monochrome ghost to your naked eye, your camera will capture every vibrant hue in all its glory.

Stay Safe on the Road

Are you planning to drive at night? Keep your eyes peeled for wildlife and other road surprises. Stick to a safe speed, and don't forget to let someone know where you're headed. It's dark out there, and safety comes first! Bringing a friend or two is a great idea—not just for company but also for that extra layer of safety.

How to dress for this frosty adventure?

Are you ready to brave the cold and catch the Northern Lights? Let's make sure you're dressed for the occasion!

Layer Like a Pro

First things first—layer up! Start with a thermal base layer, your cozy second skin that not only keeps the chill at bay but also provides a comforting shield against the cold. Next, add a warm mid-layer like a fleece or wool sweater, wrapping yourself in a cocoon of warmth. Finally, top it all off with a windproof and waterproof outer layer, ensuring you're protected from the elements. This triple-layer combo keeps you warm, dry, and secure while you're out there marvelling at the Aurora.

Keep Those Toes Toasty

Don't let cold toes ruin your Northern Lights experience! Ensure you're wearing thick, insulated socks and most importantly, sturdy, waterproof boots. Your feet will thank you when you're standing on the snowy ground, staring at the sky in awe.

Head and Hands: The Essentials

Don't forget your head and hands! A snug hat will keep your noggin warm, and gloves are a must-have. Choose gloves that let you handle your camera or smartphone without turning your fingers into popsicles. For extra cold conditions, mittens are even better—shared warmth between fingers is a game-changer for extended photography sessions.

Bonus Warmth: Hand Warmers

Here's a handy trick for extra warmth—hand warmers! These little heat packs can be slipped into your pockets, gloves, or boots for a boost of warmth when needed. It's like carrying a bit of sunshine with you, ensuring you stay comfortable during your Northern Lights adventure!

So, bundle up in layers, keep those toes toasty, and ensure your head and hands are snug. With these tips, you'll be all set to enjoy the Northern Lights without turning into an ice sculpture! Get ready to brave the cold and catch the Northern Lights with confidence and excitement!

Capturing the Aurora with Your Camera: A Fun and Easy Guide

Have you got a DSLR or mirrorless camera? Awesome! You don't need the fanciest gear—just something that can handle long exposure shots. Pick a landscape that looks cool even without the Aurora when setting up your shot. Trust me, when those lights start dancing, your photo will go from "nice" to "absolutely stunning" in no time!

Master Your Settings

Before you head out, get cozy with your camera settings. Practice using your camera in the dark so you won't fumble when the Aurora puts on its show. The more familiar you are with your gear, the better your shots will be.

Steady as She Goes: Tripod Time

A sturdy tripod is your best friend for this adventure. It doesn't have to be top-of-the-line, but sturdier ones handle windy conditions better. If yours is a bit shaky, hang something heavy from the hook under the central column—your backpack, a water bottle, or even a rock can do the trick.

Batteries and Memory Cards: Don't Get Caught Short!

Cold weather drains batteries fast, so make sure your camera is fully charged and pack extra batteries. You'll also want a high-capacity memory card or a few spares to store all your RAW shots of the Aurora.

Lens Love: Go Wide and Fast

For the best results, opt for a fast, wide-angle lens—something with an f/2.8 aperture or lower is perfect. You generally don't want to shoot the Aurora with a focal length longer than 35mm, but a 14mm lens can capture a lot of sky. Suppose you're in the mood for something different. In that case, a fisheye lens can be super fun, especially when the Aurora activity is off the charts.

Remote Control Magic

An intervalometer is a must-have for continuous shots and time-lapse videos; it lets you step back and enjoy the show! A remote shutter release or wireless remote minimizes camera vibrations from pressing the shutter button, keeping your shots crisp. Many photographers love continuous shooting mode—it lets you sit back, relax, and watch the Aurora. At the same time, your camera does all the work. The self-timer mode (set to 2 seconds) also avoids camera shake if you don't have a remote.

Infinity Focus: Get It Just Right

Focusing in the dark can be tricky since auto-focus won't help much. Here's how to nail it:

Focus on a Star: Find a star and make it as sharp as possible. If that's not an option, wind your focus to infinity (look for the sideways figure 8 symbol).

Manual Focus Without Infinity: If your lens doesn't have an infinity setting, switch to manual focus, open the aperture wide, and turn on the live view. Point your camera at the sky, find a bright star, centre it, and zoom in on the live view using your camera controls. Adjust the focus until the star is sharp, then tape down the focus and zoom ring (if you have one) to keep it in place.

Manual Mode: Take Control

Switching to manual mode gives you complete control over your camera settings—aperture, shutter speed, white balance, exposure, and ISO. This is perfect for getting the exact exposure and effect you want, letting you adapt to different lighting conditions and capture the perfect shot.

Shutter Speed: Capture the Movement

Shutter speed determines how long your camera's sensor is exposed to Light. A fast shutter speed freezes the moment, while a slow one lets in more Light and captures movement.

For bright, active Auroras: Try 3-10 seconds.
For slow-moving Auroras: Go for 12-20 seconds.
For faint Auroras: Extend to 20-25 seconds.

Since the Aurora constantly moves, a faster shutter speed can help capture more detail. Don't be afraid to experiment with your settings!

Shooting RAW: Keep It Real

Shooting in RAW mode captures all the data from your camera's sensor without compression. This gives you the highest-quality image with the most detail and dynamic range. RAW files are perfect for post-processing, allowing you to adjust exposure, white balance, and other settings without losing image quality.

ISO: Light Sensitivity Superpower

ISO is your camera's sensitivity to Light. Lower ISO numbers (like 100) are great for bright conditions, while higher numbers (like 3200) ramp up sensitivity for low Light.

For faint Auroras: Crank it up to 6400 or more.
For bright and clear Auroras, Dial it down to 400-800.
Adjust the ISO to balance light sensitivity and image noise perfectly.

White Balance: Get the Colours Right

White balance adjusts your photos' colour temperature to ensure the colours look natural.

Under a full moon: Go for a warmer temperature (5700-5900K).

Without moonlight: Aim for a cooler setting (4200-4500K).

Ultimately, it's all about what looks best to you, so don't be afraid to tweak the white balance to match your taste.

Aperture (f-stop): Let in the Light

The aperture controls how wide your lens opens when taking a photo. A wider aperture (lower f-stop number) lets in more Light, which is crucial for low-light conditions.

For Aurora photography: Aim for an aperture of f/1.8 to f/2.8. If your lens can't go that wide, try f/4. Experiment and see what works best for your shots.

The 500 Rule: Say Goodbye to Star Trails

The 500 Rule is a handy formula for determining the longest shutter speed before stars look like streaks of Light instead of twinkling dots.

The formula: 500 is divided by your lens's focal length.

For example, if you're using a 20mm lens, the math is simple: 500 ÷ 20 = 25 seconds. You can set your shutter speed to 25 seconds before those stars blur.

Remember to factor in the crop factor using a cropped sensor camera. For instance, with a 20mm lens on a camera with a 1.5x crop factor would be 500 ÷ (20 × 1.5) = 16.7 seconds. So, you can expose for about 17 seconds without getting those pesky star trails. With these tips and tricks, you're all set to capture the stunning beauty of the Northern Lights. Get out there, experiment with your settings, and enjoy the magic!

Snapping the Northern Lights with Your Smartphone

Guess what? You don't need a high-end camera to capture the stunning Aurora! Your trusty smartphone is up to the task. With night mode and extended exposure settings, you can snap vibrant photos of the Northern Lights like a pro. No fancy gear is needed—just you, your phone, and a little magic!

iPhone

Night photography can be tricky, but your iPhone makes it a breeze to capture stunning shots of the Northern Lights, even if you're a beginner. Here's how to make the most of your iPhone's capabilities:

Enable Night Mode: Night Mode kicks in automatically in low-light conditions. Look for the Night Mode icon (a moon) in the top left corner of your iPhone. This mode lets the camera sensor stay open longer, capturing more light and detail through long exposure. To get the best results, maximize the exposure time. Night Mode is available on every iPhone since the iPhone 11, and the latest models offer even better photo quality.

Mount Your iPhone on a Tripod: A stable tripod is your best bet for sharp photos, as even a tiny movement can cause blur. If you don't have a tripod, find a steady surface to rest your iPhone. Bonus tip: Use your Apple Watch to control the camera remotely so you don't accidentally shake your phone.

Use the 1x Lens: The 1x wide-angle lens is your best friend for low-light photography. It provides the brightest and clearest shots, making the Aurora look its best.

Manually Focus: Tap the screen to focus on your subject, whether it's an interesting object in the foreground or a selfie under the Northern Lights. If you capture the sky, your iPhone will automatically focus to infinity, so you're all set!

Adjust Shutter Speed: After taking a test shot, check if the Northern Lights are visible. If they're faint, increase the shutter speed by swiping up in the Camera app and tapping the Night Mode icon. A tripod will help you take longer exposures, bringing out more light and detail.

Shoot in RAW: For maximum control over your photos, shoot in RAW. Please turn it on in Settings > Camera > Formats > Apple ProRAW. This gives you better flexibility in post-processing with apps like Adobe Lightroom Mobile.

Android

Are you ready to snap jaw-dropping shots of the Northern Lights with your Android? Let's dive into the step-by-step fun!

Tripod and Phone Holder: Keep It Steady

First, pack a light, compact tripod that fits snugly in your luggage. Make sure you've got a phone holder that tightens with a screw. If you're using a spring-loaded holder, secure it with an elastic band. Trust me, you don't want your phone taking a tumble just as you're about to capture the perfect shot!

Focus for Clarity: Sharpen That Image

Tap your screen to focus on a point, like a star or something in the distance. This helps ensure your image is sharp and crystal clear. There's nothing worse than setting everything up perfectly, only to end up with a blurry photo—nightmare avoided!

Use Your Primary Lens: Go for Quality

For the best-quality photos, stick with your primary lens. Please avoid using a super-wide lens, as it's not the best in low-light conditions. Your primary lens is your secret weapon for capturing the Aurora's glory.

Shoot in RAW: Unlock Creative Freedom

Enable RAW shooting mode to give yourself more flexibility when editing your photos later. Because who doesn't love a bit of creative freedom? RAW files capture all the details to tweak your shots to perfection.

Enable Night Mode: Get the Settings Right

Turn on night mode in your Android camera app. Set your ISO to 1600 or higher for better low-light performance, and adjust the white balance to around 3200K to make your image look as natural as possible—just like a postcard!

Adjust Shutter Speed: Experiment for the Best Shot
Switch your camera to 'Professional' or 'Manual' Mode. Toggle the 'MF' icon to focus the camera and turn off the flash. Set the shutter speed for bright, colourful lights to 1-5 seconds. For dimmer lights, extend it to 20-30 seconds. It's like a mini-science experiment, and the results are worth it!

Rotate Your Device: Capture the Whole Scene

Turn your device horizontally to capture a wider scene. Why settle for less when you can have more? A landscape shot will make your Aurora photos look epic.

Samsung Galaxy Expert RAW

Say hello to Expert RAW, the camera app that transforms your Samsung Galaxy into a professional photo studio! Perfect for capturing high-quality HDR photos, this app lets you tweak your shots to perfection later. If you've got a Galaxy S20 or a newer model, head to the Galaxy Store and download it now.

You get JPEG and RAW (Linear DNG 16-bit) files when you shoot with Expert RAW. Unlike JPEGs, RAW files keep all the juicy, uncompressed image data, giving you tons of editing flexibility. It's like the difference between a microwaved meal and a home-cooked feast!

Expert RAW controls you with settings like ISO, shutter speed, white balance, exposure, and focus. It's like having a pro camera right in your pocket! Plus, with the 'Special photo options' feature, you can capture stunning astrophotography and cool multiple exposures.

How to Use Expert RAW:

1. Open the Expert RAW app.
2. Tap the settings icon.
3. Turn on "Special photo options."
4. Choose Astrophotography mode and adjust the focus, white balance, and exposure time to capture the night sky in all its glory.

Recommended Settings:

Shutter Speed: Start with 10 seconds and adjust based on how wild the Aurora is dancing.
ISO: Kick off at 800 and tweak it as needed.

White Balance: Set it to 3900K for that perfect glow.

Focus: Keep it centred for sharp images.

Everything else: Leave it on auto—sometimes, letting your phone do the work is okay.

Remember to always shoot in RAW to keep all that precious image data intact. Expert RAW gives you all the tools you need to capture stunning photos.

Editing Aurora Photos: Make the Magic Happen!

Ready to turn those stunning Aurora photos into something truly magical? Grab your iPhone or Android and dive into those editing tools! But if you want to take it up a notch, Lightroom's advanced features are where the fun begins. Let's explore some playful tricks you can use to transform your snaps into masterpieces!

White Balance Wizardry

Adjusting the white balance is like being Goldilocks—finding that "just right" setting is critical! Whether shooting under a full moon or in total darkness, the perfect white balance is all about what feels right to you. Play around until you find your sweet spot!

Exposure Magic

Do you need to brighten up the scene or add some moody darkness? The exposure tool has you covered. It's like having a dimmer switch for your entire photo, bringing out those hidden details in the shadows and highlights. Use it to make your Aurora pop!

Dehaze Delight

Have you ever taken a photo that looks a bit foggy or misty? The dehaze tool is like giving your photo a pair of glasses—everything suddenly becomes clear and vibrant. Perfect for enhancing those dreamy landscapes!

Highlights & Shadows: The Dynamic Duo

Balance is everything! Use the highlights and shadows sliders to control your photo's brightest and darkest parts. Whether bringing back details from an overexposed sky or revealing textures in the darker areas, these tools help you create a well-rounded and detailed image.

Contrast Craze

Want to add some drama or keep it soft and dreamy? The contrast slider lets you control the difference between light and dark areas.

Crank it up for depth and drama, or dial it down for a gentler look—it's all in your hands!

Blacks & Whites: The Fine-Tuners

These sliders are your secret weapons for adding depth and richness to your photos. Fine-tune the darkest and brightest parts to balance contrast and detail, making your image stand out.

Vibrance & Saturation: Colour Party

Let's talk colours! Saturation pumps up all the colours in your photo. At the same time, vibrance focuses on the more muted tones, leaving skin tones intact. These tools make your Aurora photos lively and vivid without going overboard.

Clarity & Texture: Detail Enhancers

Want to make your landscape shots sharp and crisp? Clarity boosts mid-tone contrast for that sharper look, while texture enhances fine details without messing with overall contrast. These sliders give your photos that extra oomph!

Colour Tweaks: Customize Your Palette

For true-colour aficionados, the HSL (Hue, Saturation, Luminance) panel is your playground. Tweak individual colours, adjust their brightness, or change their tone entirely. It's your colour palette—go ahead, get creative!

So, are you ready to dive into the editing magic and make your Aurora photos shine? With these fun tools at your fingertips, you'll create masterpieces in no time!

9
THE EPIC GEOMAGNETIC STORM OF MAY 2024

In May 2024, the world was graced with a celestial spectacle of unparalleled rarity—a geomagnetic storm of epic proportions that left everyone gazing in wonder. This mega G5 storm, the largest in over 20 years, illuminated the skies from May 10-11 with a breathtaking display of Aurora Australis and Aurora Borealis. Even regions that typically miss out on the aurora magic were given a front-row seat to this cosmic light show. And who do we have to thank? A colossal sunspot cluster, AR3664, is a staggering 15-16 times the size of Earth! It hosted a solar eruption party, directing its fiery fury towards our planet. This extraordinary event marked the most intense geomagnetic storm since the Halloween solar storms of 2003. It was truly a once-in-a-lifetime spectacle!

Our Sun, like many stars, goes through mood swings—periods of high and low activity. We're in the Solar Maximum Cycle, the Sun's time to shine with the most solar activity in its 11 year cycle. On May 8, 2024, a supercharged solar hotspot, AR3664, decided to show off by launching a series of Coronal Mass Ejections (CMEs)—massive bursts of solar wind and magnetic fields. These were triggered by a mighty X-Class flare (X5.8) and a few M-class flares aimed right at Earth. As these CMEs, the main ingredient in solar storms zoomed through space, they teamed up into a giant plasma party that crashed into Earth on May 10-11. This plasma, packed with charged particles, was just what we needed to light up the sky with some truly epic auroras.

The interplanetary magnetic field hit a whopping 73 nT (nanotesla). In contrast, Earth's magnetic field (Bz) took a nosedive to -50 nT, flooded with charged particles. Add in a super dense solar wind, blasting at 750–800 km/s, and we had ourselves a G5-class geomagnetic storm (Kp = 9), a top-tier space weather event. The result? The Aurora Oval, the prime region for aurora sightings, spread out like never before, lighting up the skies in places you'd never expect. People in Mexico, the Bahamas, western Africa, New Zealand, Australia, Chile, and Argentina were treated to incredible aurora displays. It was like the universe decided to throw a massive, worldwide light show!

On May 14, 2024, the most active solar region spun away from Earth, unleashing an X8.7 flare. If it had been aimed at us, we might have witnessed another record-breaking storm, keeping us all on our toes. But for now, we can bask in the glow of the unforgettable light show of May 2024 and eagerly await the next celestial spectacle, filled with anticipation and excitement. The universe never fails to surprise us, and we can't wait to see what it has in store next!

The 1859 Carrington Event: A Solar Storm on Steroids

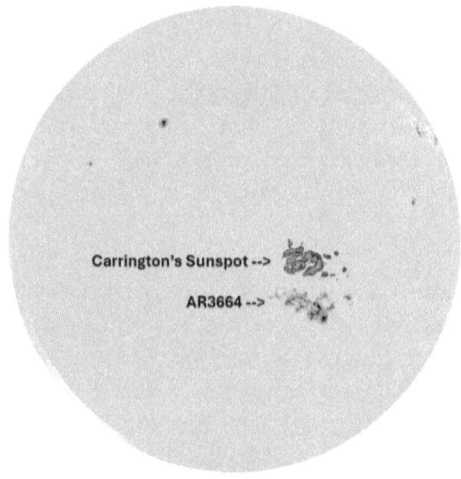

The 1859 Carrington Event was an extraordinary and unexpected solar storm that showcased nature's immense power. It began in late August 1859 when astronomers spotted giant sunspots on the Sun. On September 1, a massive solar flare erupted, a sight that was visible even in daylight, sending a wave of solar particles that reached Earth in just 17.6 hours. The impact was stunning: auroras lit up the skies as far south as the Caribbean, with people in places like Cuba, Jamaica, and Hawaii witnessing dazzling colours. In the northeastern United States, the auroras were so bright that people could read newspapers by their light at night.

However, the event also caused significant disruption, particularly to telegraph systems that malfunctioned, sparked, and even operated without connected batteries. The Carrington Event blended breathtaking beauty and chaotic disruption, making it a memorable and significant historical event.

10
THE PATIENCE AND THRILL OF AURORA HUNTING

Imagine you're out under a sky full of stars, bundled up in cozy layers with a steaming cup of hot cocoa in hand. Your camera's ready, your heart's racing with excitement, and the adventure has begun. You're hunting for the Northern Lights, the ultimate cosmic light show. But here's the catch: it's a waiting game, and patience is the key to winning. Let's dive into why this waiting makes the experience even more electrifying!

The Waiting Game: Your Ticket to the Sky's Best Show

Picture yourself standing in the crisp night air, watching the sky like a hawk. You might be out there for hours, maybe even the whole night. Auroras are like the universe's surprise party—they show up when they want to. But that's part of the thrill! The longer you wait, the more exciting it gets. Will the lights make an appearance tonight? The suspense is real, and it's all part of the fun.

Anticipation: The Spark That Keeps You Going

Every little change in the sky sends a jolt of excitement through you. Was that a glimmer of green on the horizon? Or just a shooting star? The suspense builds with each passing moment, and when the lights finally appear, it's like unwrapping the best present ever. The wait only makes the reward that much sweeter.

Relax and Soak in the Beauty

While you're waiting, there's no rush—take a deep breath and enjoy the serenity of the night. The sky is a masterpiece, dotted with stars, constellations, and maybe even a glimpse of the Milky Way. It's a perfect chance to relax, reflect, and escape from the hustle and bustle of everyday life. In those quiet moments, you'll find peace and wonder in gazing at the stars.

Perseverance: The True Test of an Aurora Hunter

Aurora hunting isn't for the faint of heart. Sometimes, you'll head out night after night with no luck. But the true aurora hunters know that persistence is vital. Every outing gets you one step closer to that magical moment. And when it finally happens, it feels like you've won a cosmic lottery—a reward worth the wait.

The Aurora Hunting Crew: Friends, Fun, and Shared Stories

One of the best parts of aurora hunting is the camaraderie that comes with it. Whether you're with friends, family, or fellow enthusiasts you meet along the way, there's something special about sharing the experience. Swapping stories, sharing tips, and enduring the wait together turns the whole adventure into a social event. Who knew waiting could be so much fun?

The Grand Finale: A Sky Full of Magic

And then, when you least expect it, the sky lights up with a breathtaking display of colours. The Northern Lights dance across the sky, shimmering in green, pink, and purple shades. It's a moment of pure awe, made even more incredible by the anticipation and effort it took to witness.

A Lesson in Nature's Timing

Aurora hunting is a reminder that nature doesn't run on our schedule—and that's okay. The best things in life often come to those who wait, and the Northern Lights are a shining example. Patience helps you connect with the natural world on a deeper level, making the experience all the more meaningful.

So next time you find yourself under a starry sky, waiting for the auroras to enter, remember: the wait is part of the adventure. And when the lights finally appear, you'll know it was all worth it.

What makes Aurora Hunting very addictive?

Imagine chasing after the sky's most enchanting light show—once you've tasted the thrill of aurora hunting, there's no going back. Let's dive into why this magical pursuit is simply irresistible!

The Thrill of the Chase

Think of yourself as a cosmic detective searching for the night sky's most mesmerizing mystery. Tracking down auroras is like piecing together an epic puzzle. When you finally catch a glimpse, a triumphant moment leaves you craving more. It's the ultimate sky chase, and you're in the driver's seat.

Nature's Light Show

Who needs Netflix when you've got the auroras? They swirl, twirl, and shimmer across the sky, putting on a show that outshines anything Hollywood can dream up. And the best part? No pesky ads interrupting the action—just pure, uninterrupted celestial magic.

The Perfect Excuse to Travel

Aurora hunting takes you to some of the most stunning corners of the planet. Whether you're exploring the icy wilds of Alaska or the cozy fjords of Norway, you're on a real-life adventure. And when you tell people you're off to hunt the Northern Lights, you instantly sound like the coolest, most laid-back explorer around.

Bonding with Fellow Hunters

Aurora hunting isn't just a solo mission—it's a team sport. Sharing tips, celebrating sightings, and swapping stories with fellow hunters build a tight-knit community. These shared experiences turn strangers into friends, making the hunt even more unforgettable.

Capturing the Magic

Getting that perfect shot of the auroras is like a hobby within a hobby. Snapping a picture of those glowing lights is a challenge, but when you nail it, the reward is priceless. Each photo becomes a cherished memory, and the drive to capture even more stunning images keeps you hooked.

The Emotional High

There's a hard-to-describe emotional rush associated with aurora hunting. You're filled with awe and wonder when the sky explodes into vibrant colours. It's a moment of pure joy that stays with you long after the lights fade, leaving you eager to chase that feeling again and again.

Bragging Rights

Let's face it: being an aurora hunter gives you serious bragging rights. Your stunning photos and epic tales of nighttime adventures will make you the envy of everyone who's ever posted a boring sunset pic. Your Instagram? Pure fire.

A Cosmic Connection

Aurora hunting connects you to the universe in a way few other experiences can. Understanding the science behind these dancing lights and witnessing them firsthand makes you feel like a tiny part of something much bigger. It's a reminder of the universe's beauty and complexity, sparking a sense of wonder that never fades.

Once you start chasing those dancing lights, there's no turning back. Happy hunting!

11
PRIME AURORA LOCATIONS - ALASKA

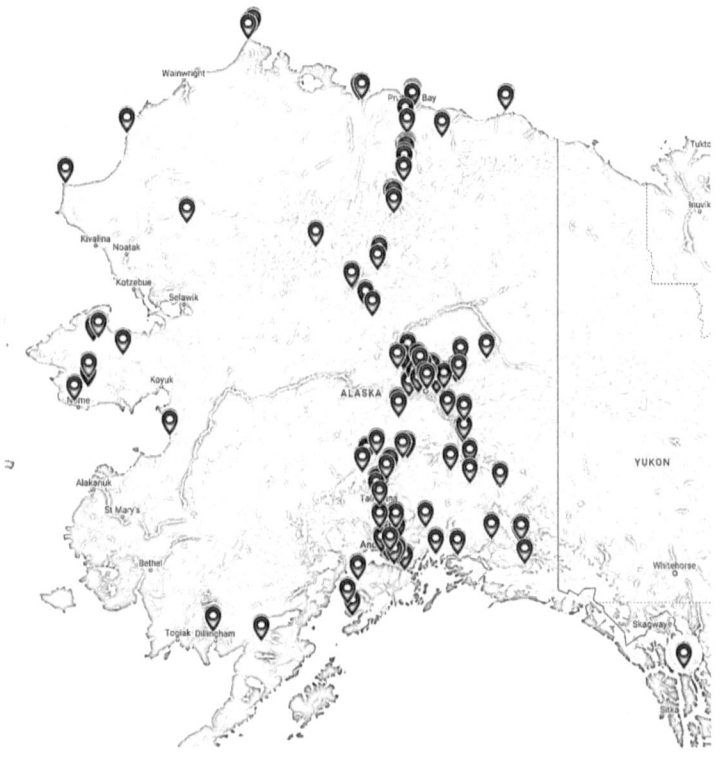

Scan the QR Code below for 130+ Aurora locations in Alaska

Anchorage, AK:
1. Anchorage Coastal Trail Beach Access, 2009 Foraker Dr, Anchorage, AK 99517
2. Arctic Valley Overlook, Arctic Valley Rd, Anchorage
3. Beluga Point, Mile 110, Seward Hwy, Anchorage, AK 99540
4. Bird Point, Anchorage, AK 99540
5. Brundie Rd Parking, Brundie Rd, Anchorage, AK 99508
6. Downtown Anchorage Viewpoint, Anchorage, AK 99502
7. Fish Creek Estuary, Fish Creek, Coastal Trail, Anchorage
8. Glen Alps / Flattop Trailhead, Parking lot, Blueberry Loop Trail, Anchorage, AK 99516
9. Kavik River Camp, Anchorage, AK 99519
10. Point Woronzof Beach Hike, 7251 Point Woronzof Rd, Anchorage, AK 99502
11. Point Woronzof Overlook, 7251 Point Woronzof Rd, Anchorage, AK 99502
12. Point Woronzof Park, 9700 Point Woronzof Rd, Anchorage, AK 99502

Fairbanks, AK:
1. Angel Rocks Trailhead, 15450 Chena Hot Springs Rd, Fairbanks, AK 99712
2. Arctic Hive, Wiseman Rd, Fairbanks, AK 99701
3. Aurora Borealis Lodge, 1906 Ridge Run Rd, Fairbanks
4. Aurora Camp, 2710 McCall St, Fairbanks, AK 99709
5. Aurora Husky Lodge, 9605 Parks Hwy, Fairbanks, AK 99709
6. Aurora Ice Museum, 17600 Chena Hot Springs Rd, Fairbanks,
7. Aurora View Point, 7893-7935 Chena Hot Springs Rd, Fairbanks, AK 99712
8. Borealis Basecamp, 2640 Himalaya Rd, Fairbanks, AK 99712
9. Chena Hot Springs Resort, 17600 Chena Hot Springs Rd, Fairbanks, AK 99712
10. Chena Hot Springs, Fairbanks, AK 99712
11. Cleary Summit Aurora Viewing Area, 2315 Fish Creek Rd, Fairbanks, AK 99712
12. Coldfoot Airport, Airport-CXF, Winter Rd, Fairbanks, AK 99701
13. Coldfoot Camp, 175 Dalton Hwy, Fairbanks, AK 99701
14. Finger Mountain, Dalton Hwy, Fairbanks, AK 99701
15. Grapefruit Rocks, Elliott Hwy, Fairbanks, AK 99790

16. Hagelbarger Viewpoint, 550-584 Hagelbarger Ave, Fairbanks, AK 99712
17. Murphy Dome, Alaska 99709
18. Northern Lights Location, 1084-1088 Ballaine Rd, Fairbanks, AK 99709
19. Scenic Pullover, 5304-5560 Parks Hwy, Fairbanks, AK 99709
20. Sirius Sled Dogs Rescue & Aurora Viewing, 922 Deraco Ln, Fairbanks, AK 99709
21. Tolovana Hot Springs, Fairbanks, AK 99708
22. Wedgewood Wildlife Sanctuary, 212 Wedgewood Dr, Fairbanks, AK 99701
23. White Mountains National Recreation Area, Elliott Hwy, Fairbanks, AK
24. Wickersham Dome, Elliott Highway, Fairbanks, Alaska
25. Wickersham Trailhead, Fairbanks, AK 99712

Girdwood, AK:
1. Begich, Boggs Visitor Center, Portage Lake Loop, Girdwood, AK 99587
2. Portage Glacier Cruises, 1500 Byron Glacier Rd, Girdwood, AK 99587
3. Scenic spot of Portage Glacier, 401 Portage Lake Loop, Girdwood, AK 99587

Willow, AK:
1. Curry lookout, Willow, AK 99683
2. Curry Ridge, Alaska 99683
3. Hatcher Pass, Willow, AK 99654
4. Summit Lake State Recreation Site Alaska, Hatcher Pass Rd, Willow, AK 99688
5. Willow Creek State Recreational Area, George Parks Hwy, Willow, AK 99688

Trapper Creek, AK:
1. Denali Mountains View Pullout, 11025 AK-3, Trapper Creek, AK 99683
2. Denali View North, Parks Hwy, Trapper Creek, AK 99683
3. Denali Viewpoint Hike, Trapper Creek, AK 99683
4. Denali Viewpoint South, Parks Hwy, Trapper Creek, AK 99683
5. Denali, Trapper Creek, AK 99683

Chitina, AK:
1. Chitina Bridge, 32 McCarthy Rd, Chitina, AK 99566
2. Kennecott Mines National Historic Landmark, Kennicott, Chitina, AK 99566
3. McCarthy Bridge, McCarthy Rd, Chitina, AK 99566
4. McCarthy Road Information Station, McCarthy Road Mile 59, Chitina, AK 99566
5. Root Glacier Trail, Chitina, AK 99566

Palmer, AK:
1. 35 Foot Viewing Tower, Palmer, AK 99645
2. Independence Mine State Historical Park, 23264 Gold Cord Rd, Palmer, AK 99645
3. Matanuska Glacier Scenic Turnout, 31849 Glenn Hwy, Palmer, AK 99645
4. Reflections Lake Trail, Palmer, AK 99645

Anderson, AK:
1. Anderson River Park, Anderson, AK 99744
2. Clear Space Force Station, 6417 Clear Anderson 6, Anderson, AK 99744

Prudhoe Bay, AK:
1. Brooks Camp, 75 Sag River Rd, Prudhoe Bay, AK 99734
2. Deadhorse Camp, Mile 412.8 Dalton Highway, Prudhoe Bay
3. The Aurora Hotel, 123 E Lake Colleen Dr, Prudhoe Bay, AK 99734
4. Prudhoe Bay General Store, #1 Old, Spine Rd, Prudhoe Bay, AK 99734

Cantwell, AK:
1. Cantwell Lodge -Longhorn Saloon & Grill, 137MP, Denali Hwy #8, Cantwell, AK 99729
2. Denali Highway, Cantwell, AK
3. Hurricane Gulch Bridge, Parks Hwy, Cantwell, AK 99729

Other locations:
1. Alagnak Wild River, King Salmon, AK 99613
2. Arctic Circle Sign, Milepost 115, Dalton Highway, AK
3. Arctic Plains north of the brooks, 93XH7446+8C, Sagwon,

AK 99791
4. Arigilivik Beach, North Slope Borough AK
5. Atchalik Historic Site, 48JX+JR, Kaktovik, AK 99747
6. Aurora Viewing Cabin, Bettles, AK 99726
7. Bettles Lodge, 1 Airline Dr, Bettles, AK 99726
8. Bering Land Bridge National Preserve, Shishmaref, AK 99772
9. Cabin Rock, Bob Blodgett Hwy, Nome, AK 99762
10. Chena Lake Recreation Area, 3780 Laurance Rd, North Pole, AK 99705
11. Chugach National Forest, Seward, AK 99664
12. Circle Hot Springs, Central, AK 99730
13. Dalton Highway Sign, Dalton Hwy, Livengood, AK 99762
14. Donnelly Dome, Donnelly Dome, Fort Greely, AK 99731
15. False Outer Point, N Douglas Hwy, Juneau, AK 99801
16. First Bible Baptist Church, 712 Sisuagvik Ave, Point Lay, AK 99759
17. Galbraith Lake Campground, Milepost 275 Dalton Highway
18. Gates of the Arctic National Park and Preserve
19. Gulkana Glacier trailhead, Dot Lake, AK 99737
20. Hot Springs Creek Bridge, Portage Rd, Central, AK 99730
21. Imuruk Lake, Imuruk Lake, Alaska
22. Lake Aleknagik State Recreation Site, Aleknagik Lake Rd, Aleknagik, AK 99555
23. Lake Benchmark Mountain Access Point, Dalton Hwy, Alaska
24. Maclaren River Lodge, Mile 42 Denali Hwy, Paxson, AK 99737
25. Mahay's Dock, 13687 E Front St, Talkeetna, AK 99676
26. Meier's Lake Roadhouse, 170 Richardson Hwy, Gakona, AK 99737
27. Mount Iliamna Viewpoint, 21875 Sterling Hwy, Ninilchik, AK 99639
28. Mt. Baldy Trailhead, 12900 Golden Eagle Dr, Eagle River, AK 99577
29. Myles Gonangnan / Aaron Paneok Memorial Hall, 270 Main Rd, Unalakleet, AK 99684
30. Nanuk Lake, Alpine, AK
31. Noatak National Preserve, 171 Third Ave, Kotzebue, AK 99752
32. Northernmost Point of the United States, Stevenson St, Alaska
33. Paxson Lake Campground Road, Paxson Lake Campground

Rd, Paxson, AK 99737
34. Pilgrim Hot Springs, Kougarok Rd, AK
35. Public Rest Area, Birch Lake Pull Off, Salcha, AK 99714
36. Quartz Lake State Recreation Area, Delta Junction, AK 99737
37. Raised Animal Pipeline Crossing, Dalton Hwy, Alaska
38. Salmon Lake Campground, Nome, AK 99762
39. Scenic Pulloff (MP 241.3), AK-4, Delta Junction, AK 99737
40. Scenic Viewpoint, Coal Mine Rd, Fort Greely, AK 99731
41. Serpentine Hot Springs and Airport, Bearing Land Bridge NP
42. Slana Ranger Station, Nabesna Rd, Slana, AK 99586
43. Stony Hill Scenic Overlook, Park Rd, Healy, AK 99743
44. Talkeetna Riverfront Park, 62°19'22. 150°07'16.2"W, E Second St, Talkeetna, AK 99676
45. The Aurora Express Camp (AEC), Nuiqsut, AK 99789
46. Twelvemile Summit, Alaska 99730
47. Utqiagvik Whale Bone Arch, Brower, Estate Dr, Utqiagvik
48. Valdez Glacier Lake, Valdez, AK 99686
49. Viewpoint Skyline Dr, 1033 Skyline Dr, Homer, AK 99603
50. Waldo Arms Hotel, 2011 Lake Rd, Kaktovik, AK 99747
51. Wevok park, Point Hope, AK 99766
52. Wrangell-St. Elias National Park & Preserve
53. Denali National Park and Preserve, Denali Park, AK 99755
54. Ester Dome, Ester, AK 99709
55. Kenai River Viewing Platform, 1591-1571 Boat Launch Rd, Kenai, AK 99611
56. The Overlook, Talkeetna, AK 99676
57. 68.899203, -148.869173
58. 69.097050, -148.829872
59. 69.150107, -148.835423
60. 69.258499, -148.768866
61. 69.285994, -148.760769
62. 69.316874, -148.721316
63. 69.731606, -148.695162
64. 69.919570, -148.777111
65. 69.974988, -148.710593
66. 70.165041, -148.456251

12 PRIME AURORA LOCATIONS - CANADA

Scan the QR Code below for 340 Aurora locations in Canada

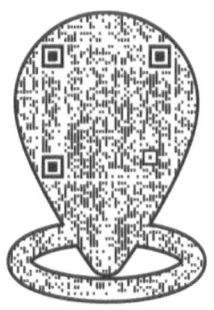

Yukon (YT)

1. 60°06'35.9"N 136°55'31.7"W
2. 60°17'39.5"N 137°00'09.8"W
3. 60°48'42.8"N 137°42'31.2"W
4. 60°49'42.8"N 137°44'37.2"W
5. 60°50'56.5"N 137°47'34.5"W
6. 60°56'18.1"N 137°59'05.6"W
7. 61°00'17.7"N 138°11'46.7"W
8. 61°10'38.8"N 135°23'28.7"W
9. 61°24'39.9"N 135°42'38.0"W
10. 61°27'05.4"N 139°14'02.0"W
11. 61°29'51.2"N 139°17'37.3"W
12. 61°38'09.5"N 139°42'06.3"W
13. 64°33'58.6"N 138°14'40.0"W
14. Arctic Circle Sign, Dempster Hwy, Yukon Y0B 1J0, Canada
15. Arthur Laing Peak, Yukon Y0B 1N0, Canada
16. Auriol Trail. Kluane National Park, Haines Rd, Haines Junction, YT Y0B 1L0, Canada
17. AuroraCentre, 194 Kluane Wagon Trl, Ibex Valley, YT Y0B 1L0, Canada
18. Bennett Beach Lookout, Carcross, YT Y0B 1B0, Canada
19. Big Creek Government Campground, Yukon Y0A 1C0, Canada
20. Carcross Airstrip Parking, YT-2, Carcross, YT Y0B 1B0, Canada
21. Dalton Trail Lodge, Dalton Trail Lodge
22. Dezadeash Campground, Haines Rd, Yukon Y0B 1L0, Canada
23. Discovery Yukon Lodgings, Km 1818, Alaska Hwy, Koidern, YT Y0B 1A0, Canada
24. Dredge No. 4 National Historic Site, Upper Bonanza Creek Road, Dawson City, YT Y0B 1G0, Canada
25. Dry Creek Rest Area, Yukon Y0B 1A0, Canada
26. Eagle Bay Park Lookout, Whitehorse, YT Y1A 6K1, Canada
27. Eagle Plains, YT Y0B 1N0, Canada
28. Fish Lake, Yukon Y0B, Canada
29. Five Finger Rapids Lookout, Yukon Y0B 1C0, Canada
30. Grizzly Lake Trailhead, Dempster Hwy, Yukon Y0B 1N0, Canada
31. Historical Downtown Carcross Sign, 3225 Klondike Hwy,

Carcross, YT Y0B 1B0, Canada
32. Hot Springs Campground & Resort Suites, box 20423 KM 10, Takhini Hot Springs Rd, Whitehorse, YT Y1A 7A2, Canada
33. Kluane Lake Gravel Viewpoint, Yukon Y0B 1H0, Canada
34. Lake Laberge Campground, 61.076°N 135, YT Y0B 1Y0, Canada
35. Lazulite Park, Whitehorse, YT Y1A 6S9, Canada
36. McIntyre Creek Lookout, PVM2+H7, Whitehorse, YT Y0B 1Y0, Canada
37. Midnight Dome Viewpoint, Dome Rd, Yukon Y0B 1N0, Canada
38. Miles Canyon Suspension Bridge, Whitehorse, YT, Canada
39. Miles Canyon, Whitehorse, YT Y1A 6L4, Canada
40. Millennium Trail Nest, Whitehorse, YT Y1A 6L4, Canada
41. Ogilvie Ridge Viewpoint, Dempster Hwy, Yukon Y0B 1G0, Canada
42. Our Lady of Grace Catholic Mission, 65 Yukon 1, Beaver Creek, YT Y0B 1A0, Canada
43. Pickhandle Lake Recreation site, Yukon 1, Beaver Creek, YT Y0B 1A0, Canada
44. Pine Lake Campground, Yukon Y0B 1L0, Canada
45. Pringle lake, Pringle Lake, YT Y0B 1L0, Canada
46. Rest Stop, Yukon Y0A 1B0, Canada
47. Rock Glacier Trailhead, 1H0, Haines Rd, Destruction Bay, YT Y0B 1H0, Canada
48. Ross River Suspension Bridge, Ross River, YT Y0B 1S0, Canada
49. Rotary Centennial Bridge, 3J5, Nisutlin Dr, Whitehorse, YT, Canada
50. Scenery view point, Carcross, YT Y0B 1B0, Canada
51. Shakat Tun Parking, Unnamed Road, 1H0, Destruction Bay, YT Y0B 1H0, Canada
52. Shea's lookout trail, GM8C+95, Marsh Lake, YT Y0B 1Y0, Canada
53. Soldier's Summit Trailhead, Yukon Y0B 1L0, Canada
54. Spruce Beetle Trail, Yukon Y0B 1L0, Canada
55. Teslin Lake Lookout Platform, 56FM+MM, Teslin, YT Y0A 1B0, Canada
56. The Gunnar Nilsson & Mickey Lammers Research Forest, Whitehorse, YT Y0B 1Y0, Canada
57. Top of the World Hwy, Yukon, Canada

58. Twin Lakes Campground, Yukon Y0B 1C0, Canada
59. Twin Lakes, YT-2, Yukon Y0B 1C0, Canada
60. Welcome to Beaver Creek Sign, 94GF+CJ, Beaver Creek, YT Y0B 1A0, Canada
61. Welcome to the Yukon sign, Yukon 1, Watson Lake, YT Y0A 1C0, Canada
62. Welcome to Yukon Sign, YT-2, Atlin, YT Y0B 1B0, Canada
63. Whitehorse Aurora Cabins, 229 Takhini River Rd, Yukon Y0B, Canada
64. WindmillViewPoint, PQXG+4C, Whitehorse, YT Y1A 5Y9, Canada
65. Yukon Energy Viewpoint Trail, Whitehorse, YT Y0B 1Y0, Canada
66. Yukon Lake Cabins, Silver City Rd, Silver City, YT Y0B 1H0, Canada
67. Yukon River Campground, Dawson City, YT, Canada

Northwest Territories (NT)

26. 62°30'31.9"N 114°48'28.3"W
27. 62°36'01.2"N 115°11'35.6"W
28. 62°41'29.5"N 115°29'25.2"W
29. 62°43'51.0"N 115°39'48.9"W
30. 7th Aurora Lodge, 7 Madeline Lake E, Lutselk'e, NT X0E 1A0, Canada
31. Arctic Ocean Sign - Tuktoyaktuk, Beaufort Rd, Tuktoyaktuk, NT X0E 1C0, Canada
32. Aurora Borealis Lookout, Fort Smith, Unorganized, NT X0E 0Y0, Canada
33. Aurora Village, Cassidy Point, Yellowknife, NT X1A 2P4, Canada
34. Boundery Creek, nwt, Mackenzie Hwy Wrigley, Fort Smith, Unorganized, NT X0E 0Y0, Canada
35. Cinnamon Island Scenic Viewpoint Trailhead, GP3H+HH, Yellowknife, NT X0E 1A0, Canada
36. End of the Road, Beaufort Rd, Tuktoyaktuk, NT X0E 1C0, Canada
37. Gwich'in Territorial Park, Inuvik, Unorganized, NT X0E 1L0, Canada
38. Hay River public beach, Hay River, NT X0E 0R9, Canada
39. Inuvik sign, 25 Carn St, Inuvik, NT X0E, Canada

40. Jackfish Lake Scenic Viewpoint, Yellowknife, NT X0E 0Y0, Canada
41. Jak Territorial Park, Dempster Hwy, Inuvik, NT X0E 0T0, Canada
42. Madeline Lake Crest Trailhead, Ingraham Trail, Fort Smith, Unorganized, NT X0E 1A0, Canada
43. Madeline Lake Territorial Park Day Use Area, Ingraham Trail, Fort Smith, Unorganized, NT X0E 1A0, Canada
44. North Arm Territorial Park Day Use Area, Behchokǫ, NT X0E 0Y0, Canada
45. Per Lunder Trail head, North Slave Region, NT X0E 1A0, Canada
46. Pingo National Landmark Viewpoint, Inuvik Tuktoyaktuk Hwy No 10, Inuvik, Unorganized, NT X0E, Canada
47. Pontoon Lake Territorial Park, Ingraham Trail, Fort Smith, Unorganized, NT X1A 3T4, Canada
48. Prelude Lake Scenic Viewpoint, Ingraham Trail, Fort Smith, Unorganized, NT X0E 0Y0, Canada
49. Prospector Trail Scenic Viewpoint, Ingraham Trail, Yellowknife, NT X1A 3T4, Canada
50. Prosperous Lake Territorial Park Day Use Area, Fort Smith, Unorganized, NT X0E 1A0, Canada
51. Pumphouse Beach, Hay River, NT X0E 0R9, Canada
52. Queen Elizabeth Territorial Park, Fort Smith, NT X0E 0P0, Canada
53. Ranney Hill Trail, Fort Smith, Unorganized, NT X0E 1A0, Canada
54. Reid Lake Territorial Park, Fort Smith, Unorganized, NT X0E 1A0, Canada
55. Tibbitt Lake Loop, Ingraham Trail, Fort Smith, Unorganized, NT X0E 1A0, Canada
56. Tithegeh Chii Vitaii lookout (Gwich'in Park Lookout Trailhead), Dempster Hwy, Inuvik, NT X0E 1L0, Canada
57. Tsiigehtchic Tourist Centre, Tsiigehtchic, NT X0E 0B0, Canada
58. Welcome to Canada's Highway to the Arctic Ocean sign, Inuvik Tuktoyaktuk Hwy No 10, Inuvik Region, NT X0E 1L0, Canada
59. Welcome to Northwest Territories Sign, NT-8, Fort McPherson, NT X0E 0J0, Canada
60. Welcome to Tuktoyaktuk Sign, Tuktoyaktuk, NT X0E 1C0,

Canada
61. Yellowknife River Territorial Park Day Use Area, Yellowknife, NT X0E 0Y0, Canada
62. オーロラ鑑賞, Fort Smith, Unorganized, NT X0E 1A0, Canada

Nunavut (NU)

1. Arctic Circle Monument, Naujaat, NU X0C 0H0, Canada
2. Coral Harbour Airport, Coral Harbour, NU X0C 0C0, Canada
3. Char River Bridge, Unnamed Road, Rankin Inlet, NU X0C 0G0, Canada
4. Gibbs Fjord, Qikiqtaaluk Region, NU, Canada
5. Grise Fiord Guest House, P.O. Box 75, Grise Fiord, NU X0A 0J0, Canada
6. Grise Fiord Hotel, Grise Fiord, NU X0A 0J0, Canada
7. Holy Cross Monument, G5RF+XC, Kugaaruk, NU X0B 1B0, Canada
8. Hudson Bay Company Blubber Station, Pangnirtung, NU, Canada
9. John John Lake, Rankin Inlet, NU X0C 0G0, Canada
10. Katannilik Territorial Park, Qikiqtaaluk Region, NU, Canada
11. Kivalliq Regional Visitor Centre, 131 Sivulliq Ave, Rankin Inlet, NU X0C 0G0, Canada
12. Marble Island, Marble Island, Kivalliq Region, NU, Canada
13. Nickel Mine, Rankin Inlet, NU X0C 0G0, Canada
14. Ovayok Territorial Park, Kitikmeot Region, NU X0B 0C0, Canada
15. Qamaviniktalik (Rankin Inlet Historical Sites), Kivalliq Region, NU X0C 0G0, Canada
16. Somerset Island, Somerset Island, Nunavut, Canada
17. Turaarvik Inns North, Mivvik Street, Rankin Inlet, NU X0C 0G0, Canada

British Columbia (BC)

1. 56°44'56.4"N 121°51'23.7"W
2. 57°08'25.5"N 122°41'32.9"W
3. Alaska Hawk Nestle Inn, 233 Alaska Hwy, Prophet River, BC V0C 2V0, Canada
4. Alaska Highway Memorial, Ross McLean Rotary Park, Charlie Lake, BC V0C 1H0, Canada

5. Allen's Lookout, BC-97, Northern Rockies B, BC V0C, Canada
6. Boulder Canyon, Northern Rockies B, BC V0C 1Z0, Canada
7. Borrow Pit 4 Recreation Site, Northern Rockies A, BC V0C 2V0, Canada
8. Borrow Pit 8 Recreation Site, Northern Rockies A, BC V0C 2V0, Canada
9. Boya Lake, Boya Lake, Stikine Region, BC V0C 2Z0, Canada
10. Dease Lake, Dease Lake, BC V0C 1L0, Canada
11. Dinosaur Lake Campground, Dinosaur Lake Rd, Hudson's Hope, BC V0C 1V0, Canada
12. Estuary Boardwalk, 37a Stewart Hwy, Stewart, BC V0T 1W0, Canada
13. Haida Heritage Centre, #2 2 Beach Rd, Skidegate, BC V0T 1S1, Canada
14. Jack of Clubs Lake, Jack of Clubs Lake, Wells, BC V0K 2R0, Canada
15. Kinuseo Falls, Lower Viewpoint, Kinuseo Falls Access Rd, Peace River D, BC V0J 2Z0, Canada
16. Kiskatinaw River Bridge, BC-97, Farmington, BC V0C 1N0, Canada
17. Liard River Hot Springs Provincial Park, 497 Alaska Hwy, Liard River, BC V0C 1Z0, Canada
18. Liard River Suspension Bridge, BC-97, Liard River, BC, Canada
19. Mile 0 Campground, 1901 Alaska Hwy, Dawson Creek, BC V1G 1P7, Canada
20. Mile 202 Rest Stop, BC-97, Trutch, BC V0J 3N0, Canada
21. Minette Bay Lodge, Village 2255, Kitamaat Village Rd, Kitimat, BC V8C 2P4, Canada
22. Morfee Lakes, Morfee Lakes, Mackenzie, BC V0J 2C0, Canada
23. Morley Lake Recreation Site, Yukon 1, Stikine Region, BC V0W 1A0, Canada
24. Mount Sproatt, Mount Sproatt, Squamish-Lillooet, BC V0N 2L2, Canada
25. Muncho Lake Provincial Park, Alaska Hwy, Northern Rockies B, BC V0C, Canada
26. Northern Rockies Lodge, Mile 462, Alaska Hwy, Muncho Lake, BC V0C 1Z0, Canada
27. Prophet River Wayside Provincial Park, Peace River B, BC V0C 2V0, Canada

28. Quesnel Lake Landing Recreation Site, Cariboo F, BC V0J 1J0, Canada
29. Sikanni Brake Check - South, Alaska Hwy, Sikanni Chief, BC V0C, Canada
30. Sikanni River Campground & RV Park, Alaska Hwy, Pink Mountain, BC V0C 2B0, Canada
31. Spirit Bear Lodge, 300 Raven Rd, Klemtu, BC V0T 1L0, Canada
32. Stone Mountain Provincial Park, Northern Rockies B, BC V0C 2X0, Canada
33. Stone's Sheep Trail, Northern Rockies B, BC V0C 1Z0, Canada
34. Wapta Lake, Wapta Lake, Columbia-Shuswap, BC V0A 1G0, Canada
35. Yukon BC border and Mile 585, BC-97, Northern Rockies B, BC V0C 1W0, Canada

Alberta (AB)

1. 59°34'24.4"N 117°11'37.3"W
2. 59°02'19.1"N 117°42'20.1"W
3. Banff National Park, Improvement District No. 9, AB T0L, Canada
4. Banff Town Sign, 101 Mt Norquay Rd, Banff, AB T1L 1C3, Canada
5. Bison loop road, Unnamed Road, Ardrossan, AB T8G 2A6, Canada
6. Blackfoot Lake Staging Area, Sherwood Park, AB T8G 1G2, Canada
7. David Thompson Monument, 10419 Churchill Dr, Lac la Biche, AB T0A 2C2, Canada
8. Dormition Skete, 53504, Range Rd 101, Wildwood, AB T0E 2M0, Canada
9. Dry Island Buffalo Jump Provincial Park, Hwy 585, Elnora, AB T0M 0Y0, Canada
10. Elk Island Beaver Pond Trail, Range Rd 200, Fort Saskatchewan, AB T8L 4B6, Canada
11. Elk Island National Park, 54401 Range Rd 203, Fort Saskatchewan, AB T8L 0V3, Canada
12. Elk Island Visitor Parking, Improvement District No. 13, AB T8G 2A6, Canada

13. Fairview Lookout, Improvement District No. 9, AB T0L, Canada
14. Flat Lake, AB T0A 3B0, Canada
15. Goose Lake Campground, 83036 Township Rd 615, Lone Pine, AB T0G 1M0, Canada
16. Holy Transfiguration Orthodox Church, Lamont County, AB T0B 4E0, Canada
17. Horseshoe Canyon, Township Rd 284, Kneehill County, AB T0M 2A0, Canada
18. Horseshoe Canyon Lookout, Unnamed Road, Elkwater, AB T0J 1C0, Canada
19. Islet Lake, Islet Lake, Beaver County, AB T8G, Canada
20. Jasper National Park Of Canada, Jasper, AB T0E 1E0, Canada
21. Kananaskis, Kananaskis, AB T0L, Canada
22. Lake Louise, Lake Louise Lakeshore Trail, Lake Louise, AB T0L, Canada
23. McDougall Memorial United Church, Bow Valley Trail, Bighorn No. 8, AB T0L 1N0, Canada
24. Moraine Lake, Moraine Lake, Improvement District No. 9, AB T0L, Canada
25. Moraine Lake Lodge, 1 Moraine Lake Rd, Lake Louise, AB T0L 1E0, Canada
26. Okotoks Erratic, AB-7, Foothills County, AB T0L 0H0, Canada
27. Pyramid Island, Pyramid Island, AB T0E 1E0, Canada
28. Red Rock Coulee, Orion, AB T0K 1S0, Canada
29. Rosalind Historic House, AB-854, Rosalind, AB T0B 3Y0, Canada
30. Rowley Train Station, Main St, Rowley, AB T0J 2X0, Canada
31. Schuman Lake, Schuman Lake, Woodlands County, AB T0G 1M0, Canada
32. Skoki Lodge, 1 Whitehorn Dr, Lake Louise, AB T0L 1E0, Canada
33. Spaca Moskalyk Ukrainian Catholic Church, Range Rd 160, Mundare, AB T0B 3H0, Canada
34. St. Mary's Russo-Greek Orthodox Church of Shishkovtzy, Lamont

Saskatchewan (SK)

1. 55°07'36.6"N 107°46'25.5"W

CHASING NORTHERN LIGHTS

2. 56°16'19.0"N 108°54'19.3"W
3. Adanac Cemetery, 410 Round Valley, Round Valley No. 410, SK S0K 4L0, Canada
4. Anglin Lake, Anglin Lake, SK S0J 0N0, Canada
5. Annie Laurie Lake, Annie Laurie Lake, Saskatchewan S0A 3B0, Canada
6. Athabasca Sand Dunes Provincial Park, Laronge, SK S0J 1L0, Canada
7. Battle of Tourond's Coulee, Unnamed Road, Alvena, SK S0K 0E0, Canada
8. Buffalo Narrows Airport, Buffalo Narrows, SK S0M 0J0, Canada
9. Buffalo Pound Lake, Buffalo Pound Lake, Saskatchewan, Canada
10. Candle Lake, SK, Canada
11. Canund Bay Saskatchewan, Wollaston Lake, SK S0J 3C0, Canada
12. Cranberry Flats Conservation Area, Range Rd 3055, Saskatoon, SK S7T 1A3, Canada
13. Frenchman Valley Campground, Val Marie, SK S0N 2T0, Canada
14. Greig Lake, SK S0M, Canada
15. Grey Owl's Cabin Trail, Kingsmere Rd, Waskesiu Lake, SK S0J 2Y0, Canada
16. Hanging Heart Lakes, Hanging Heart Lakes, Prince Albert National Park, SK S0J 2Y0, Canada
17. Holy Trinity Anglican Church, Saskatchewan, Canada
18. Lower Fishing Lake, Lower Fishing Lake, Saskatchewan S0J 3E0, Canada
19. Madge Lake, Madge Lake, Saskatchewan S0A, Canada
20. Manitou Springs Resort and Mineral Spa, 302 MacLachlan Ave, Manitou Beach, SK S0K 4T1, Canada
21. Moonie Beach, 7V2G+M4, Wadin Bay, SK S0J 2P0, Canada
22. Nut Point Campground, La Ronge provincial park, Saskatchewan, La Ronge Ave, La Ronge, SK S6V 6G1, Canada
23. Nut Point Trail, Ave, La Ronge, SK S0J 1L0, Canada
24. Nistowiak Falls, Nistowiak Falls, Saskatchewan S0J 2P0, Canada
25. Rocky Hill (great view), 8RG2+C7, Fond-du-Lac, SK S0J 0W0, Canada

26. Shady Lake Trail, Prince Albert National Park, SK S0J 2Y0, Canada
27. Stony Rapids Viewpoint, Unnamed Road, Stony Rapids, SK S0J, Canada
28. Tobin Lake, Tobin Lake, SK, Canada
29. Tobin Lake Leisure, 700 Spruce Place Resort Village of, Tobin Lake, SK S0E 1E0, Canada
30. Village Of Love, Love, SK S0J 1P0, Canada
31. Waskesiu Lake, Waskesiu Lake, SK S0J, Canada
32. Wolseley Swinging Bridge, 208 Sherbrooke St, Wolseley, SK S0G 5H0, Canada

Manitoba (MB)

1. 55°41'13.0"N 97°54'28.1"W
2. Aurora Domes, 152 Kelsey Blvd, Churchill, MB R0B 0E0, Canada
3. Baldy Mountain Viewing Tower, Unnamed Road, Boggy Creek, MB R0L 0G0, Canada
4. Beluga Boat, 180 La Vérendrye Ave, Churchill, MB R0B 0E0, Canada
5. Blue Lakes Campground, MB-366, Manitoba R0L 0G0, Canada
6. Cape Merry, Churchill, MB R0B 0E0, Canada
7. Caribou River Park Reserve, Manitoba, Canada
8. Centre of Canada Park, Taché, MB R0A 0Y0, Canada
9. Cliff Beach, R5G3+47, Flin Flon, MB R0B 0C0, Canada
10. Courage Lake, Taché, MB R0A 0Y0, Canada
11. Cranberry Portage, Cranberry Portage, MB, Canada
12. Falcon Lake Beach Campground, Manitoba R0E 2H0, Canada
13. Fisher Bay, Fisher Bay, MB R0C 0S0, Canada
14. Flin Flon, MB, Canada
15. Flin Flon Airport (YFO), Airport Rd, Flin Flon, MB R8A 0T7, Canada
16. Hecla Provincial Park, 2R0, MB-8, Riverton, MB R0C 2R0, Canada
17. Hecla Village Self-Guiding Trail, Hecla, MB R0C 2R0, Canada
18. Inuit Stone Sculpture, 162 La Vérendrye Ave, Churchill, MB R0B 0E0, Canada
19. Lindsay Tower, 2R0, MB-8, Gull Harbour, MB R0C 2R0, Canada

20. Little Limestone Lake, Moose Lake 31j, MB R0B 0Y0, Canada
21. Little Steep Rock Trail, Grahamdale, MB R0C 0Y0, Canada
22. Moonie Beach, 7V2G+M4, Wadin Bay, SK S0J 2P0, Canada
23. Nopiming Provincial Park, MB-314, Bird River, MB, Canada
24. Paint Lake Provincial Park, 59 Elizabeth Drive, Thompson, MB R8N 1X4, Canada
25. Pinawa Dam Provincial Heritage Park, MB-520, Pinawa, MB R0E 1L0, Canada
26. Polar Bear Alley, QX7W+22, Churchill, MB R0B 1P0, Canada
27. Prince of Wales Fort National Historic Site, Prince of Wales Fort, Churchill, MB R0B 0E0, Canada
28. Sand Lakes Provincial Wilderness Park, Manitoba, Canada
29. Sasagiu Rapids Lodge 2013 Ltd, Sasagiu Rapids Provincial Park, Wabowden, MB R0B 1S0, Canada
30. South Indian Lake, South Indian Lake, MB, Canada
31. Steep Rock Marina and Beach, Grahamdale, MB, Canada
32. Tadoule Lake, Tadoule Lake, MB R0B 2C0, Canada
33. Tobin Lake, Tobin Lake, SK, Canada
34. Viking Lodge, 351 Public Rd SE, Cranberry Portage, MB R0B 0H0, Canada
35. Wasagaming, MB R0J, Canada
36. West Hawk Lake, MB R0E 2H0, Canada
37. Whiteshell Provincial Park, Hwy 1, Eastern Manitoba, MB R0E 0N0, Canada
38. York Factory National Historic Site, York Factory, MB R0B 0E0, Canada

Ontario (ON)

1. 50°58'00.9"N 93°46'00.4"W
2. Agawa Bay, ON P0S 1K0, Canada
3. Biscotasi Lake, Biscotasi Lake, Sudbury, Unorganized, North Part, ON, Canada
4. Cascades Conservation Area, 1157 Balsam St, Thunder Bay, ON P7G 1Y2, Canada
5. Cochenour Cabin, 21 Cochenour Crescent, Cochenour, ON P0V 1L0, Canada
6. Dawson Trail Campgrounds, Dawson Trail, Rainy River, Unorganized, ON P0W, Canada
7. Fushimi Lake, Unorganized North Cochrane District, ON P0L, Canada

8. Fushimi Lake Provincial Park, Neely Rd, Hearst, ON P0L 1N0, Canada
9. George Lake, George Lake, Killarney, ON P0M 2A0, Canada
10. Ivanhoe Lake Provincial Park, 170 Ivanhoe Lake Rd, Foleyet, ON P0M 1T0, Canada
11. Lake of Two Rivers Campground beach, Unorganized South Nipissing District, ON K0J 2M0, Canada
12. Little Cove Beach, 240-242 Little Cove Rd, Tobermory, ON N0H 2R0, Canada
13. Little Current River, Unorganized North Cochrane District, ON, Canada
14. Maple Mountain, Maple Mountain, Unorganized West Timiskaming District, ON P0J 1G0, Canada
15. Missinaibi Lake, Missinaibi Lake, Ontario, Canada
16. Northernmost Point of Ontario, Kenora, Unorganized, ON P0V 2P0, Canada
17. Overhanging Point, Bruce Trail, Northern Bruce Peninsula, ON N0H 2R0, Canada
18. Pipestone River Landing, Balmertown, ON P0V 2Y0, Canada
19. Severn River Provincial Park, Kenora, Unorganized, ON P0V 1B0, Canada
20. Sunset Lodge on Red Lake, Sunset Rd, Red Lake, ON P0V 2M0, Canada
21. The Grotto, Bruce Peninsula National Park, Bruce Trail, Tobermory, ON N0H 2R0, Canada
22. Thunder Bay Lookout, Thunder Bay, Unorganized, ON P0T, Canada
23. Viewpoint, 3 Dickinson Ave, Port Rowan, ON N0E 1M0, Canada
24. White River Suspension Bridge, Thunder Bay, Unorganized, ON P0T 1R0, Canada
25. Winisk River Provincial Park, Peawanuck, ON P0L 2H0, Canada
26. World's Largest Snowman, ON-11, Beardmore, ON P0T 1G0, Canada
27. Wright's Wilderness Camp, 200 Weavers Rd, Red Lake, ON P0V 2M0, Canada

Newfoundland and Labrador (NL)

1. Bonne Bay Marine Station, 1 Clarke's Rd, Norris Point, NL

A0K 3V0, Canada
2. Boney Shore Walking Trail, Unnamed Road, Red Bay, NL A0K 4K0, Canada
3. Brimstone Head, Brimstone Head, Fogo Island, NL A0G 2B0, Canada
4. Captain James Cook National Historic Site, Mayfair Ave, Corner Brook, NL A2H 6M7, Canada
5. Coal Silos, St. Anthony, NL A0K 4S0, Canada
6. Cow Head Lighthouse, 189 Main St, Cow Head, NL A0K 2A0, Canada
7. Cow Head Wharf, Unnamed Road, 2A0, Cow Head, NL A0K 2A0, Canada
8. Dr. Henry N. Payne Community Museum & Craft Shop, 143 Main St, Cow Head, NL A0K 2A0, Canada
9. Griffins Harbour, Newfoundland and Labrador, Canada
10. Grebe's Nest, Wabana, NL A0A 4H0, Canada
11. Grenfell Historical Society, 1 Maraval Dr, St. Anthony, NL A0K 4S0, Canada
12. Hidden Falls, 363 NL-460, West Bay Centre, NL A0N 2E0, Canada
13. Long Point Lighthouse & Twillingate Lighthouse Heritage Museum, Lighthouse Rd, NL-340, Crow Head, NL A0G 4M0, Canada
14. Net Loft Museum, Rigolet, NL, Canada
15. Port Hope Simpson Wharf, NL A0K 4E0, Canada
16. Red Bay National Historic Site & World Heritage Site, Red Bay, NL A0K 4K0, Canada
17. Shallow Bay Beach, Gros Morne National Park Of Canada, Cow Head, NL A0K 2A0, Canada
18. Shankar Labrador Sea Island, Newfoundland and Labrador A0P 1P0, Canada
19. Torngat Mountains National Park, Torngat Mountains, Nain, NL A0P 1L0, Canada
20. Tourist Viewing area, Newfoundland and Labrador A0R 1A0, Canada
21. Western Brook Pond, Western Brook Pond, Newfoundland and Labrador, Canada
22. White Elephant Museum, 16 Andersen St, Makkovik, NL A0P 1J0, Canada

Quebec (QC)

1. ASTROLab, 189 Rte du Parc, Notre-Dame-des-Bois, QC J0B 2E0, Canada
2. Belvédère de l'Île-Aux-Pins, Parc National de la Mauricie, Saint-Roch-de-Mékinac, QC G0X 2E0, Canada
3. Belvédère Robert-Bourassa, Rte Billy-Diamond, Jamésie, QC J0Y 2X0, Canada
4. Cap-Bon-Ami, QC G0E, Canada
5. Inuksuk, Kasuqvik St, Nunavik, QC J0M, Canada, Canada
6. Kuururjuaq National Park (provincial park), P.O. 30, Kangiqsualujjuaq, QC J0M 1N0, Canada
7. Kuujjuaq Beach, 4J34+86, Kuujjuaq, QC J0M 0A4, Canada
8. Mont Dos de Baleine, X3X7+53, Marsoui, QC G0E 1Z0, Canada
9. Mont Jacques-Cartier, La Haute-Gaspésie Regional County Municipality, QC G0E 1Z0, Canada
10. Mont Naapaayaakuuchii, Eeyou Istchee Baie-James, Jamésie, QC J0Y 2X0, Canada
11. Nunavik, QC, Canada
12. Observatoire Populaire du Mont-Mégantic, La Patrie, QC J0B 1Y0, Canada
13. Observatoir LG4, Eeyou Istchee Baie-James, Jamésie, QC J0Y 2X0, Canada
14. Pingualuk Lake, Nunavik, QC J0M 1K0, Canada
15. Pont sur la rivière Utahunanis, Rte de l'Évacuateur, Jamésie, QC J0Y 2X0, Canada
16. point de vue de la grande Rivière, Radisson, QC, Canada
17. Refuge Mines Madeleine, La Haute-Gaspésie Regional County Municipality, QC G0E 1S0, Canada
18. The Lookout, Jamésie, QC J0Y 2X0, Canada
19. Vide-Bouteille, Saint-Roch-de-Mékinac, QC G0X 2E0, Canada
20. 53.692161, -77.742359
21. 53.328380, -77.395843
22. 53.522650, -76.079096
23. 53.075531, -77.407604
24. 52.930060, -77.275137
25. 52.788622, -67.265229
26. 52.762208, -67.447470
27. 47.140606, -76.619462

13 PRIME AURORA LOCATIONS - CONTIGUOUS UNITED STATES

Scan the QR Code below for **151** Aurora locations in contiguous United States

Washington (WA):

1. Deception Pass Bridge, North Whidbey, Oak Harbor, WA 98277
2. Ala Spit County Park, Geck Rd, Oak Harbor, WA 98277
3. Kukutali Preserve State Park Heritage Site, Kiket Island Rd, La Conner, WA 98257
4. Mt Erie Viewpoint, 1300 Erie Mountain Dr, Anacortes, WA 98221
5. Panorama Point Overlook, Ashford, WA 98304
6. Mount Rainier National Park, Washington
7. Sunrise Visitor Center, Sunrise Park Rd, Ashford, WA 98304
8. Emmons Vista, W975+25 Mount Rainier National Park, Sunrise, WA 98304
9. Diablo Lake Vista Point, State Rte 20, Rockport, WA 98283
10. Ross Lake Overlook, Rockport, WA 98283
11. Washington Pass, Washington Pass, Washington 98862
12. Anacortes Ferry Terminal, 2100 Ferry Terminal Rd, Anacortes, WA 98221
13. Guemes Island Ferry Terminal, 500 I Ave, Anacortes, WA 98221
14. Zuanich Point Park, 2600 N Harbor Loop Dr, Bellingham, WA 98225
15. Park Butte Lookout, FS road 13, Sedro-Woolley, WA 98284
16. Lookout Mountain Lookout, Marblemount, WA 98267
17. Hidden Lake Lookout, Cascade River Rd, Marblemount, WA 98267
18. Lighthouse Marine Park Lookout, XWC8+HJ, Point Roberts, WA 98281
19. Cape Flattery Observation Deck, Makah, Indian Reservation, Sekiu, WA 98357
20. Neah Bay Scenic View Point, Boom Rd, Neah Bay, WA 98357
21. Cascade Park, 8301 Valley Rd NE, Moses Lake, WA 98837

Idaho (ID):

1. Heyburn State Park, 57 Chatcolet Lower Rd, Plummer, ID 83851
2. Priest Lake, Idaho
3. Navigation Campground, Coolin, ID 83821

CHASING NORTHERN LIGHTS

4. Plowboy Campground, Coolin, ID 83821
5. Hill's Resort, 4777 W Lakeshore Rd, Priest Lake, ID 83856
6. Boise National Forest, Idaho 83637
7. Robinson Lake Campground, 330 Robinson Lake Campground Rd, Bonners Ferry, ID 83805
8. Historical Scenic Spot, US-95, Bonners Ferry, ID 83805
9. Lakeview Public Dock, 625 Lakeview Rd, Bayview, ID 83803
10. Lake Coeur d'Alene, Idaho
11. Hilltop Station, 12342 ID-21, Boise, ID 83716
12. Teton River, Idaho 83440
13. Lookout PO, 1000 East Bunco Road, Athol, ID 83801
14. Schweitzer, Sandpoint, ID 83864
15. Island Park Dam, Island Park, ID 83429
16. Mt Harrison Lookout, 885R+HC, Elba, ID 83342
17. Camas Prairie Scenic Viewpoint, ID-46, Fairfield, ID 83327
18. Bonneville Point, Idaho 83716

Montana (MT):

1. Lake McDonald, Glacier National Park, Glacier Rte 1 Rd, West Glacier, MT 59936
2. Lake McDonald Lodge, 288 Lake McDonald Ldg Lp, West Glacier, MT 59936
3. Apgar Amphitheater, Apgar Lp Rd, West Glacier, MT 59936
4. Apgar Village Lodge & Cabins, Lake View Dr, West Glacier, MT 59936
5. Kintla Lake, Polebridge, MT 59928
6. Kintla Lake Ranger Station, Polebridge, MT 59928
7. Bowman Lake, Polebridge, MT 59928
8. Goat Haunt Ranger Station, Browning, MT 59417
9. Grinnell Glacier Overlook, Garden Wall Trail, West Glacier, MT 59936
10. Point Salish Park, Polson, MT 59860
11. Finley Point Unit - Flathead Lake State Park, 31453 S Finley Point Rd, Polson, MT 59860
12. Trinity Lutheran Camp, 450 Pierce Ln, Bigfork, MT 59911
13. 48.939610, -104.573397
14. 48.968633, -104.572170
15. 48.910656, -104.573386
16. 48.823717, -104.571197
17. 48.928875, -105.409698

18. 48.824262, -105.421052
19. 48.912262, -106.388244
20. 48.635750, -106.479680
21. 48.991954, -107.830424
22. 48.856955, -110.059486
23. 48.798071, -111.859387

North Dakota (ND):

1. Pembina Gorge State Recreation Area Trailhead, Langdon, ND 58249
2. Sully Creek State Park, 1465 36th St, Medora, ND 58645
3. Theodore Roosevelt National Park, North Dakota
4. Round Lake Access, 2qc7+m59, Minnewaukan, ND 58351
5. Lakeside Haven Campground, Eastbay, St Michael, ND 58370
6. Pelican Lake West Causeway, ND-19, Minnewaukan, ND 58351
7. Pelican Lake East Causeway, ND-19, Minnewaukan, ND 58351
8. Devils Lake State Parks, 152 S Duncan Rd, Devils Lake, ND 58301
9. Fort Stevenson State Park, 1252A 41st Ave NW, Garrison, ND 58540
10. Fort Stevenson Visitor Center, 1252A 41st Ave NW, Garrison, ND 58540

14 PRIME AURORA LOCATIONS - GREENLAND

Scan the QR Code below for 70+ Aurora locations in Greenland

Ilulissat, Greenland:

1. Ilulissa fjord, Greenland
2. Ilulissat Icefjord, Greenland
3. Randonnées à Ilulissat, 6V44+9JF, Ilulissat, Greenland
4. Ilulissat Icefjord, Unnamed Road, 6V43+854, Ilulissat,
5. Ilulissat Isfjord, Ilulissat 3952, Greenland
6. Ilulissat Isfjordscenter, Sermermiut Aqq. B 2089, Ilulissat
7. Zion's Church, 6V9R+W4J, Oqaluffiup Aqq., Ilulissat 3952,
8. Knud Rasmussen skulptur, Noah Mølgaard'ip Aqq. 12 3952, Ilulissat, Greenland
9. Glacier Lodge Eqi, Kussangajaannguaq 7, Ilulissat 3952,
10. Hotel Arctic, Mittarfimmut Aqq. B-1128, Ilulissat 3952,
11. Ilulissat Airport, Mittarfimmut Aqqutaa B-1138, Ilulissat 3952,
12. Eqi camp, Greenland

Kangerlussuaq, Greenland:

1. Distance Roadsign - North pole 3hrs, 2894+PFW, Tankeqarfiup aqq., Søndre Strømfjord, Greenland
2. Old Camp, Aqisseq 266, Søndre Strømfjord, Greenland
3. Kangerlussuaq Fjord, X6P9+P9C, Kangerlussuaq, Greenland
4. Point 660, 5X23+W57, Greenland
5. Tacan, X9WP+M3, Kangerlussuaq, Greenland
6. Hotel Kangerlussuaq, 2894+VV8, Tankeqarfiup aqq., Søndre Strømfjord, Greenland
7. Kangerlussuaq Camping, 279X+8G4, Kangerlussuaq,

Sisimiut, Greenland:

1. Arctic Circle Viewpoint - Sisimiut, Nasiffimmut 1086, Sisimiut
2. Saqqaq Kultur, W8M4+Q7, Sisimiut 3911, Greenland
3. Sisimiut, Grønland, W8JP+H6G, Kussangasoq, Sisimiut
4. Aasivissuit – Nipisat. Inuit Hunting Ground between Ice and Sea, Makkorsip Aqq 2, Sisimiut 3911, Greenland
5. Startingpoint of the Prästefjeldet trail, X834+25P, Asummiunut, Sisimiut 3911, Greenland

Tasiilaq, Greenland:

1. Bone Stone Viewpoint, Jens Emilip Aqqulaa 221, Tasiilaq,

2. Sledge Viewpoint, Ittimiini 464, Tasiilaq, Greenland
3. Flower Valley, J962+PW2, Tasiilaq, Greenland
4. Tasiilaq Church, J978+R4M, Kaaralip Aqq., Tasiilaq,
5. Hotel Angmagssalik, J958+MV9, Tasiilaq, Greenland
6. Trawellodge Greenland, Ittimiini 1228, Tasiilaq, Greenland

Nuuk, Greenland:

1. Kuanninnguit, Paradise Valley, 692G+7HM, Nuuk,
2. Udsigten Nuuk, 5CPM+4J, Nuuk, Greenland
3. Startpunkt Wanderweg am Seeufer, 58GX+94F, 3905,
4. Good view at sunset, Tuukkaq 6, Nuuk 3900, Greenland
5. Isikkivik view, 5878+6F, Nuuk 3905, Greenland
6. Wasserfall, 6WH8+CH, Igdlúnguaq, Greenland

Narsarsuaq, Greenland:

1. Hotel Narsarsuaq, 5H4H+P4C, Narsarsuaq, Greenland
2. Narsarsuaq Marina, Unnamed Road Greenland, 4HW8+22R, Narsarsuaq, Greenland
3. Hostel Narsarsuaq, Narsarsuaq 3920, Greenland

Igaliku, Greenland:

1. Igaliku Bygdehotel, XHQG+72G, Igaliku 3920, Greenland
2. Igaliku Church, XHPF+RXQ, Igaliku 3920, Greenland
3. Randonnée à Igaliku., Unnamed Road, 2H3Q+37G, Igaliku,

Uummannaq, Greenland:

1. Brown house, MVF5+X95, Uummannaq 3961, Greenland
2. Cafemma Ummannaq, Aqqusinersuaq 799, Uummannaq
3. Uummannaq Helistop, MVJQ+678, Uummannaq, Greenland
4. FC Malamuk, MVPM+36X, Uummannaq, Greenland

Upernavik, Greenland:

1. Café de Upernavik, Niuertup Otto-P Aqq BNR-10, Upernavik
2. Upernavik Tourist Service, QRJX+78R, Road, Upernavik,
3. Arsaattarfik, QVR5+4M, Upernavik, Greenland
4. Gina's Guesthouse - Upernavik, Road 1602, Upernavik 3962,

5. Upernavik Airport, QVQ9+XQW, Upernavik, Greenland

Kulusuk, Greenland:

1. Arctic Hiking and Expeditions, B 1375, Kulusuk 3915,
2. Church of Kap Dan, HRH7+3WV, Unnamed Road, Kulusuk, Greenland
3. Hotel Kulusuk, B-1500, Greenland
4. Kulusuk Airport, HVF8+R82, Kulusuk, Greenland

Qassiarsuk, Narsaq, Greenland:

1. Sillisit Sheep Farm, Sillisit B.nr 226, Qassiarsuk, Narsaq 3921,

Qaanaaq, Greenland:
1. Qaanaaq Hotel, FQ99+P97, Qaanaaq, Greenland

Sarfannguit, Greenland:

1. Qaammat Pavilion, V4WR+86, Sarfannguit, Greenland

Other Locations:

1. 67.047439, -50.523513
2. 67.055835, -50.468231
3. 67.077774, -50.344936
4. 67.091529, -50.278643
5. 67.130940, -50.158944
6. 67.143331, -50.125434
7. 67.146800, -50.082432
8. 67.150850, -50.071609
9. Aattartoq lodge, Greenland
10. ACF 57, CQM4+JMV, unnamed Road, Sarqaq, Greenland
11. Igloo Lodge, Greenland
12. Købmand, CPPH+6MF, Kapisillit, Greenland
13. Prinz Christian Sund, Greenland
14. Stone & Man - Woman head, PX95+X4V, Qaqortoq, Greenland
15. Hvalsey Church, Greenland

15 PRIME AURORA LOCATIONS - ICELAND

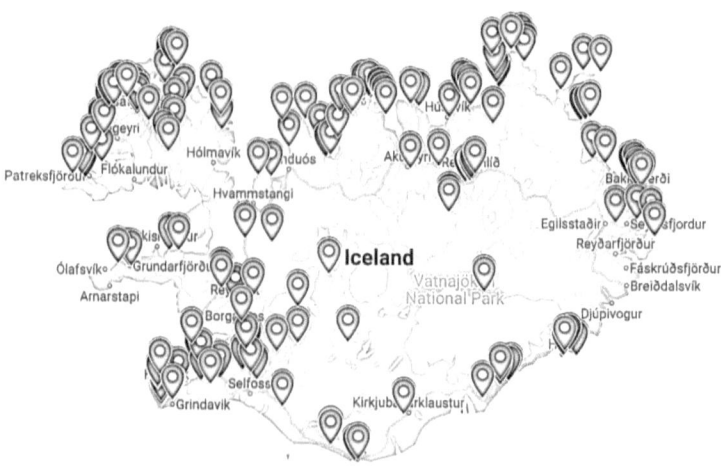

Scan the QR Code below for 170+ Aurora locations in Iceland

Westfjords

1. Bolafjall Útsýnispallur, 5MH8+HXX, 416 Bolungarvik, Iceland
2. Drangajökull útsýnisstaður, 3H96+HRW, Melgraseyri, Iceland
3. Drangajökull, Drangajökull, 512, Iceland
4. Gamla laugin Reykjanesi, Reykjanesskóli, 401, Iceland
5. Hornbjargsviti campsite, CJ6C+C54, 401 Horn, Iceland
6. Hornstrandir Nature Reserve, Aðalstræti 10, Ísafjörður, Iceland
7. Hornvík campsite, CGG5+5G6, 401 Horn, Iceland
8. Hringsdalur, Hringsdalur, 466, Iceland
9. Minnibakki Beach, Skálavíkurvegur, 416, Iceland
10. Observation Deck, Urðarvegur 34, 400 Ísafjörður, Iceland
11. Olafsviti Lighthouse, JR5Q+W9G, 451 Hnjótur, Iceland
12. Óshólar Lighthouse, Djúpvegur, 416, Iceland
13. Sæluvogur, Borgarfjarðarhöfn, 720 Bakkagerði, Iceland
14. Samúel Jónsson's Art Farm, Unnamed Road, Q2P5+QPP, 466 Selárdalur, Iceland
15. Sauðanes Lighthouse (Súgandafjörður), 489V+48Q, 431 Suðureyri, Iceland
16. Sicily flag, 52PX+RJR, 580 Siglufjörður, Iceland
17. Siglunes Lighthouse, 55VH+2QJ, 581 Hvanneyri, Iceland
18. Sigríðarstaðir, 3V48+QVP, Djúpvegur, 400 Ísafjörður, Iceland
19. Skarfasker útsýnispallur, 4V9H+QQ, 410 Hnífsdalur, Iceland
20. Svalvogaviti, W553+XR7, 471 Hraun, Iceland
21. Straumnes lighthouse, 3JGW+V67, 566 Fell, Iceland
22. Tungurif - Golden Beach, Örlygshafnarvegur, 451, Iceland
23. Vatnsfjörður - kirkja og fiskihjallar, Iceland, Vatnsfjordhur, Unnamed Road
24. Viking hovel, 4CFM+H2R, Unnamed Road, 431 Suðureyri, Iceland
25. Wheel Sculpture, 3WJ3+Q3, 410 Ísafjörður, Iceland

North Iceland

1. Æðarsker, 3CVP+MQ, Ólafsfjörður, Iceland
2. Aldeyjarfoss, Sprengisandsleið, 645, Iceland
3. Ásbyrgi, 2F2P+MQW, 671 As, Iceland

4. Barnafoss, Möðruvellir 5, Möðruvallavegur, 320, Iceland
5. Bird Watching, Norðausturvegur, 676, Iceland
6. Black beach, 744, 550 Sauðárkrókur, Iceland
7. Borgarfjarðarhöfn, G6RW+V55, 721 Bakkagerði, Iceland
8. Botnstjörn, Ásbyrgi, XFXP+CH7, 671 As, Iceland
9. Camping 66.12 NORTH, Mánárbakki 641, 641 Húsavík, Iceland
10. Cliff viewpoint, 85, 671, Iceland
11. Dalatangi, 7CCF+3P8, 715 Skálanes, Iceland
12. Digranes Lighthouse, 3749+X6P, 686 Bakkafjörður, Iceland
13. Djúpavík, Iceland
14. Fjörður Beach, Fjörður, 616, Iceland
15. Flateyjardalur Beach, 44F2+6PX, 607 Flateyjardalsheiði, Iceland
16. Fossdalsfoss, 49FM+FPQ, Ólafsfjörður, Iceland
17. Gamla bryggjan, 25QV+F8H, Hafnartangi, 685 Bakkafjörður, Iceland
18. Geitafoss, MFP5+268, 645 Fossholl, Iceland
19. Grettislaug Campsite in Reykhólar, Hvammur, Hesteyri 550, Sauðárkrókur, Iceland
20. Grótta Island Lighthouse, Iceland, Gróttuviti, 170 Seltjarnarnes, Iceland
21. Haganesvík, 3VH9+5W, Haganes, Iceland
22. Hegranesviti Lighthouse, QF95+W3, 551 Sjafarborg, Iceland
23. Hrafnabjargafoss, 8MQ6+V6M, 645 Svartarkot, Iceland
24. Húsavík Wooden Church, Garðarsbraut 11, 640 Húsavík, Iceland
25. Illugastadir seal watching, Illugastadhir, Iceland
26. Kálfshamarsviti, 2H88+VRR, 546 Kálfshamarsvík, Iceland
27. Kópasker strönd, Norðausturvegur, 671, Iceland
28. Kópaskersviti, 870, Kópaskersviti, 671 Kópasker, Iceland
29. Mígandifoss, 3F8G+G4P, Hrisey, Iceland
30. Mývatn Nature Baths, Jarðbaðshólar, 660 Mývatn, Iceland
31. Njarðvíkurskriður, H593+GC, 721 Njardhvik, Iceland
32. Norðfjarðarhornviti Lighthouse, 5F8P+9W, 741 Neskaupstadur, Iceland
33. Raufarhöfn Campsite, C3X5+45F, Skólabraut, 675 Raufarhöfn, Iceland
34. Rifstangi, GRP4+P28, 671 Blikalon, Iceland
35. Samúel Jónsson's Art Farm, Unnamed Road, Q2P5+QPP, 466 Selárdalur, Iceland

36. Sauðanes Lighthouse (Súgandafjörður), 489V+48Q, 431 Suðureyri, Iceland
37. Sauðaneskirkja, 6PWQ+F97, 681 Sauðanes, Iceland
38. Sauðanesviti, 52PX+QQ, 581 Siglufjörður, Iceland
39. Skagaströnd Lookout, RM9V+369, 546 Skagaströnd, Iceland
40. Skinnalón farm, GWF8+363, 671 Asmundarstadhir, Iceland
41. Staðarbjörg Basalt Columns, VHWQ+2MW, Hofsós, Iceland
42. Stafnesviti, X6CX+93G, 246, Iceland
43. Stokksnes, Stokksnesvegur 9720, Iceland
44. Straumnes lighthouse, 3JGW+V67, 566 Fell, Iceland
45. Svalvogaviti, W553+XR7, 471 Hraun, Iceland
46. The Arctic Henge, F26Q+V4F, 676 Raufarhöfn, Iceland
47. Tjaldsvæði, Vallarvegur, 806, Iceland
48. Trollaskagi, Aðalgata 27, 581 Siglufjörður, Iceland
49. Ullarfoss, 4VMV+V44, 500 Staður, Iceland
50. Viking hovel, 4CFM+H2R, Unnamed Road, 431 Suðureyri, Iceland
51. Wheel Sculpture, 3WJ3+Q3, 410 Ísafjörður, Iceland

East Iceland

1. Borgarfjarðarhöfn, G6RW+V55, 721 Bakkagerði, Iceland
2. Dalatangi, 7CCF+3P8, 715 Skálanes, Iceland
3. Digranes Lighthouse, 3749+X6P, 686 Bakkafjörður, Iceland
4. Djúpavík, Iceland
5. Fjörður Beach, Fjörður, 616, Iceland
6. Flateyjardalur Beach, 44F2+6PX, 607 Flateyjardalsheiði, Iceland
7. Njarðvíkurskriður, H593+GC, 721 Njardhvik, Iceland
8. Norðfjarðarhornviti Lighthouse, 5F8P+9W, 741 Neskaupstadur, Iceland
9. Raudinupur Cape, GF55+7JQ, 671 Grjotnes, Iceland
10. Sæbólskirkja, Ingjaldssandsvegur, 426, Iceland
11. Sauðanes Lighthouse (Súgandafjörður), 489V+48Q, 431 Suðureyri, Iceland
12. Siglunes Lighthouse, 55VH+2QJ, 581 Hvanneyri, Iceland
13. Sigríðarstaðir, 3V48+QVP, Djúpvegur, 400 Ísafjörður, Iceland
14. Skógafoss, Gönguleið um Fimmvörðuháls, 861, Iceland
15. Skútustaðagígar, HXC8+943, 660 Skútustaðir, Iceland
16. Staðarbjörg Basalt Columns, VHWQ+2MW, Hofsós, Iceland

17. Stapavík, J22J+2M4, 701 Njardhvik, Iceland
18. Straumnes lighthouse, 3JGW+V67, 566 Fell, Iceland
19. Svalvogaviti, W553+XR7, 471 Hraun, Iceland
20. Tjaldsvæði, Vallarvegur, 806, Iceland
21. Vogaseatours, XHMX+8XC, 421 Vogavegur, 190 Vogar, Iceland
22. Wheel Sculpture, 3WJ3+Q3, 410 Ísafjörður, Iceland

South Iceland

1. Alternative carpark to Jökulsárlón, 781, Iceland
2. Aurora Igloo, Stekkatún 1, 851 Hella, Iceland
3. Breiðárlón, 3J3M+MC9, 785 Breiðárlón, Iceland
4. Diamond Beach, Diamond Beach, 781, Iceland
5. Fjaðrárgljúfur, 881, Iceland
6. Fosstorfufoss, Iceland, Gönguleið um Fimmvörðuháls
7. Gljúfursárfoss, Gljúfursá, Gljúfur, 691, Iceland
8. Gjáin utan við Sýrdalsvoga, 49X2+CM, Vík, Iceland
9. Grábrók, Grábrók, 311, Iceland
10. Grundarfjörður harbour view and Kirkufjell, Snæfellsnesvegur, 350, Iceland
11. Gullfoss Waterfall Eastside, Gullfoss Parking, 806, Iceland
12. Gullfoss Waterfall Lookout, above, Gullfoss Parking, 806, Iceland
13. Húsavík Wooden Church, Garðarsbraut 11, 640 Húsavík, Iceland
14. Hvalsneskirkja, Hvalnes, 246, Iceland
15. Illugastadir seal watching, Illugastadhir, Iceland
16. Kirkjufell reflection, Grundarfjarðarbær,351, 351, Iceland
17. Kirkjufell Viewpoint, WPC7+RXG, 351 Grundarfjörður, Iceland
18. Kirkjufellsfossar, WMGQ+FFJ, 351 Grundarfjörður, Iceland
19. Klettasel Villa, Klettasel, 785 Hof, Iceland
20. Lavator Dimmuborgir, Dimmuborgavegur, 660, Iceland
21. Lake Mývatn panoramic point, H3G2+2HX, 660 Skútustaðir, Iceland
22. Lindarbakki, G5GR+47P' 720' Bakkagerði, Iceland
23. Lísafoss, Snæfellsnesvegur, 371, Iceland
24. Mígandifoss, 3F8G+G4P, Hrisey, Iceland
25. Minnibakki Beach, Skálavíkurvegur, 416, Iceland
26. Njarðvíkurskriður, H593+GC, 721 Njardhvik, Iceland

27. Norðfjarðarhornviti Lighthouse, 5F8P+9W, 741 Neskaupstadur, Iceland
28. Northern Light View Point, 5X7P+32P, 170 Seltjarnarnes, Iceland
29. Northern Lights Lookout, X73V+WXV, 246 Hafnir, Iceland
30. Northern Lights View Point, 23P8+GJP, Göngustígur, 221 Hafnarfjörður, Iceland
31. Northern Lights, Sveitarfélagið Vogar, 191, 191, Iceland
32. Northern Light Inn & Max's Restaurant, 1 Norðurljósavegur (1 Northern Lights Road, 241 Grindavik, Iceland
33. Pláneturnar á Reykjanesi, R8J2+PHX, 230 Reykjanesbær, Iceland
34. Raudinupur Cape, GF55+7JQ, 671 Grjotnes, Iceland
35. Rifstangi, GRP4+P28, 671 Blikalon, Iceland
36. Sauðaneskirkja, 6PWQ+F97, 681 Sauðanes, Iceland
37. Sauðanesviti, 52PX+QQ, 581 Siglufjörður, Iceland
38. Seals, Whales and canoes, Djúpvegur, 401, Iceland
39. Skagaströnd Lookout, RM9V+369, 546 Skagaströnd, Iceland
40. Skógafoss, 861, Iceland
41. Skógafoss, Gönguleið um Fimmvörðuháls, 861, Iceland
42. Steinbogafoss, Gönguleið um Fimmvörðuháls, 861, Iceland
43. Stokksnes, Stokksnesvegur 9720, Iceland
44. Straumnes lighthouse, 3JGW+V67, 566 Fell, Iceland
45. Svalvogaviti, W553+XR7, 471 Hraun, Iceland
46. Tjaldsvæði, Vallarvegur, 806, Iceland
47. Twinheads, 23HX+CX, Bakkafjörður, Iceland
48. Ullarfoss, 4VMV+V44, 500 Staður, Iceland
49. Urdartindur Guesthouse And Cottages, Nordurfjördur 1, 524 Nordurfjördur, Iceland
50. Viewpoint over Jökulsárlón, Unnamed Road, 781, Iceland
51. Viking hovel, 4CFM+H2R, Unnamed Road, 431 Suðureyri, Iceland
52. Víkurfjara Black Sand Beach, CX7Q+PR4, Vik, Iceland

Capital Region (Reykjavík and Surroundings)

1. Aurora Cabins Höfn Iceland, Hafnavegur, 780 Höfn í Hornafirði, Iceland
2. Aurora Igloo, Stekkatún 1, 851 Hella, Iceland
3. Blue Lagoon, Blue Lagoon, 241, Iceland
4. Borealis Hotel, 805 Selfoss, Iceland

5. Bridge Between Continents, V89F+8QH, 233 Hafnir, Iceland
6. Dimmuborgir Parking, Dimmuborgavegur, 660, Iceland
7. Drangaskörð, 57H3+W6J, 524 Drangar, Iceland
8. Fitjarfoss, 52, 311, Iceland
9. Fosstorfufoss, Iceland, Gönguleið um Fimmvörðuháls
10. Glanni Waterfall, QF33+F2C, 311 Bifröst, Iceland
11. Grábrók, Grábrók, 311, Iceland
12. Grundarfjörður harbour view and Kirkufjell, Snæfellsnesvegur, 350, Iceland
13. Gunnuhver Hot Springs, Möðruvellir, Möðruvallavegur 4, 241, Iceland
14. Hallgrimskirkja, Hallgrímstorg 1, 101 Reykjavík, Iceland
15. Heavier Mountain, Seyðisfjarðavegur, 701, Iceland
16. Hidden Crevasse in Thingvellir Park, 550, 806, Iceland
17. Höfði útsýni 2, 848, 660, Iceland
18. Hvannagjá, 550, 806, Iceland
19. Hveravellir, Hveravellir, 541, Iceland
20. Viewing point, 4RFM+JH, 805 Úlfljótsvatn, Iceland

16 PRIME AURORA LOCATIONS - FAROE ISLANDS

Scan the QR Code below for 41 Aurora locations in Faroe Islands

Trøllanes, Faroe Islands

1. Kallur Lighthouse, Kalsoy, 95CP+3M7, Trøllanes 798, Faroe Islands
2. Eastern Ridge Viewpoint, Kalsoy, 95CV+JQP, Trøllanes 798, Faroe Islands
3. James Bond Gravestone, Trøllanes 798, Faroe Islands
4. Kallur lighthouse parking, 9665+786, Trøllanes 798, Faroe Islands

Mikladalur, Faroe Islands

1. The Seal Woman (Kópakonan), 16 Bakkavegur, Mikladalur 797, Faroe Islands
2. Mikladalurfossur, 86PP+755, Mikladalur 797, Faroe Islands

Viðareiði, Faroe Islands

1. Cape Enniberg, Cape Enniberg, 750, Faroe Islands
2. Praktfuldt udsigtspunkt, Kirkjugøta, Viðareiði, Færøerne, 9F64+4CG, Viðareiði 750, Faroe Islands
3. Malinsfjall, 8FV6+69J, Viðareiði 750, Faroe Islands
4. Vidareidi Viewpoint, 8FWQ+3X5, Viðareiði 750, Faroe Islands

Kunoy, Faroe Islands

1. Skarðsbygd, 89F2+M87, Kunoy 785, Faroe Islands

Borðoy, Faroe Islands

1. Svartidalurfoss, 7F2J+F92, Borðoy 727, Faroe Islands
2. Klakkur trailhead, 69GR+MC2, Bordoy, Klaksvík 700, Faroe Islands
3. Klakkur, 69PM+P73, Klaksvík 700, Faroe Islands

Dalur, Faroe Islands

1. Dalur Camping, 1 Dalsvegur, Dalur 235, Faroe Islands

Skálavík, Faroe Islands

1. Skálhøvdi, R9H7+P34, Skálavík 220, Faroe Islands

Sandur, Faroe Islands

1. Ship capsize memorial, R4V4+XV2, Sandur 210, Faroe Islands

Skopunar, Faroe Islands

1. Trailhead Líraberg, W32H+QC8, Skopunar 240, Faroe Islands

Vágar, Faroe Islands

1. Skarðsáfossur, Vágar, 3HRW+P85, Bøur, Faroe Islands
2. Múlafossur Waterfall, 4H57+2QG, Gasadalur 387, Faroe Islands
3. Sunset Viewpoint, 4H47+CXP, Gasadalur 387, Faroe Islands
4. Bøur panoramic viewpoint, 3JPM+36G, Bøur 386, Faroe Islands
5. Bøsdalafossur Waterfall, 2QF6+G74, Sandavágur 370, Faroe Islands

Streymoy, Faroe Islands

1. Slættanes, 5Q44+264, Slættanes 360, Faroe Islands
2. Pollurin Waterfall, 7R25+7H6, Streymoy 436, Faroe Islands
3. Mindesmærke for sømænd, 33, 440 Víkavegur, Haldórsvík 440, Faroe Islands
4. Fossá, Fossá, 360, Faroe Islands
5. Kollafjarðar kirkja, 438X+Q8W, Við Sjógv, Kollafjørður 410, Faroe Islands
6. Vestmanna scenic point, 5V5V+59, Vestmanna 350, Faroe Islands
7. Viewpoint over Kvívík, 4WF9+XQ2, 340, Faroe Islands

Fuglafjørður, Faroe Islands

1. Fuglafjørður Viewpoint, 65QJ+72J, Fuglafjørður 530, Faroe

Islands
2. Fuglafjarðar, Faroe Islands, 756C+RF, Hellurnar 695, Faroe Islands

Sumba, Faroe Islands

1. Akraberg Lighthouse, 18 Akrabergsvegur, Sumba 970, Faroe Islands

Sandvík, Faroe Islands

1. Ásmundarstakkur, J2PF+Q52, Faroe Islands
2. Ásmundarstakkur trailhead, J2HV+XQ, Sandvík 860, Faroe Islands

Other Locations

1. Rinkusteinar, Faroe Islands
2. Trælavatn - the Slave Lake, 656J+2P5, Trælavatn, Faroe Islands
3. Gøtu kirkja, 57V3+9F5, Gøtugjógv 511, Faroe Islands
4. Lervik webcam, 11, 520 Nýggjagerði, Leirvík 520, Faroe Islands
5. Hole in the Cliff, 825, Faroe Islands
6. Hvannhagi, 800, Faroe Islands

17 PRIME AURORA LOCATIONS - IRELAND

Scan the QR Code below for 40 Aurora locations in Ireland

Ardmalin, Malin Head, Co. Donegal, Ireland

1. Malin Head, Ardmalin, Malin Head, Co. Donegal
2. Northernmost Point of Contiguous Ireland, 9JMH+JC, Malin Head, Co. Donegal, Ireland
3. Pólifreann or Hells Hole, Ardmalin, Co. Donegal
4. Lloyds Signal Tower- Malin Head, Unnamed Rd,, Ardmalin, Co. Donegal
5. Cliff of Pracha, Ardmalin, Co. Donegal, Ireland
6. Portmór or Kitters Beach, Unnamed Road, Ardmalin, Co. Donegal, Ireland
7. Esky Bay, Unnamed Road, Ardmalin, Co. Donegal

Ballygorman, Co. Donegal, Ireland

1. Ballygorman Beach, Ireland

Falmore, Co. Donegal, Ireland

1. Tremone Bay Beach, Ballycharry, Falmore, Co. Donegal, Ireland

Stroove, Co. Donegal, Ireland

1. Shrove viewpoint, Unnamed Road, Stroove, Co. Donegal, Ireland
2. Stroove Beach, Stroove, Co. Donegal, Ireland

Culdaff, Co. Donegal, Ireland

1. Culdaff Beach, 2 Shore Rd, Culdaff, Co. Donegal, Ireland

Fanad, Co. Donegal, Ireland

1. Fanad, Fanad, Arryheernabin, Co. Donegal, Ireland
2. Fanad Head Lighthouse, Cionn Fhánada Eara Thíre na Binne, Arryheernabin, Baile Láir, Co. Donegal, F92

YC03, Ireland
   3. Fanad Head Lighthouse Visitors Centre and Car Park, Fanad Head, Shannagh, Co. Donegal, Ireland
   4. Great Pollet Sea Arch, Stooey, Co. Donegal, Ireland
   5. Mowi Ireland, Rinmore, Fanad, Cooladerry, Letterkenny, Co. Donegal, Ireland
   6. White Shore Beach, Eelburn Caravan Park, Rinmore, Co. Donegal, Ireland
   7. Malgorm Point, 7739+WG, Rinboy, Ballyhoorisky, Co. Donegal, Ireland
   8. Martins Tower, Ballyhooriskey, Fanad, Co. Donegal, Ireland

Mamore Gap, Co. Donegal, Ireland
   1. Gap of Mamore, Mamore Gap, Urrismenagh, Co. Donegal, Ireland

Tullagh, Co. Donegal, Ireland
   1. Tullagh Strand, Tullagh Strand, Co. Donegal, Ireland

Pollan, Co. Donegal, Ireland
   1. Pollan Strand, Pollan Strand, Co. Donegal, Ireland

Carrickabraghy, Co. Donegal, Ireland
   1. Carrickabraghy Castle, Unnamed Road, Carrickabraghy, Carrickabraghy, Co. Donegal, Ireland

Melmore, Co. Donegal, Ireland
   1. Eire 78 - Melmore, 66Q2+PP, Melmore, Co. Donegal, Ireland
   2. Rosguill Holiday Park, Melmore Road, Gortnalughoge, Letterkenny, Co. Donegal, F92 W965, Ireland
   3. Trá na Rossan view, Glebe, Co. Donegal, Ireland
   4. Rosguill Peninsula, Unnamed Road, Glenoory, Co. Donegal, Ireland

Mayo, Ireland
   1. Minaun Heights, Dookinelly (Thulis), Co. Mayo, Ireland

2. Cross Loop walk, Belmullet, Cross (Wallace) East, Co. Mayo, Ireland
3. Downpatrick Head, Knockaun, Ballycastle, Co. Mayo, Ireland

Horn Head, Co. Donegal, Ireland
1. Wild Atlantic Way Discovery Point @Horn Head, Unnamed Road, Muntermellan, Co. Donegal, Ireland

Tramore, Co. Donegal, Ireland
1. Tramore, Tramore, Co. Donegal, Ireland

Knockfola, Co. Donegal, Ireland
1. Bloody Foreland Arch, Unnamed Road, Knockfola, Co. Donegal, Ireland

Tororragaun, Co. Donegal, Ireland
1. Sea Arches, Tororragaun, Co. Donegal, Ireland

Gola, Co. Donegal, Ireland
1. Sand Beach, Gola, Ballindrait, Co. Donegal, Ireland

Glencolumbkille, Co. Donegal, Ireland
1. Cloghanmore Megalithic Tomb, Malin More, Glencolumbkille, Co. Donegal, Ireland

Maghera, Co. Donegal, Ireland
1. Maghera Beach, Unnamed Road, Maghera, Co. Donegal, Ireland
2. Caves of Maghera, Maghera, Ardara, Co. Donegal, Ireland

Mullaghderg, Co. Donegal, Ireland
1. Mullaghderg Beach, The Banks, Mullaghderg, Co. Donegal, Ireland

Other Locations
1. Martins Tower, Ballyhooriskey, Fanad, Co. Donegal

CHASING NORTHERN LIGHTS

18 PRIME AURORA LOCATIONS - UK

Scan the QR Code below for 210 Aurora locations in UK

Caernarfon, UK

1. Aberafon Camping and Caravan Site, Gyrn Goch, Caernarfon LL54 5PN, UK
2. Aberdesach Beach, Clynnog-fawr, Aberdesach, Caernarfon LL54 5EW, UK
3. Traeth Trefor, Beach Rd, Caernarfon LL54 5LB, UK

Ballymena, UK

1. Access to Hidden Village of Galboly, 125 A2, Ballymena BT44 0JT, UK
2. Ardclinis Church, 125 Garron Rd, Ballymena BT44 0JT, UK
3. Bachelor's Walk, Straidkilly Rd, Ballymena BT44 0BZ, UK
4. Kilranney Chapel, Torr Rd, Cushendun, Ballymena BT44 0PU, UK
5. Madman's Window, Larne, Ballymena BT44 0BA, UK
6. Whitebay, Ballymena BT44 0DA, UK
7. Ballygally Beach, 262 Coast Rd, Ballygalley, Larne BT40 2QX, UK
8. Carnlough Beach, Carnlough Beach, Larne BT44 0HR, UK

Lairg, UK

1. Achininver Beach, Lairg IV27 4YT, UK
2. Achnahaird Beach, Achnahaird Beach IV26 2YT, UK
3. Ard Neackie Lime Kilns, Heilam, Lairg IV27 4UL, UK
4. Balnakeil Church, Durness, Lairg IV27 4PX, UK
5. Drumbeg Viewpoint, Lairg IV27 4NW, UK
6. Bettyhill Viewpoint, Thurso KW14 7SQ, UK
7. Borve Castle, Farr, Thurso KW14 7TA, UK
8. Durness bay, Unnamed Road, Lairg IV27 4PR, UK
9. Geological Information Point, Road End, Lairg IV27 4QF, UK
10. Old Man of Stoer, Lairg IV27 4JG, UK

11. Puffin Viewpoint, 9RP3+P9, Tarbet, Lairg IV27 4TE, UK
12. Sandwood Bay Beach, Sandwood Bay Beach, Lairg IV27 4RU, UK
13. Scourie Beach, Scourie, Beach, Lairg IV27 4TG, UK
14. Stoer Lighthouse, Stoer Lighthouse, Lairg IV27 4JH, UK
15. Visit Cape Wrath, Braemar, Lairg IV27 4PZ, UK

Isle of Skye, UK

1. Amar River Viewpoint, A863, Isle of Skye IV56 8FX, UK
2. An Corran Beach, Unnamed Road, 9JT, Portree IV51 9JT, UK
3. Clan MacLeod Memorial Cairn, Trumpan, Isle of Skye IV55 8GW, UK
4. Fairy Pools, Isle of Skye IV47 8TA, UK
5. Neist Cliff Viewpoint, Unnamed Road, Isle of Skye IV55 8WU, UK
6. Neist Point Cliff Lighthouse Viewpoint, Skye, Isle of Skye IV55 8WT, UK
7. Neist Point Lighthouse, Isle of Skye IV55 8WU, UK
8. Rigg Viewpoint, Isle of Skye IV51 9HX, UK
9. Rob and Chris Wright Lookout and Bench, Skye, Isle of Skye IV55 8GT, UK
10. Rubha Hunish, Rubha Hunish, Isle of Skye, Portree IV51, UK
11. The Brother's Point, near, Culnacnoc, Isle of Skye IV51 9JJ, UK
12. The Lump, 6 Bayfield Rd, Portree IV51 9EW, UK
13. Waternish Lighthouse, Skye, Isle of Skye IV55 8GW, UK

Isle of Harris, UK

1. Ardvourlie Woodland, Aird a' Mhulaidh, Isle of Harris HS3 3AB, UK

Girvan, UK

1. Ardmillan Beach, Girvan KA26 0HP, UK
2. Ardwell Bay, 6443+WM, Girvan, UK
3. Girvan Beach, Girvan KA26 9AJ, UK
4. Turnberry Lighthouse, South Ayrshire, Girvan KA26 9PD, UK

Isle of Man

1. Ballaugh Beach Carpark, Unnamed Road, Isle of Man IM7, Isle of Man
2. Blue Point, 9GVF+3FM, Andreas, Isle of Man IM7, Isle of Man
3. Corrin's Tower, Corrin's Tower, Isle of Man IM5, Isle of Man
4. Glen Mooar Beach Car Park, 79CV+RQ4, Kirk Michael, Isle of Man IM6, Isle of Man
5. Glen Wyllin Beach, Glen Wyllin, Isle of Man IM6, Isle of Man
6. Maughold Lighthouse, Maughold Lighthouse, Maughold Village, IM7, Isle of Man
7. Milner's Tower, 36VC+2V6, Bradda East, Isle of Man
8. Point of Ayre Lighthouse, A16, Isle of Man IM7, Isle of Man
9. Port Lewaigue Beach, 8J5W+RG2, Ramsey, Isle of Man IM7, Isle of Man
10. Sulby Reservoir, y, Tholt-e-Will Plantation, A14, Isle of Man IM7, Isle of Man
11. The Ayres National Nature Reserve, Isle, CH4Q+C2M, Isle of Man IM7, Isle of Man
12. The Great Laxey Wheel, Mines Rd, Laxey, Isle of Man IM4 7NL, Isle of Man

Isle of Colonsay, UK

1. Balnahard Beach, Isle of Colonsay PA61 7YT, UK
2. Dùn Uragaig, Colonsay, Isle of Colonsay PA61 7YT,

UK
3. Kiloran Bay, Colonsay, Isle of Colonsay PA61 7YT, UK
4. South Western Colonsay beaches, 2PXV+WJ, Isle of Colonsay PA61 7YR, UK

Omagh, UK

- Barnes Gap, Gorticashel Rd, Omagh BT79 8EN, UK

Orkney, UK

1. Bay of Swartmill Beach Car Park & Picnic Area, 73XM+84, Skelwick, Orkney KW17 2DD, UK
2. Broch of Burrian, North Ronaldsay, Orkney KW17 2BE, UK
3. Broch of Gurness, Aikerness, Evie, Orkney KW17 2NH, UK
4. Castle o'Burrian, Orkney KW17 2DE, UK
5. Fisherman's Huts, Mainland, Orkney KW17 2NB, UK
6. Kelp Pits, 9JMG+X6, Hollandstoun, Orkney KW17 2BG, UK
7. Kitchener Memorial, Mainland, Orkney KW17 2ND, UK
8. Midhowe Broch, Orkney KW17 2PS, UK
9. Natural Arch, Westray, Orkney KW17 2DN, UK
10. Northern View, Unnamed Road, Orkney KW17 2BU, UK
11. Noup Head Lighthouse, Unnamed Road, Orkney KW17 2DW, UK
12. Parking at Saviskaill Bay, Rousay, Orkney KW17 2PS, UK
13. Pine Cone of Stones, 9H65+VC, Hollandstoun, Orkney KW17 2BE, UK
14. Skiba Geo, Northside, Birsay, Orkney KW17 2LX, UK
15. Start Point Lighthouse, Orkney KW17 2BP, UK
16. White Mill Circular Walk & Beach, Unnamed Road, Orkney KW17 2AZ, UK

Shetland, UK

1. Breckon Sands, Breckon Sands, Shetland ZE2 9DD, UK
2. Broch of Mousa, Shetland ZE2 9HP, UK
3. Burrafirth Beach Viewpoint, R45C+GF, Burrafirth, Shetland ZE2 9EQ, UK
4. Burrafirth viewing point alternative, R43C+22, Burrafirth, Shetland ZE2 9EQ, UK
5. Fugla Ness Lighthouse, 4M43+G2, Hamnavoe, Shetland ZE2 9LA, UK
6. Geopark Shetland, Shetland ZE2 9PP, UK
7. Holes of Scraada, Shetland ZE2 9RS, UK
8. Minn Beach, Shetland ZE2 9UY, UK
9. Northernmost Point Of UK, V46G+6C, Skaw, Shetland ZE2 9EQ, UK
10. Point of Fethaland Lighthouse, Shetland Island, Shetland ZE2 9RY, UK
11. Scousburgh Sands, Mainland, Shetland ZE2 9JE, UK
12. Skaw Beach, Unst, Shetland ZE2 9EF, UK
13. St Ninian's beach, Unnamed Road, Bigton, Shetland ZE2 9JA, UK

Isle of Lewis, UK

1. Butt of Lewis Lighthouse, Lewis and Harris HS2 0XH, UK
2. Calanais Standing Stones, 12m west of Stornoway off the A859 Isle of Lewis, Isle of Lewis HS2 9DY, UK
3. Dalmore Beach, Carloway, Isle of Lewis HS2 9AD, UK
4. Dùn Èistean, Isle of Lewis HS2 0XF, UK
5. Eoropie Beach, Ness, Isle of Lewis HS2 0XH, UK
6. Galson Campsite - Campervan Bays, 5 Tom Na Ba, South Galson, Isle of Lewis HS2 0SG, UK
7. Mangersta Sea Stacks, Isle of Lewis HS2 9HA, UK
8. Port Stoth, Isle of Lewis HS2 0XH, UK
9. Shawbost Beach, N Shawbost, Isle of Lewis HS2 9BQ, UK

10. St Columba's Church (Eaglais na h-Aoidhe), Isle of Lewis HS2 0PB, UK
11. St Moluag's Church, Isle of Lewis HS2 0XA, UK
12. Swainbost Beach, FPR8+JR, Swainbost, Isle of Lewis HS2 0TG, UK
13. Traigh Mhòr, North Tolsta, Isle of Lewis HS2 0NH, UK
14. The Blackhouse, Arnol, 42 Arnol, Bragar, Isle of Lewis HS2 9DB, UK

Islay, UK

1. Cultoon Stone Circle, Islay, Isle of Islay PA47 7SZ, UK
2. Currie Sands Beach, Unnamed Road, Isle of Islay PA47 7SY, UK
3. Ruvaal Lighthouse, Isle of Islay PA46 7RB, UK
4. Saligo Bay Beach, Isle of Islay PA44 7PU, UK
5. Sanaigmore Beach, Sanaigmore, Isle of Islay PA44 7PT, UK

Eyemouth, UK

1. Eyemouth Beach, High St, Eyemouth TD14 5EU, UK
2. Fast Castle, 1-6 Dowlaw Rd, Eyemouth TD14 5TY, UK
3. St Abb's Head, Eyemouth TD14 5QG, UK

Bideford, UK

1. Angels Wings, Clovelly, S W Coast Path, EX39, Bideford EX39 5TA, UK
2. Blackchurch Rock, Westward Ho!, Bideford EX39 5TA, UK
3. Hartland Point, Hartland, Bideford EX39 6AU, UK

North Uist, UK

1. St Kilda viewing point, Isle of North Uist HS6 5DF, UK

2. Traigh Iar, North Uist, Isle of North Uist HS6 5BS, UK

Dunbar, UK

1. Dunbar Esplanade, Dunbar EH42 1AR, UK
2. Tyninghame Beach, Tyninghame Beach, Dunbar EH42 1XW, UK

North Berwick, UK

1. Tantallon Castle, North Berwick EH39 5PN, UK
2. The Lookout Cabin, North Berwick EH39 4SS, UK

Wick, UK

1. Castle Sinclair Girnigoe, Wick KW1 4QT, UK
2. Duncansby Head Lighthouse, Wick KW1 4YS, UK
3. Ness Broch, Wick KW1 4XX, UK
4. Noss Head Lighthouse, Unnamed Road, Wick, Wick KW1 4QT, UK

Penzance, UK

1. Bosigran Castle Promontory Fort, Zennor, Penzance TR20 8YX, UK
2. Gurnard's Head, Zennor, Saint Ives TR26 3DE, UK
3. National Trust - Cape Cornwall, 7NN, S W Coast Path, Penzance TR19 7NN, UK
4. Portheras Cove, Pendeen, Penzance TR19 7TU, UK

Cemaes Bay, UK

1. Coronation Tower King Edward VII, Llanbadrig, Cemaes Bay LL67 0LN, UK
2. Maes Parcio Bryn Aber, Unnamed Road, Cemaes Bay LL67 0DY, UK
3. Traeth Porth Wen Beach, Traeth Porth Wen Beach, Llanbadrig, Cemaes Bay LL67 0LN, UK

Newquay, UK

1. Holywell Bay, Holywell Bay, Newquay TR8 5PG, UK
2. Kelsey Head, S W Coast Path, Newquay TR8 5SE, UK
3. Pentire Point West, S W Coast Path, Newquay TR8 5SE, UK

Stranraer, UK

1. Corsewall Lighthouse Hotel, Corsewall Point, Kirkcolm, Stranraer DG9 0QG, UK

Elgin, UK

1. Burghead Pictish Fort, 83 Bath St, Burghead, Elgin IV30 5TZ, UK
2. Hopeman East Beach, Hopeman East Beach, Hopeman, Elgin IV30 5RX, UK
3. Covesea Lighthouse & Royal Navy and Royal Air Force Heritage Centre, Covesea, Lossiemouth IV31 6SP, UK

Orkney, UK

1. Bay of Swartmill Beach Car Park & Picnic Area, 73XM+84, Skelwick, Orkney KW17 2DD, UK
2. Broch of Burrian, North Ronaldsay, Orkney KW17 2BE, UK
3. Broch of Gurness, Aikerness, Evie, Orkney KW17 2NH, UK
4. Castle o'Burrian, Orkney KW17 2DE, UK
5. Fisherman's Huts, Mainland, Orkney KW17 2NB, UK
6. Kelp Pits, 9JMG+X6, Hollandstoun, Orkney KW17 2BG, UK
7. Kitchener Memorial, Mainland, Orkney KW17 2ND, UK
8. Midhowe Broch, Orkney KW17 2PS, UK
9. Natural Arch, Westray, Orkney KW17 2DN, UK
10. Northern View, Unnamed Road, Orkney KW17 2BU,

UK
11. Noup Head Lighthouse, Unnamed Road, Orkney KW17 2DW, UK
12. Parking at Saviskaill Bay, Rousay, Orkney KW17 2PS, UK
13. Pine Cone of Stones, 9H65+VC, Hollandstoun, Orkney KW17 2BE, UK
14. Skiba Geo, Northside, Birsay, Orkney KW17 2LX, UK
15. Start Point Lighthouse, Orkney KW17 2BP, UK
16. White Mill Circular Walk & Beach, Unnamed Road, Orkney KW17 2AZ, UK

Shetland, UK

1. Breckon Sands, Breckon Sands, Shetland ZE2 9DD, UK
2. Broch of Mousa, Shetland ZE2 9HP, UK
3. Burrafirth Beach Viewpoint, R45C+GF, Burrafirth, Shetland ZE2 9EQ, UK
4. Burrafirth viewing point alternative, R43C+22, Burrafirth, Shetland ZE2 9EQ, UK
5. Fugla Ness Lighthouse, 4M43+G2, Hamnavoe, Shetland ZE2 9LA, UK
6. Geopark Shetland, Shetland ZE2 9PP, UK
7. Holes of Scraada, Shetland ZE2 9RS, UK
8. Minn Beach, Shetland ZE2 9UY, UK
9. Northernmost Point Of UK, V46G+6C, Skaw, Shetland ZE2 9EQ, UK
10. Point of Fethaland Lighthouse, Shetland Island, Shetland ZE2 9RY, UK
11. Scousburgh Sands, Mainland, Shetland ZE2 9JE, UK
12. Skaw Beach, Unst, Shetland ZE2 9EF, UK
13. St Ninian's beach, Unnamed Road, Bigton, Shetland ZE2 9JA, UK

Other Locations

1. Bow Fiddle Rock, AB56 4NN, UK

2. Brancaster Beach, Brancaster, King's Lynn PE31 8AX, UK
3. Campselker, Bootle Station, Selker LA19 5XQ, UK
4. Cairnbulg Boathaven, M3J4+65, Fraserburgh AB43 8WT, UK
5. Cairngorms National Park, United Kingdom
6. Cley Beach, X28X+85, Holt NR25 7TE, UK
7. Clodgy Point, St Ives, Saint Ives TR26 3AB, UK
8. Corgarff Viewpoint, Aberdeenshire, Strathdon AB36 8YP, UK
9. Cove Harbour, 6 W End, Cove, Cockburnspath TD13 5XD, UK
10. Cove Light Anti Aircraft Battery WW2, Achnasheen IV22 2LT, UK
11. Cula Bay, 7 Nunton, Isle of Benbecula HS7 5LU, UK
12. Culzean Country Park Visitor Centre, Maybole KA19 8JX, UK
13. Cumbria Coast, Sandwith, Whitehaven CA28 9UY, UK
14. Drigg Sand Dunes & Beach, Holmrook CA19 1XL, UK
15. Dunstanburgh Castle, Dunstanburgh Rd, Craster, Alnwick NE66 3TT, UK
16. Eilean Donan Lookout, Bridge Road End, Kyle IV40 8DX, UK
17. Electric Brae, A719, Maybole KA19 8JR, UK
18. Findhorn Beach, Findhorn Beach, North Shore, Findhorn, Forres IV36 3YQ, UK
19. Fleswick Bay, Fleswick Bay, St Bees, Whitehaven CA28 9UY, UK
20. Glencoe Viewpoint, A82, Ballachulish PH50 4SF, UK
21. Glenfinnan Viewpoint, 2 Erracht, A830, Banavie, Fort William PH37 4LT, UK
22. Heddon's Mouth, Barnstaple EX31 4PY, UK
23. Holy Island Causeway, Holy Island, Berwick-upon-Tweed TD15 2PB, UK
24. Holywell Bay, Holywell Bay, Newquay TR8 5PG, UK
25. Kelsey Head, S W Coast Path, Newquay TR8 5SE, UK
26. Loch Duich Viewpoint, Carr Brae, Kyle IV40 8HA, UK
27. Loch Lochy Viewpoint, A82, Spean Bridge PH34 4DZ,

UK
28. Maen Porth Llong, WM5X+VW, Haverfordwest, UK
29. Moryn, Porthdinllaen, Morfa Nefyn, Pwllheli LL53 6DB, UK
30. Nairn Beach, Nairn Beach, Nairn IV12 4EA, UK
31. Penbryn Beach, Unnamed Road, 6QL, Llandysul SA44 6QL, UK
32. Porth Bach, V73M+RH, Pwllheli LL53 8LP, UK
33. Porth Ysgaden, Porth Ysgaden, Tudweiliog, Pwllheli LL53 8PD, UK
34. Queen's View, Queens View Visitor Centre, B8019, Pitlochry PH16 5NR, UK
35. RSPB Dunnet Head, Dunnet Head Lighthouse, Brough, Thurso KW14 8XS, UK
36. Salthouse Beach, Beach Rd, Holt NR25 7XW, UK
37. Sand Dunes, Norfolk Coast Path, King's Lynn PE31 8JJ, UK
38. Sheringham Beach, Promenade, Sheringham NR26 8LS
39. Siccar Point, Siccar Point, Cockburnspath TD13 5YS, UK
40. Tantallon Castle, North Berwick EH39 5PN, UK
41. The Blackhouse, Arnol, 42 Arnol, Bragar, Isle of Lewis HS2 9DB, UK
42. The Bone Caves, Tain, Lairg IV27 4HL, UK
43. The Hebridean Way Start Point, Vatersay, Isle of Barra HS9 5YW, UK
44. The Lookout Cabin, North Berwick EH39 4SS, UK
45. The Rumps, Wadebridge PL27 6QY, UK
46. Tintagel Castle, Castle Rd, Tintagel PL34 0HE, UK
47. Tor Ness lighthouse, Hoy, Stromness KW16 3NZ, UK
48. Torr Head, Ballycastle BT54 6RQ, UK
49. Torrisdale beach, GPGX+59, Bettyhill, Thurso KW14 7SS, UK
50. Tresaith Waterfall, Afon Saith, Cardigan SA43 2JL, UK
51. Uamh An Duin, 2GVX+GM, Isle of Barra HS9 5YD, UK
52. Weybourne beach, 3 Beach Ln, Weybourne, Holt NR25 7AH, UK

19 PRIME AURORA LOCATIONS - SVALBARD

Scan the QR Code below for 36 Aurora locations in Svalbard

Longyearbyen, Svalbard and Jan Mayen

1. Isbjørnskiltet i Adventdalen, Unnamed Road, 6P96+39W, Longyearbyen 9170
2. Longyearbyen Harbour, SJ, 6HHX+HQF, Longyearbyen 9170, Svalbard and Jan Mayen
3. Longyearbyen Camping, Hotellneset, Longyearbyen 9171, Svalbard and Jan Mayen
4. Svalbard Satellite Station, 69HW+HQ4, Longyearbyen 9170, Svalbard and Jan Mayen
5. Gjestehuset 102, Guest House 102, Nybyen 9170 Longyearbyen SJ, Longyearbyen 9171
6. Coal Miners' Cabin, 6H2R+RP4, Vei 100, Longyearbyen 9171, Svalbard and Jan Mayen
7. Sverdrupbyen, Longyearbyen, 6H3J+G34, Longyearbyen 9170, Svalbard and Jan Mayen
8. Nybyen, 5HXQ+QCG, Longyearbyen 9170
9. Svalbard Church, Postboks 533 Longyearbyen, Longyearbyen 9171, Svalbard and Jan Mayen
10. Gruve 3, 6CQX+46W, Longyearbyen 9170
11. Vestpynten Lighthouse, 7C28+PR, Longyearbyen 9170, Svalbard and Jan Mayen
12. EISCAT Svalbard Radar, SJ, Gruve 7-fjellet, Longyearbyen, Longyearbyen 9170, Svalbard and Jan Mayen
13. Gruvefjellet, Gruvefjellet, 9170, Svalbard and Jan Mayen

Pyramiden, Svalbard and Jan Mayen

1. Hotel Pyramiden, M84H+3C2, Pyramiden 9170, Svalbard and Jan Mayen
2. Pyramiden City Identification Sign, M83W+PWF, Pyramiden 9170, Svalbard and Jan Mayen
3. Lenin Statue, M845+7FG, Pyramiden 9170, Svalbard and Jan Mayen

Ny-Ålesund, Svalbard and Jan Mayen

1. Ny-Ålesund Museum, Unnamed Road, WWGJ+538, Ny-Ålesund 9173, Svalbard and Jan Mayen
2. Roald Amundsen Monument, Unnamed Road, WWFJ+G42, Ny-Ålesund 9173, Svalbard and Jan Mayen
3. Ny-Ålesund Geodetiske Observatorium, WVH9+MF, Ny-Ålesund 9173, Svalbard and Jan Mayen

Other Locations in Svalbard and Jan Mayen

1. Camp Barentz, 9170, Svalbard and Jan Mayen
2. Svalbard Global Seed Vault, 9170, Svalbard and Jan Mayen
3. Isfjord Radio Adventure Hotel, Kapp Linné, 9170, Svalbard and Jan Mayen
4. Wilczekodden-Hus, XHW2+6GM, 9170, Svalbard and Jan Mayen
5. Ariebreen, 9170, Svalbard and Jan Mayen
6. Russian State Meteorological Service, 3659+RQ5, Barentsburg 9178, Svalbard and Jan Mayen
7. Ny-London, 9170, Svalbard and Jan Mayen
8. Von Post Glacier, 9170, Svalbard and Jan Mayen
9. Sassen-Bünsow Land National Park, 9170, Svalbard and Jan Mayen
10. South Spitsbergen National Park, South Spitsbergen National Park
11. Camp Bolterdalen, 5XC2+H4H, 9170, Svalbard and Jan Mayen
12. Svalbard Husky AS, CFCMWF2M+GH, 9170, Svalbard and Jan Mayen
13. Nordenskjøld-Land-Nasjonalpark, 31.5903709, 74.2990391 SJ, 5400, Svalbard and Jan Mayen

Unnamed Coordinates

1. 78.198399, 15.839638
2. 78°12'20.1"N 15°35'37.3"E
3. 78°14'48.5"N 15°23'06.3"E
4. 78°12'54.6"N 15°37'04.7"E

20 PRIME AURORA LOCATIONS - NORWAY

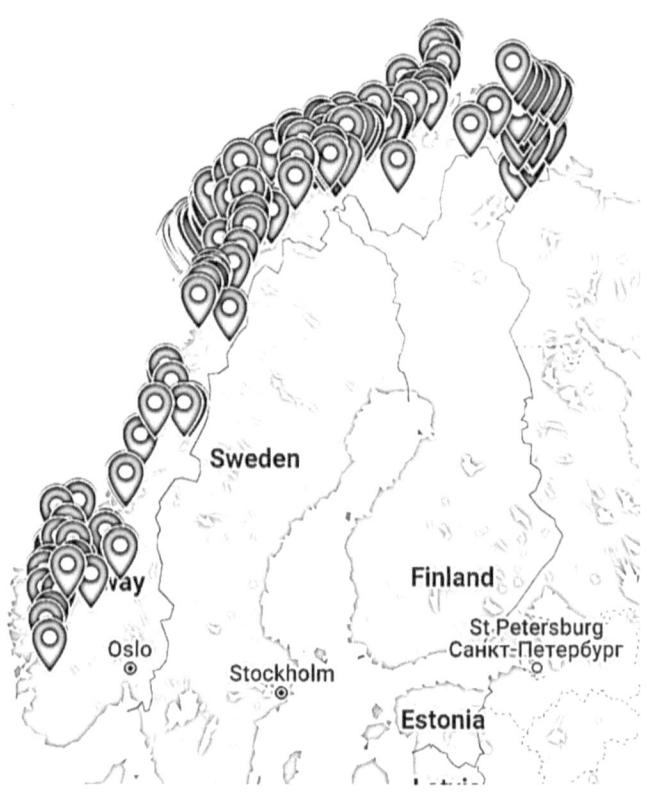

Scan the QR Code below for 251 Aurora locations in Norway

Å, Norway
1. Å i lofoten point, VXGG+84, Å, Norway
2. Ågvatnet Lookout, Moskenes Municipality, Norway
3. Andstabben viewpoint, VWHR+2X, Å, Norway
4. Punkt widokowy na Å, VXJ8+4J, Å, Norway

Andenes, Norway
1. Andenes Viewpoint (Aurora Borealis), Andøya, Andøy

Andoy, Norway
1. Sandvika strand i Børra, Andoy, Norway

Aurland, Norway
1. Skjerdalsvegen 3, Skjerdalsvegen 3, 5745 Aurland, Norway

Balestrand, Norway
1. Gaularfjellet Utsikten (Viewpoint), Rv13, 6899 Balestrand

Ballstad, Norway
1. Hill with monument, Hattvikveien 7, 8373 Ballstad, Norway
2. Stokkvika, CH5P+5P, Mulstrand, Norway

Beito, Norway
1. Smørkollen Viewpoint, Fv51, 2952 Beito, Norway

Billingen, Norway
1. Billingen Viewpoint, Billingen, Skjåk, Norway

Bleik, Norway
1. Bleik sandstrand, Fv976, 8481 Bleik, Norway

Bodø, Norway
1. Badeplass (passer fint for småbarn), Soløyvannet badeplass
2. Bestefarsvarden, Bratten 7, 8014 Bodø, Norway
3. Hovdsundet, Hovdsundet, Bodø, Norway
4. Keiservarden viewpoint, 8016 Bodø, Norway
5. Langsanden, Langsanden, Gildeskål, Norway
6. Lopsfjellet, Bodø Municipality, Norway
7. Mjelle, Unnamed Road, 8016, 8016 Bodø, Norway
8. Ørnvassbu, 8050 Bodø, Norway

Bø i Vesterålen, Norway
1. Nordahlstranda, Nordahlstranda 11, 8470 Bø i Vesterålen

Bø, Norway
1. Fjærvollsanden, Fjærvollsanden, Bø, Norway
2. Ingvalds Garasje, Moloveien 4, 8475 Straumsjøen, Norway
3. Skiftesanden Beach, Langøya, Bø, Norway
4. Uværshula Bø, Fv820 304,8470, Bø, Norway

Bøstad, Norway
1. Borga Eggum, Eggumsveien 850, 8360 Bøstad, Norway
2. Eggum naturreservat, Eggum, Norway
3. Head, Eggumsveien, 8360 Bøstad, Norway
4. Hvit strand - Eggum, Eggumsveien 825, 8360 Bøstad, Norway
5. Waterfall/Powerstation, 7MVC+FV, Eggum, Norway

Bøverdalen, Norway
1. Nufshaug Scenic ViewPoint, Fv55, 2687 Bøverdalen, Norway

Botnhamn, Norway
1. Jekthavna, Laukvikveien 423, 9373 Botnhamn, Norway
2. Sandsneset view, Fv274, 9373 Botnhamn, Norway
3. Stranda i Laukvika, Laukvikveien, 9373 Botnhamn, Norway

Bø, Norway
1. Båen, Vestvågøy, Norway

Bugøynes, Norway
1. View on Bugøynes / Pykeija, Fv355, 9935 Bugøynes, Norway

Burfjord, Norway
1. Park for caravan, with ocean view, Fv364 21, 9161 Burfjord,

Båtsfjord, Norway
1. Båtsfjord View Point, Hindberggata 21A, 9990 Båtsfjord,
2. Persfjorden-Syltefjorden, Fv341 1, 9990 Båtsfjord, Norway

Brunstranda, Flakstad, Norway
1. Brunstranda, Brunstranda, Flakstad, Norway

Eggum, Norway

1. Henningsvær Port Viewpoint

Eidfjord, Norway
1. Hardanger Bridge Viewpoint, Eidfjordvegen 571, 5783 Kinsarvik, Norway

Ersfjordbotn, Norway
1. Klokka ti, MJPG+7G, Ersfjordbotn, Norway

Flakstad, Norway
1. Flakstadbruene, 8380 Flakstad, Norway
2. Flakstadsanden, Flakstadsanden, Flakstad, Norway
3. Morpheus Beach, 38FW+H8, Flakstad Municipality, Norway
4. Skagsanden beach, Skagsanden beach, 8380 Flakstad, Norway

Flata, Norway
1. Amazing viewpoint, VR3G+V8, Flata, Norway

Fredvang, Norway
1. Kvalvika Beach Trail Head, Fv808, 8387 Fredvang, Norway
2. Mulstøa, 8387 Fredvang, Norway
3. Orca Rock, 8382 Vikten, Norway
4. Parking Kvalvika Beach, Moskenesøya, Flakstad, Norway
5. Roren, Fredvang, Norway
6. Vestervika Beach, Vestervika, 8387, 8380 Fredvang, Norway
7. Viewpoint Rock, 33PR+QP, Fredvang, Norway

Geiranger, Norway
1. Punto Panoramico sul Geirangerfjord, Fv63 24, 6216 Geiranger, Norway

Gildeskål, Norway
1. The Forgotten Town, Gildeskål Municipality, Norway
2. Thaihuset, Gildeskål Municipality, Norway

Grunnførfjord, Norway
1. Egg breaking stone, 9G46+C7, Grunnførfjord, Norway

Gryllefjord, Norway
1. Gryllefjord observasjonskurve, Fv86, 9380 Gryllefjord, Norway

Hamna, Norway
1. View Point, G2RH+F3, Hamna, Norway

Hamningberg, Norway
1. Hamningberg Vista Point, 9990 Hamningberg, Norway
2. Hamningberg, Norway

Hammerfest, Norway
1. Glimmevannet Hytta, Hammerfest Municipality, Norway

Hjerkinn, Norway
1. viewpoint SNØHETTA, Hjerkinnhusvegen 33, 2661 Hjerkinn, Norway

Husøy, Senja, Norway
1. Husøy Lighthouse, Løkta 4, 9389 Husøy i Senja, Norway

Innhavet, Norway
1. Sagvassdalen, Unnamed Road 8260, 8260 Innhavet, Norway

Jotunheimen, Norway
1. Viewpoint, Jotunheimen fjellstue, Lom, Norway

Kabelvåg, Norway
1. Kabelvåg breakwater, Norway, Vikabakken 23, 8310 Kabelvåg, Norway

Kvaløysletta, Norway
1. Arsa Aurora viewing spot, Fjordvegen 330, 9100 Kvaløysletta, Norway
2. Aurora watching point. Northern lights., Ersfjordvegen 5, 9100 Kvaløysletta, Norway
3. Nice Spot for Aurora, Fjordvegen 330, 9107 Kvaløysletta, Norway

Karlsøy, Norway
1. Karlsøy Brygge, Karlsoy, 9138 Karlsøy, Norway

Kiberg, Norway
1. Easternmost Point of Norway, 73Q7+JJ, Kiberg, Norway

Kirkenes, Norway
1. Fjellvatn badeplass, Bergstien 42, 9901 Kirkenes, Norway
2. Skoltefossen Waterfall, 69°41'36. 29°22'09., 9th Ave, Norway
3. Snowhotel Kirkenes Outside Views, Sandnesdalen 9910, 9910 Bjørnevatn, Norway
4. Svartakslevannet, svartaksla, 9911 Kirkenes, Norway

Kjøpsvik, Norway
1. Korshamn Fort, Korshamn, 8543 Kjeldebotn, Norway
2. Stortindrampen, Bakkanveien 5, 8590 Kjøpsvik, Norway

Kongsfjord, Norway
1. Veinesodden batteri, 9982 Kongsfjord, Norway

Kvalsund, Norway
1. Repparfjord Camping and Misjonssenter, Cuovvarjohkka 1, 9620 Kvalsund, Norway
2. Repparfjordfossen, E6 142, 9620 Kvalsund, Norway

Kviby, Norway
1. Aussichtspunkt Altafjord,Lerresfjordveien 8, 9519 Kviby, Norway

Kvænangsveien, Norway
1. Badderen Bukt, Kvænangsveien, Badderen, Norway
2. Parking with a view and tourist info, Kvænangsveien 1346, 9162 Sørstraumen, Norway

Lakselvdal, Norway
1. Northern Light Dog Adventure AS, Lakselvdalvegen 375, 9045 Lakselvbukt, Norway

Laukvik, Norway
1. Laukvik Lighthouse, 8315 Laukvik, Norway

Laupstad, Norway
1. Sildpolltjønna Ship Wreck Lofoten Norway, E10 48, 8316 Laupstad, Norway

Leknes, Norway

1. Dragon's Eye, Uttakleivveien, 8370 Leknes, Norway
2. Gudinnegrava, Einangen 14, 8370 Leknes, Norway
3. Gårdsvatnet observation tower, Leknes, Norway
4. Lakselva River Viewpoint, 8370 Leknes, Norway
5. Uttakleiv Beach, Uttakleiv strand, Uttakleivveien 238, 8370 Leknes, Norway
6. Vik Beach, Fv826 8370, 8370 Leknes, Norway

Lyngvær, Norway
1. Lofot Fjordview, 783H+HQ, Lyngvær, Norway

Limingen, Norway
- Viewpoint Børgefjell - Vekterklumpen, Vekterklumpen, 7898 Limingen, Norway

Lyngen, Norway
- Blåvatnet, Blåvatnet, Lyngen kommune, Norway
- Lysverkdammen, 9060 Lyngen, Norway

Lyngseidet, Norway
- Ørnes Beach, Sandvikveien 381, 9060 Lyngseidet, Norway
- Yykeä eli Lyngen -keinu, Sandvikveien 381, 9060 Lyngseidet, Norway

Mortsund, Norway
- Mortsund Fotopoint, 3JMX+8C, Mortsund, Norway

Målselv, Norway
- Målselvfossen Lachsfenster, Målselv Municipality, Norway

Magerøya, Norway
- Jalgavarri, Magerøya, Nordkapp, Norway

Masi, Norway
- Rasteplass Pikefossen, 9525 Masi, Norway

Mestervik, Norway
- Hamnvåg Ytre, Hamnvågneset 47, 9055 Mestervik, Norway
- The Rock and the Brigde, Malangsveien 1761, 9055 Mestervik, Norway

Molde, Norway

- Molde Panorama, Vardevegen, 6412 Molde, Norway

Napp, Norway
- Viewing point Storvatnet, E10, 8382 Napp, Norway

Namsskogan, Norway
- Gamla Steinfjällsvägen, Gaallinenjaevrie, 7890 Namsskogan, Norway

Narvik, Norway
- Narvik mountains, Narvik Municipality, Norway
- Observasjons deck, Rombaksveien 104, 8517 Narvik, Norway

Nærøysund, Norway
- Setervatnet, Setervatnet, Nærøysund, Norway

Nordkapp, Norway
- Cuerno del Cabo Norte, Nordkapp Municipality, 9764 Nordkapp, Norway
- Knivskjelodden Trail, 9764 Nordkapp, Norway
- Midnight Sun Monument, North Cape, E69, 9764 Nordkapp, Norway
- Northernmost Point of Europe excluding Svalbard, Novaya Zemlya and Franz Josef Land, 5MMG+78, 9764 Tunes, Norway

Nordlenangen, Norway
- XLyngen, Lenangsveien 2344, 9068 Nordlenangen, Norway

Nyvågar, Austvågøya, Norway
- Nyvågar - Photo Point, Austvågøya, Norway

Olderfjord, Norway
- Olderfjord - Leaibevuotna - Leipovuono, E69 1480, 9713 Olderfjord, Norway

Porsanger, Norway
- The trolls of Trollholmsund, Porsanger Municipality, Norway

Ramberg, Norway
- Flakstadøya View Point, E10, 8382 Ramberg, Norway

- Fotopoint, Nusfjordveien 112, 8380 Ramberg, Norway
- Korsordsstolen på Skagsanden, Flakstadveien 279, 8380 Ramberg, Norway
- Lofoten Beach Camp, Kjerkveien 45, 8380 Ramberg, Norway
- Nusfjord Lighthouse, Nusfjordveien 180, 8380 Ramberg, Norway
- Public Parking Midnight Sun Viewpoint, 8380 Ramberg, Norway
- Ramberg Beach Red Cottage, E10 190, 8380 Ramberg, Norway
- Ramberg Promenade, 8380 Ramberg, Norway
- Prosjektlofoten, Vestersia 35, 8380 Ramberg, Norway

Reine, Norway
- Bunes Beach, Moskenesøya, Moskenes, Norway
- Bunes beach viewpoint, Bunes beach, 8390 Reine, Norway
- Fotospot Hamnoy, E10 18, 8390 Reine, Norway
- Hamnøy Scenic Viewpoint, Olenilsøya, 8390 Reine, Norway
- Hammerskaft, 8390 Reine, Norway
- Horn, Hammerskaft, 8390 Reine, Norway
- Olenilsøya kystfort, 8390 Reine, Norway
- Reine - Photo Point, 8390 Reine, Norway
- Reine Lighthouse, Unnamed Road, 8390 Reine, Norway
- Reine utsiktspunkt, Unnamed Road, 8390, Reine, Norway
- Reine Viewpoint, E10 235, 8390 Reine, Norway
- Sakrisoy viewpoint, Moskenes - Værøy 184, 8390 Reine, Norway
- Sakrisøya, Sakrisøya, Moskenes, Norway
- Small Parking Place, E10 15, 8390 Reine, Norway

Repvåg, Norway
- Kåfjird, Kåfjord 5, 9768 Repvåg, Norway

Russenes, Norway
- Skarvbegtunel, E69, 9713 Russenes, Norway
- Sunken Boat, E6 228, 231, 9713 Russenes, Norway

Røldal, Norway
- Hyttehaugen (Viewpoint), Fv520 420, 5760 Røldal, Norway

Rotsund, Norway

- Spåkenes coastal fort, 9153 Rotsund, Norway
- Utsikt mot Uløy, Fv866 102, 9153 Rotsund, Norway

Saltdal, Norway
- View point over mountain river, Saltdal Municipality, Norway

Senja, Norway
- Hamn Lighthouse, Senja, Norway
- Husfjellet, Husfjellet, Senja, Norway

Skjervøy, Norway
- Aurora hot spot / viewing point, 2XFJ+JP, Skjervøy municipality, Norway
- Viewing point, Engnesveien 98, 9180 Skjervøy, Norway

Senjahopen, Norway
- Blaues Licht Aurora Viewing Point, GF6M+8J, Senjahopen, Norway

Skaland, Norway
- Tungenes, Fylkesvei 862 558, 9385 Skaland, Norway
- Bergsbotn utsiktsplattform, Fylkesvei 862, 9385 Skaland, Norway

Skarsvåg, Norway
- Kirkeporten in Skarsvåg, Skutnesveien 4, 9763 Skarsvåg, Norway
- Salo Cin North Cape Fjord viewpoint, Mefjorden 1, 9763 Skarsvåg, Norway

Skibotn, Norway
- Rovijoen putous, 9143 Skibotn, Norway
- Skibotnbenken, Skibotsveien 376, 9143 Skibotn, Norway
- Skibotndissa, 9143, Storfjord kommune, Norway

Skjolden, Norway
- Sengjaberget viewpoint, 6876 Skjolden, Norway

Sogndal, Norway
- Flatbreen / Supphellebreen, Sogndal Municipality, Norway

Sollia, Norway

- Sohlbergplassen, Rv27 730, 2477 Sollia, Norway

Sortland, Norway
- Mount Strandheia, Sortland Municipality, Norway

Sørstraumen, Norway
- Utsiktspunkt, E6 6, 9162 Sørstraumen, Norway

Storfjord, Norway
- Rastebykaia, Storfjord Municipality, Norway
- Salmenes lighthouse - Salmenes fyr - Salminiemen majakka, Horsnesveien, Storfjord kommune, Norway

Straumen, Norway
- Straumen fjord View Point, Fv618 8226, 8226 Straumen, Norway

Svanvik, Norway
- 96-høyden utsiktstårn, NIBIO Svanvik, 9926 Svanvik, Norway
- Appelsinsteinen, Sor-Varanger, Norway
- Grense Jakobselv, Norway
- Noatun (Pasvik) - privat, 9926 Svanvik, Norway
- Skrøytnes Fugletårn, NIBIO Svanhovd, 9926 Svanvik, Norway
- Vardenhytta, Sor-Varanger, Norway

Svolvær, Norway
- Austnesfjorden, E10, 8300 Svolvær, Norway
- Djevelporten, Svolværveien, 8300 Svolvær, Norway
- Fiskehjeller, 6HG9+GH, Svolvær, Norway
- Moloen I Svolvær, Gunnar Bergs vei 25, 8300 Svolvær, Norway
- Svolvær Beach, E10, 8300 Svolvær, Norway
- View Point Svolvær, E10 1 17, 8300 Svolvær, Norway

Sørvågen, Norway
1. Kaimauer, Å-veien 108, 8392 Sørvågen, Norway
2. Kollfjellet, E10 225, 8392 Sørvågen, Norway
3. Stokkvika, 8392 Sørvågen, Norway
4. Viewpoint at Å, Unnamed Road, 8392 Sørvågen, Norway

5. Vittö, Musdalen 13, 8392 Sørvågen, Norway

Strønstad, Norway
   1. Hessand beach, Fv888 22, 8317 Strønstad, Norway
   2. Strønstadvika Beach, Fv888 35, 8317 Strønstad, Norway

Tana, Norway
   1. Perhovapa, Tana Municipality, Norway

Tingvoll, Norway
   1. Stølvatnet lake view point, Hafellvegen 15, 6630 Tingvoll, Norway

Tromsø, Norway
   1. Top of Tromsø, J234+9Q, Tromsø Municipality, Norway
   2. Tromsdalstinden, Tromsdalstinden, Tromsø Municipality, Norway
   3. Tromsø city view point, Tromsø, Norway
   4. Tromsø Viewpoint, 9020 Tromsø, Norway
   5. Utsiktspunkt, Tromsø, Norway
   6. Aurora watching car park. Northern lights., Snarbyeidet snuplass, Tromsø, Norway

Tovik, Norway
   1. Seven Magic Points (Skulpturlandskap Nordland), Fylkesvei 825 46, 9445 Tovik, Norway

Trondheim, Norway
   1. Djupvika, Trondheim, Norway
   2. Nidelva utsiktspunkt, Trondheim, Norway

Unstad, Norway
   1. Hanna's cairn, 7G6W+HM, Unstad, Norway
   2. Näköala Paikka, 7J46+64, Unstad, Norway
   3. Unstad Beach, Unstad Beach, Vestvågøy, Norway
   4. Viewpoint Sortland & Steinsfjorden, 7J29+MX, Unstad, Norway

Vikten, Norway
   1. Vikten beach, Norway

Vadsø, Norway
1. Ekkerøy Bird Cliff, Unnamed Road, 9804 Vadsø, Norway
2. Skihytta Vadsø, Vadso, Norway

Valldal, Norway
1. Valldøla River View Point, Fv63 200, 6210 Valldal, Norway

Vardø, Norway
1. Klondyke - Vardø view point, Vårbergveien 9950, 9950 Vardø, Norway
2. Valen, Vardø, 9950 Vardo, Norway
3. Vardø E75, Fridtjof Nansens gate 1, 9950 Vardø, Norway
4. Vardø Lighthouse, Vardøya, 9950 Vardø, Norway

Vikafjellsvegen, Norway
1. Vikfjell view, Vikafjellsvegen 1284, 6893 Vik i Sogn, Norway

Viksanden, Norway
1. Vikasanden, Fv355 2-11, 9151, 9157 Storslett, Norway

Volda, Norway
1. Haukøykrysset rasteplass, Tømmeråstunellen, Norway

Voss, Norway
1. Gårdsveien View Point, 786H+HQ, Lyngvær, Norway

Øksfjord, Norway
1. Perletur, Hytteveien, 9552 Øksfjord, Norway

Other Locations
1. Torvdalshalsen Viewpoint, Torvdalshalsen Viewpoint

21 PRIME AURORA LOCATIONS - SWEDEN

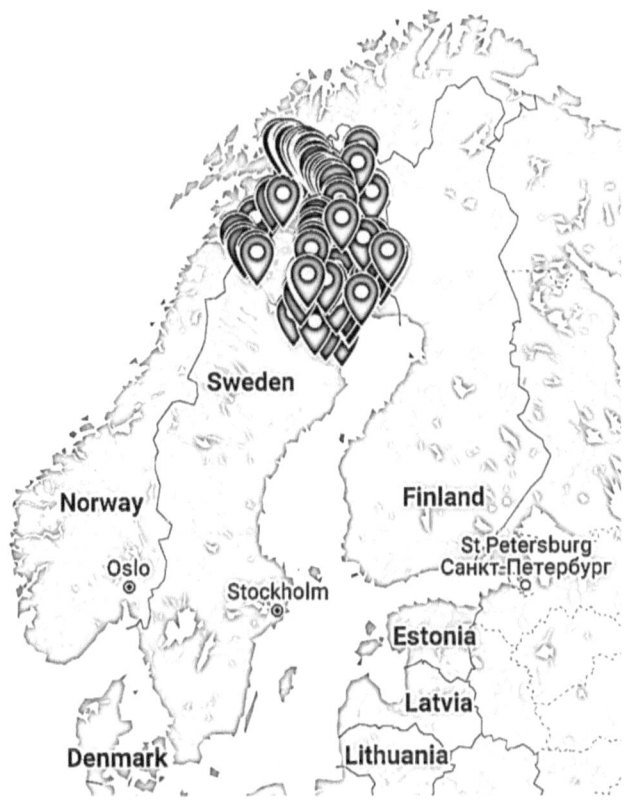

Scan the QR Code below for 127 Aurora locations in Sweden

Abisko

1. Lake Torneträsk Pier, ABISKO STRAND 1, 981 07 Abisko
2. Aurora Sky Station, Abisko Turist Station, 981 07 Abisko
3. Sensing the Arctic, 9Q5Q+MG, 981 07 Abisko Östra, Sweden
4. Abisko Arkparadis, Träskvägen, 981 07 Abisko, Sweden
5. Abisko Mountain Lodge, Lapportsvägen 30, 981 07 Abisko
6. Camping ground STF Abisko Turiststation, 9Q5R+4Q, 981 07 Abisko Östra, Sweden
7. View point for Abisko, Lapportsvägen 40, 981 07 Abisko, Sweden
8. Northern Lights View, Unnamed Road, 981 07 Abisko, Sweden
9. Báddosdievvá (Paddus Trail), 981 07 Abisko, Sweden
10. Abisko National Park, Kiruna, Sweden
11. Abisko's Tungspets, 981 07 Abisko, Sweden
12. Kungsleden, 981 07 Abisko, Sweden

Kiruna

1. STF Kebnekaise Fjällstation, Kebnekaise Fjällstation, 981 99 Kiruna, Sweden
2. ICEHOTEL, Marknadsvägen 63, 981 91 Jukkasjärvi, Sweden
3. Camp Ripan, Campingvägen 5, 981 35 Kiruna, Sweden
4. Aurora River Camp, Poikkijärvivägen 55, 981 92 Kiruna
5. Top of Luossabacken, Unnamed Road, 981 34 Kiruna, Sweden
6. Máttaráhkká Northern Light Lodge, Nordkalottvägen, 981 00 Kiruna, Sweden
7. Camp Alta Kiruna, Jullebovägen 2, 981 92 Kiruna, Sweden
8. Arctic Gourmet Cabin, kaalasjärvi 1100, 981 99 Kiruna
9. Stordalen Mire, 981 95 Kiruna, Sweden
10. Tjuonavagge, 981 95 Kiruna, Sweden
11. Čuonjávággi, 981 07 Kiruna, Sweden
12. Vuoskojaure, Kiruna Municipality, 981 95 Kiruna, Sweden
13. Pessisjokka rastplats, 981 95 Kiruna, Sweden
14. Rastplats med utsikt över Torneträsk - E10, E10, 981 95 Kiruna, Sweden
15. Rastplats Kaisepakte, Kaisepakte station, 981 95 Kiruna, Sweden

16. Rastplats, Rastplats, 981 95 Kiruna, Sweden
17. Stenbacken Rest Area, Rastplats, 981 95 Kiruna, Sweden
18. E10 Parking, E10 1455, 981 94 Kiruna V, Sweden
19. E10 1455 Parking, E10 1455, 981 94 Kiruna V, Sweden
20. Kiruna information point, R9W6+MV, 981 41 Kiruna, Sweden
21. Rautas Naturrastplats, E10, 981 95 Kiruna, Sweden
22. E10, E10, 981 34 Kiruna, Sweden

Riksgränsen

1. Niehku Mountain Villa, Lokvändarvägen 20, 981 94 Riksgränsen, Sweden
2. Arctic Lodge, Katterjokk, 981 94 Riksgränsen, Sweden
3. Katterjokk Turiststation, 981 94 Riksgränsen, Sweden
4. Låktatjåkko Mountain Lodge, 981 93 Björkliden, Sweden
5. Kåppas Cabin Village, Björkliden 70, 981 93 Björkliden
6. Silverfallet, Björkliden, E10, 981 93 Björkliden, Sweden
7. Outback Abisko - Björkliden, Björkliden, 981 93 Björkliden
8. Naturrastplats, E10, 981 93 Björkliden, Sweden
9. Torneträsk Lake, 981 93 Björkliden, Sweden
10. Tornhamn Parking, 68.386472, 18.727534
11. Laktajakk Vattenfall, E10, 981 94 Riksgränsen, Sweden
12. Svensk Fjällsphinx, 981 94 Riksgränsen, Sweden
13. Camping Lapland Resort, E10, 981 94 Riksgränsen, Sweden

Luleå

1. Pine Bay Lodge, Gussövägen 390, 975 98 Luleå, Sweden
2. Småskjærodden marina, 944 91 Munksund, Sweden
3. Soltrappan, Unnamed Road, 972 41 Luleå, Sweden

Harads

1. Tree Hotel, Edeforsvägen 2A, 961 78 Harads, Sweden
2. Arctic Bath, Ramdalsvägen 10, 961 78 Harads, Sweden

Gällivare

1. Lappeasuando Lodge, Lappeasuando 3, 982 93 Gällivare, Sweden

2. Nikkaluokta InfoPoint, 981 99 Gällivare, Sweden
3. Sjöfallsudden, 982 99 Gällivare, Sweden
4. Naturum Laponia, Naturum Laponia, 982 99 Gällivare
5. STF Vaimok, Vaimok, 982 99 Gällivare, Sweden
6. Spijkka, Sarek National Park, 982 99 Gällivare, Sweden
7. Stora Sjöfallet, F8GF+R5, 982 99 Vietas, Sweden
8. Sandviken Fjällgård, SANDVIKEN 1, 938 97 Arjeplog
9. Naturrastplats Koulitisjaure, 95, 930 90 Arjeplog, Sweden
10. Ruonekgårttje, 938 97 Arjeplog, Sweden
11. Sädva kraftstation, Ringselet, 938 97 Arjeplog, Sweden
12. Kyrkans Fjällgård Jäkkvik, Byvägen 4, 938 95 Jäkkvik, Sweden

Jukkasjärvi

1. Reindeer Lodge, Paksuniemivägen 188, 981 91 Jukkasjärvi, Sweden

Kangos

1. Pinetree Lodge, Särkimukka 27, 980 63 Kangos, Sweden
2. Lapland Guesthouse, Norra Byavägen 132, 980 63 Kangos

Lannavaara

1. Aurora Mountain Lodge, Guldvaskarvägen 4, 958 93 Lannavaara, Sweden
2. Lannavaara Lodge AB, Byvägen 82, 985 93 Lannavaara

Porjus

1. Hapsasjaure ställplats, Unnamed Road, 982 60 Porjus, Sweden
2. Harsprångsfallet minnesten, VRHC+7G, 982 60 Harsprånget, Sweden

Överkalix

1. Grand Arctic Resort, Bulandsgatan 4, 956 31 Överkalix

Other Locations:

1. Klinten, 952 93 Klinten, Sweden

2. Starten till klintstigen, Unnamed Road, 932 37 Skellefteå
3. Strömfors strand och badplats 🏖️ 🏖️, Strömforsvägen 6, 936 91 Boliden, Sweden
4. Svansele vildmarkscenter, Svansele 11, 936 93 Boliden
5. Arvidsjaur wooden tower, Smedsvägen 18, 933 32 Arvidsjaur
6. Ostseemole, 941 43 Piteå, Sweden
7. Bredviksberget, Bonäsvägen, 943 31 Öjebyn, Sweden
8. Sågforsbron, 946 92 Åträsk, Sweden
9. Vidsels hjärta, 31, 942 95 Vidsel, Sweden
10. Moskosel Damm, V9RR+C5, 933 90 Moskosel, Sweden
11. Ställplatser Åberget, XF68+97, 933 90 Åberget, Sweden
12. Kängsön campground, KÄNGSÖN 560, 955 31 Råneå
13. Östersjöns nordligaste punkt, 952 44 Töre, Sweden
14. Polarkreis, E10, 956 98 Lansjärv, Sweden
15. Röduppledens färja, 956 92 Kalixälven, Sweden
16. Sanningslandet, STUBBLANDET 33, 956 98 Lansjärv
17. Onkijärvi friluftsområde, Unnamed Road, 957 32 Övertorneå
18. Fäbod Koivumaa, Övertorneå C, 957 32 Övertorneå, Sweden
19. Sarek National Park, Jokkmokk, Sweden
20. Storforsens nature reserve, 942 95 Vidsel, Sweden
21. E10 Parking, E10, 981 95 Kiruna, Sweden
22. Sjön moskajärvi, Storvägen 21, 982 04 Skaulo, Sweden
23. Vattenkraftverk Ligga, RV5W+MM, 962 95 Aspudden
24. Laponia ställplats, Unnamed Road, 962 95 Jokkmokk, Sweden
25. Akkats konstverks parkering, 962 95 Jokkmokk, Sweden
26. Tårrajaur ställplats/rastplats, 962 96 Jokkmokk, Sweden
27. Ljusselfoss Rast Truck-park, E45, 933 90 Moskosel, Sweden
28. Ställplats leipojärvi, 26V6+RM, 982 92 Leipojärvi, Sweden

22 PRIME AURORA LOCATIONS - FINLAND

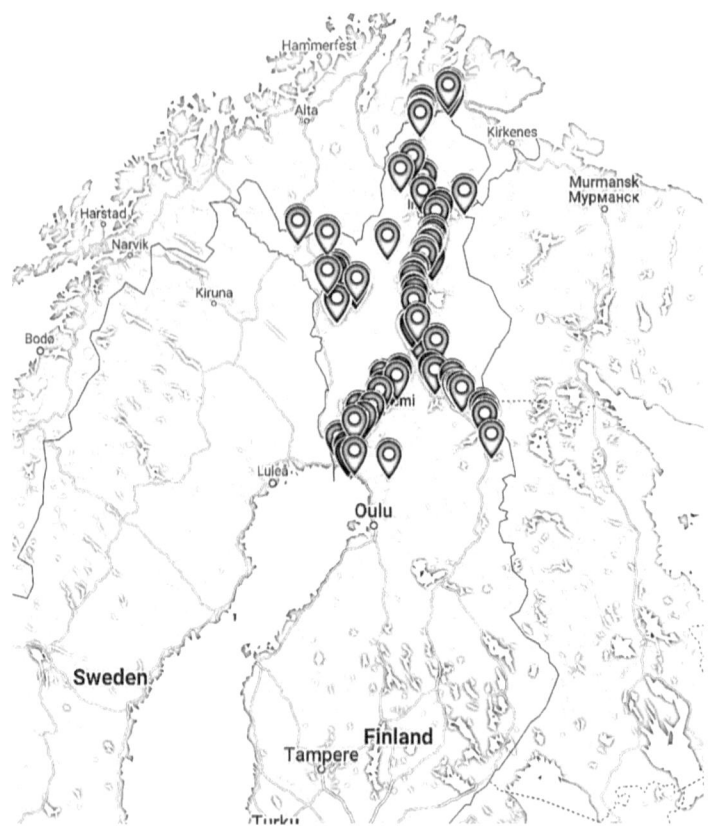

Scan the QR Code below for 102 Aurora locations in Finland

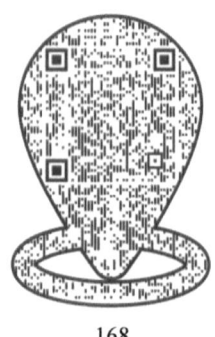

Utsjoki, Finland

1. Scenic Viewpoint, Pulmankijärventie 1303, 99990 Utsjoki, Finland
2. Pulmankijärvi Scenic Road, Pulmankijärventie 717, 99990 Utsjoki, Finland
3. The northernmost point in Finland, the EU, Nuorgamintie 4624 4640, 99990 Nuorgam, Finland
4. Ailikastunturi Scenic Spot, Ailikkaantie 239, 99980 Utsjoki, Finland
5. Umpisuunvuopaja plateau - Aurora observation spot, 9710, 322 392, 99910 Inari, Finland
6. Kielajoki, 99910 Kielajoki, Finland
7. Muotkatunturi Wilderness Area, Utsjoki, Finland
8. Aurora Cottage, Nuorgamintie 4475, 99990 Utsjoki, Finland
9. Utsjoki Church, Utsjoentie 564, 99980 Utsjoki, Finland
10. St Ulrica Culture and Silence Path, Utsjoentie 567, 99980 Utsjoki, Finland
11. Hotelli Pohjan Tuli, Hietaniementie 40, 99980 Utsjoki, Finland

Inari, Finland

1. Aurora Day Hut, 99830 Inari, Finland
2. Kaunispää Triangulation Tower, 9692, 99830 Inari, Finland
3. Saariselkä Sign, Kaunispääntie 260, 99830 Saariselkä, Finland
4. Aurora Hostel Virtaniemi, Nellimintie 5043, 99800 Inari, Finland
5. Inari Igloos, Aurora Cabins, Inarintie 2, 99870 Inari, Finland
6. Aurora Island, Kenkäheinä, Koppelo, 99800 Ivalo, Finland
7. Aurora Village Oy, Aurorakuja 38, 99800 Inari, Finland
8. Aurora Collection, Koivutie 2, 99830 Inari, Finland
9. Sielikkö Aurora Log Apartments, Sielikkö 1, 99830

Inari, Finland
10. Northern Light Cabin, 99830 Inari, Finland
11. Northern Lights Village Saariselkä, Rovaniementie 3222E, 99830 Saariselkä, Finland
12. Kuukkeli Log Houses Aurora Resort, Kiveliöntie 8, 99830 Saariselkä, Finland
13. River Villa Aurora, Kittiläntie 8435, 99800 Inari, Finland

Kittilä, Finland

1. LEVINHUIPPU, Tunturitie 480, 99130 Kittilä, Finland
2. Santa's Cabin, Unnamed Road, 99130 Kittilä, Finland
3. Aurora Pyramid Glass Igloos, Palosaarentie 30, 99140 Kittilä, Finland
4. Aurora Dome & Glamping, Torassiepintie 212, 99300 Särkijärvi, Finland
5. Punainenhiekka Day Trip Hut, Majavaojantie, 99380 Kittilä, Finland

Sodankylä, Finland

1. Pyhä-Nattanen, Sompiojärventie, 99690 Sodankylä, Finland
2. Ahvenlampi Campfire Place, Unnamed Road, 99555, Sodankylä, Finland
3. Madetkoski Scenic Caravan Park, Ivalontie 5350, 99680 Sodankylä, Finland
4. Porttikoski, Kurkiaskantie 870, 99550 Sodankylä, Finland
5. Aurora Cabins, Muotkantie 200, 99830 Sodankylä, Finland
6. Alanampa, Sodankyläntie 3848, 97520 Rovaniemi, Finland

Enontekiö, Finland

1. Tarvantovaara Wilderness Area, Enontekiö, Finland

2. Bird Watching Tower Yrjö Kokko, Ounastie 1257, 99400 Enontekiö, Finland

Kolari, Finland

1. Tahkokuru Lappish Hut, 95970 Äkäslompolo, Finland
2. Ylläs swing, Sannanrannantie, 95970 Kolari, Finland
3. Äkäslompolo Bird Watching Tower, J577+M2, 95970 Helukka, Finland
4. Kesänkijoki Bridge, 95970 Kolari, Finland

Rovaniemi, Finland

1. Santa Claus Secret Forest – Joulukka, 96910 Rovaniemi, Finland
2. Kuninkaanlaavu Lean-to, 96900 Rovaniemi, Finland
3. Häkinvaaran kami, Kammintie, 96900 Rovaniemi, Finland
4. Northern lights, Katajarinteentie 26, 96900 Rovaniemi, Finland
5. Aurora Nest – Eco Glass Igloo, Lismankuja 33, 96900 Rovaniemi, Finland
6. Könkäänvaara lookout, Sodankyläntie 2034, 96900 Rovaniemi, Finland
7. Apukka Resort - Glass Igloos Hotel, Tutkijantie 28, 96900 Rovaniemi, Finland
8. Olkkajärven venesatama, Sodankyläntie 1654, 96900 Rovaniemi, Finland
9. Aurora Hunting Olkkajärvi, Sodankyläntie 1654, 96900 Rovaniemi, Finland
10. Aurora Hut igloo, Ketavaarantie 21, 96900 Rovaniemi, Finland

Tornio, Finland

1. Heinijänkä Bird Watching Tower, Heinijänkäntie 91, 95460 Tornio, Finland

Kemi, Finland

1. Kiikeli Observation Tower, Kemi, Finland
2. Murhaniemi Lean-to Shelter, Murhaniementie 176, 94900 Kemi, Finland

Muurola, Finland

1. Kätkävaara Aurora Apartments, Kätkävaarantie 1225, 97140 Muurola, Finland

Tervola, Finland

1. Kemijoki Holiday, Louentie 720, 95300 Tervola, Finland

Kuusamo, Finland

1. Holiday Club, Rukan lomakylä, 93830 Kuusamo, Finland
2. Lähiruka Ltd, Kesätie 27, 93825 Kuusamo, Finland
3. The Salpa Line fortification zone, Lahtela Vanttajankannas, Lämsänkyläntie 62, 93700 Kuusamo, Finland

Other Locations

1. 69.865284, 27.006085
2. 69.861865, 27.005520
3. 69.811407, 27.006685
4. 69.806106, 27.001217
5. 69.801633, 26.997024
6. 69.784529, 26.998782
7. 68.322176, 27.323811
8. 68.314675, 27.314062
9. 68.304470, 27.298171
10. 68.282812, 27.286730
11. 68.196424, 27.100286

12. 68.183273, 27.092949
13. 68.147387, 27.094939
14. 67.983617, 26.869228
15. 67.950737, 26.774463
16. 67.932947, 26.767946
17. 67.911716, 26.749115
18. 67.857211, 26.720243
19. 67.754439, 26.765042
20. 67.735439, 26.758915
21. 67.696405, 26.798158
22. 67.584996, 26.753622
23. 67.311563, 26.696434
24. 66.272059, 25.335068
25. 66.082663, 24.795622
26. 65.684972, 24.783386
27. 65.619212, 25.925851
28. 67.369297, 26.901340
29. 67.107224, 27.518042
30. 66.775515, 27.333190
31. 66.715930, 27.458679
32. 66.627018, 28.032641
33. 66.653905, 28.025296
34. 66.551431, 28.128587
35. 66.539810, 28.192761
36. 66.529251, 28.235448
37. 66.489832, 28.346312
38. 66.284654, 29.015982

23 PRIME AURORA LOCATIONS - RUSSIA

Scan the QR Code below for 103 Aurora locations in Russia

Murmansk Oblast, Russia

1. Staryy Mayak, Unnamed Road, Vayda-Guba, Murmanskaya oblast', Russia, 184402
2. Mayak, Murmansk Oblast, Russia, 184402
3. Vayda-Guba, Murmansk Oblast, Russia, 184402
4. Dva Brata, Unnamed Road, Murmanskaya oblast', Russia, 184402
5. "Bereg Ryzhikh Kamney", Unnamed Road, Murmanskaya oblast', Russia, 184402
6. Орудие батареи №10, Unnamed Road, Poselok, Murmanskaya oblast', Russia, 184402

7. Эко Village Arctic Краб, 51:03:0010102:29 полуостров Средний, Murmanskaya oblast', Russia, 184410
8. WhaleCoast Glamping, Urban settlement, Murmansk, Murmanskaya oblast', Russia, 183038
9. Zagadochnyye Krugi V Linhammar, Linhammar, Murmansk Oblast, Russia, 184402
10. Hill of Glory, Pechenga, Murmansk Oblast, Russia, 184411
11. Kola Superdeep Borehole, Murmansk Oblast, Russia, 184430
12. Vodopad Na Reke Titovka, Unnamed Road, Staraya Titovka, Murmanskaya oblast', Russia, 184402
13. Zhivopisnoye Mesto U Vodopada, Unnamed Road, Staraya Titovka, Murmanskaya oblast', Russia, 184402
14. Stoyanka, Murmansk Oblast, Russia, 184310
15. Батарея береговой обороны №199, Murmansk Oblast, Russia, 184630
16. Stone Beach, Unnamed Road, Мурманская обл., Russia, 184630
17. Batareyskiy Vodopad, Teriberka, Murmansk Oblast, Russia, 184630
18. Poklonnyy Krest, 633F+64, Teriberka, Murmansk Oblast, Russia, 184630
19. Kamennyy Plyazh, Teriberka, Murmansk Oblast, Russia, 184630
20. Teriberka Plyazh, 634W+48, Teriberka, Murmansk Oblast, Russia, 184630
21. Grotik, Unnamed Road, Murmanskaya oblast', Russia, 184630
22. Guba Zavalishina, Unnamed Road, Teriberka, Murmanskaya oblast', Russia, 184630
23. Konets Vsekh Dorog, Unnamed Road, Teriberka, Murmanskaya oblast', Russia, 184630
24. Stella Monchegorsk, R-21, 1937, Monchegorsk, Murmanskaya oblast', Russia, 184511
25. Perevalochnaya Vysota El'morayork, Murmansk Oblast, Russia, 184580
26. Shuonijoki Falls, Murmansk Oblast, Russia, 184420
27. Vodopad Na Reke Lavna, р. Лавна, Мурманская обл., Russia, 183005
28. Vodopad Na R. Bol'shaya Lavna, Рядом с пос, Междуречье, Мурманская обл., Russia, 183005
29. Ruchey, Olenegorsk, Murmansk Oblast, Russia, 184530
30. Stela "Kol'skaya Aes", Apatity, Murmansk Oblast, Russia,

184230
31. Baza Otdykha Travyanaya, ул. Травяная губа, 25А, Zelenoborsky, Murmanskaya oblast', Russia, 184021
32. Stela Apatity, Apatity, Murmansk Oblast, Russia, 184209
33. Volosyanaya mountain, 47K-010, Kandalaksha, Murmanskaya oblast', Russia, 184041
34. Seydozero, Murmansk Oblast, Russia, 184592
35. Shtol'nya Podzemnogo Yadernogo Vzryva, Kirovsk, Murmansk Oblast, Russia, 184256
36. Black Padun waterfall, p., Kolvitsa, Murmanskaya oblast', Russia, 184015
37. Territoriya Otdykha Zhemchuzhina Khibin, оз Малый Вудъявр, Kirovsk, Murmanskaya oblast', Russia, 184250
38. Snezhnaya Derevnya, Ulitsa Botanicheskiy Sad, Kirovsk, Murmanskaya oblast', Russia, 184250
39. Kamennyy Labirint "Vavilon", Kandalaksha, Murmansk Oblast, Russia, 184042
40. Kitsa Dss, Kitsa, Murmansk Oblast, Russia, 184331
41. Recreation center Karavella, Pushnoy, Murmansk Oblast, Russia, 184340
42. Dom U Ozera, Unnamed Road, Murmanskaya oblast', Russia, 184340
43. Glamping Russia Discovery, Murmanskaya oblast', Russia, 184402
44. Baza Otdykha "Ozerko", Unnamed Road, Murmanskaya oblast', Russia, 184310
45. Titovka, Titovka, Murmansk Oblast, Russia, 184413
46. VicTori, Gvardeyskiy Prospekt, 5, Nikel', Murmanskaya oblast', Russia, 184650
47. Skul'ptura Zhdushchaya, Ulitsa Chumbarova-Luchinskogo, Murmansk, Murmanskaya oblast', Russia, 183040
48. Monument to the Heroes, Severomorsk, the defenders of the Arctic (Alyosha), Ulitsa Sgibneva, 11, Severomorsk, Murmanskaya oblast', Russia, 184606
49. Pamyatnik Voinam - Artilleristam, Ulitsa Sgibneva, 11, Severomorsk, Murmanskaya oblast', Russia, 184606
50. Marine Station, пл. Приморская, 1, Severomorsk, Murmanskaya oblast', Russia, 184604
51. Gostinitsa Oazis G. Gadzhiyevo, Ulitsa Kolyshkina, 55, Gadzhiyevo, Murmanskaya oblast', Russia, 184670
52. Severnoye Siyaniye, Ulitsa Biryukova, 5к1, Ofis 105,

Snezhnogorsk, Murmanskaya oblast', Russia, 184682
53. Rybolovno-turusticheskaya baza, Ulitsa Vokuyeva, 2, Lovozero, Murmanskaya oblast', Russia, 184592
54. Туристическая База "Медвежий угол", Туры в Ловозеро, Bear Corner
55. Turbaza "Yulinskaya Salma", ул. Вокуева, д.13, кв.1, Ловозеро, Murmanskaya oblast', Russia, 184592
56. parking Tour, Murmansk Oblast, Russia, 184592
57. Touristic Center Yulinskaya Salma, Murmansk Oblast, Russia, 184592
58. Lovo Baza 2, Murmansk Oblast, Russia, 184592
59. Evecta, Ulitsa Sovetskaya, 1/2, Lovozero, Murmanskaya oblast', Russia, 184592
60. Khaski-Park "Lesnaya Yelan'", Murmansk Oblast, Russia, 184580
61. Sam Syyt, квартал 58-й выдел 11, Мончегорск, Murmanskaya oblast', Russia, 184227
62. Pamyatnik Ekipazhu Korablya Meridian, Pochtovaya Ulitsa, Mishukovo, Murmanskaya oblast', Russia, 184335

Arkhangelsk Oblast, Russia

1. Национальный парк Русская арктика, Северный, Arkhangelsk Oblast, Russia
2. Gora Severny Nunatak, Arkhangelsk Oblast, Russia
3. Hotel Number 5, Советская ул., 6, Белушья Губа, Ненецкий Ао@Архангельская, Arkhangelskaya oblast', Russia
4. Stolitsa Pomorya Hotel (Capital of Pomorye), Naberezhnaya Severnoy Dviny, 88, Arkhangel'sk, Arkhangelskaya oblast', Russia, 163004
5. Turisticheskaya Kompaniya "Zimneye More", Россия, Архангельская область, Мезенский район, село Койда, дом 178, Koida, Arkhangelskaya oblast', Russia, 164763

Republic of Karelia, Russia

1. Stela "Polyarnyy Krug", E105, Respublika Kareliya, Russia, 186691
2. Memorial to war dead, Louhi, Republic of Karelia, Russia, 186660
3. The National Park Paanajärvi, пос. Пяозерский, Респ.

Карелия, Russia, 186667
4. Tolloreka, Tolloreka, Republic of Karelia, Russia, 186942
5. Gostevoy Dom Yuryakhmya, Republic of Karelia, Russia, 186904
6. Gostevoy Dom, Republic of Karelia, Russia, 186904
7. Eko Otel' Bol'shaya Medveditsa, Медвежьегорск, Респ. Карелия, Russia, 186353
8. St. Nicholas Church, Никифоровых пер, д. 1, Povenets, Respublika Kareliya, Russia, 186326
9. Baza Otdykha Nasegozero, Popov Porog, Republic of Karelia, Russia, 186410

Nenets Autonomous Okrug, Russia

1. Hanaway-sia, Zapolyarny District, Nenets Autonomous Okrug, Russia, 166715
2. Park Zakhrebetnaya Kur'ya, Naryan-Mar, Nenets Autonomous Okrug, Russia, 166002
3. "Avantage" hotel, Ulitsa Stroiteley, 8, Naryan-Mar, Nenetskiy, Russia, 166700

Sakha Republic, Russia

1. Ust'-Lenskiy Zapovednik, Sakha Republic, Russia, 678421

Chukotka Autonomous Okrug, Russia

1. Eastern point of the world, 38JX+6P Наукан, Чукотский автономный округ, Russia, 689310
2. Stantsiya Svyazi, Шоссе на Лаврентия, Lavrentiya, Chukotskiy, Russia, 689300
3. Goryachiy Istochnik "Lorinskiye Klyuchi", Chukotka Autonomous Okrug, Russia, 689315
4. Chukotka hotel, Ulitsa Rul'tytegina, 2в, Anadyr, Chukotskiy, Russia, 689000
5. Pamyatnik Pervomu Revkomu Chukotki, Ulitsa Lenina, 47, Anadyr, Chukotskiy, Russia, 689000
6. Munitsipal'naya Gostinitsa, Улица Советская, 32, Pevek, Chukotskiy, Russia, 689400
7. Mike Hawk's Big Hotel, Chukotka Autonomous Okrug, Russia, 689275

8. Leningradsky, Leningradsky, Chukotka Autonomous Okrug, Russia, 689380
9. Profilaktoriy Baes, р-н, Chukotskiy, Russia, 689450

Yamalo-Nenets Autonomous Okrug, Russia

1. STL 2.1.2 Dormitory, Yamalo-Nenets Autonomous Okrug, Russia, 629705
2. Gostinitsa Seyakha, Yamalo-Nenets Autonomous Okrug, Russia, 629705
3. Hotel "Nord House", р-н, Yamalo-Nenetskiy, Russia, 629700
4. Yalemd, Ямальский ул. Советская, 4, Yar-Sale, Yamalo-Nenetskiy, Russia, 629700
5. Yamburg, Yamburg, Yamalo-Nenets Autonomous Okrug, Russia, 629740
6. Gostinnitsa Nubr, Yamalo-Nenets Autonomous Okrug, Russia, 629306

Komi Republic, Russia

1. Vorkuta, Vorkuta, Komi Republic, Russia
2. Baza Otdykha "Yuzhnyy", Vorkuta, Komi Republic, Russia, 169901
3. 67-Parallel', Ленина ул. 45, зд. бывш. Печорниипроект, Воркута, Коми респ., 169900, Vorkuta, Respúblika Kómi, Russia, 169905

Krasnoyarsk Krai, Russia

1. Zapovednik Bolsjoj Arktitsjeski, Krasnoyarsk Krai, Russia, 663333
2. Bol'shoy Arkticheskiy Gosudarstvennyy Prirodnyy Zapovednik, Bol'shoy Arkticheskiy Gosudarstvennyy Prirodnyy Zapovednik
3. Taymyrskiy Gosudarstvennyy Prirodnyy Zapovednik, Taymyrskiy Gosudarstvennyy Prirodnyy Zapovednik

Other Locations

1. Eastern-most point of Europe, Cape Flissingsky, Russia

24
FAQS ON NORTHERN LIGHTS

Are Aurora Forecasts as reliable as your local weatherman's predictions?

Let's put it this way: If you trust your local weatherman when he says there's a "slight chance" of rain and end up drenched without an umbrella, you're prepared for Aurora forecasts! These dazzling light shows are the celestial equivalent of your weather guy saying, "It might snow, but it might also be sunny, or maybe a bit of both." Predicting auroras is like trying to guess if your cat will jump in the box or the bag—it's a beautiful mystery wrapped in science and sprinkled with a bit of cosmic whimsy. The unpredictability of these forecasts, akin to a surprise party thrown by Mother Nature, keeps us all on our toes, ready for the next cosmic surprise.

Aurora forecasts are like a cosmic heads-up, hinting about when and where the Northern Lights might put on a show. But let's be honest, they're not 100% foolproof. These predictions rely on solar activity, like flares and coronal mass ejections (CMEs). We can forecast solar tantrums, but sometimes, they're more unpredictable than a cat in a room full of laser pointers. The forecasts use the Kp index, a nifty measure of geomagnetic activity, to predict aurora visibility. A higher Kp index means you might be in for a treat. However, just like trying to predict the perfect moment to pop popcorn, the exact timing and intensity can be a bit hit or miss because geomagnetic storms keep us guessing.

Even with precise solar and geomagnetic data, local factors like weather and light pollution can make or break your aurora-spotting plans. You'll need clear, dark skies far from city lights for the best view. So, while aurora forecasts are helpful, remember to check real-time data and local weather conditions to increase your chances of witnessing this natural wonder. This local knowledge can be the key to a successful aurora-spotting adventure.

Can we predict Auroras, or are they just Mother Nature's surprise party?

Well, imagine if Mother Nature decided to throw a rave and only sent out invites to the cool kids—sometimes we get a heads-up, and other times, it's a total surprise bash! We can make educated guesses based on solar flares and those fancy-sounding coronal mass ejections (CMEs). But predicting the exact moment when the sky will light up with auroras is like trying to predict a cat's next move. Just when you think you've got it figured out, bam! They change their mind.

Think of auroras as the universe's way of keeping us on our toes. Scientists use the Kp index to give us a hint, like checking the weather before a picnic. A higher Kp index means a better chance of seeing those stunning lights. But just like the weather, it's never a sure thing.

Do the Northern Lights pose any threat to us, or are they just harmless sky glitter?

The Northern Lights are simply Mother Nature's harmless sky glitter. They might resemble alien laser beams or epic sci-fi special effects, but these colorful light shows are all about beauty, not danger. So, sit back, relax, and enjoy the show without any worry.

The dazzling display is a testament to the beauty and mystery of the universe. It's caused by charged particles from the sun colliding with our atmosphere, creating breathtaking colours that dance across the night sky. They won't zap, shrink, or transport you to another dimension (though that would be pretty cool). Instead, they inspire awe and wonder, reminding us of the beauty and mystery of the universe.

Can you see the Northern Lights every night in Tromso, or is that just tourist bait?

Well, let's spill the Arctic beans: while Tromso is one of the best spots to catch the Northern Lights, it's not a guaranteed nightly show. It's more like a fabulous, elusive rockstar—the Northern Lights don't perform on demand, but when they do, it's a spectacle! The unpredictability adds a thrill to the chase, making the experience all the more exciting.

Tromso sits right in the middle of the auroral oval, the prime Northern Lights zone, so you've got a good chance of spotting them. But just like waiting for your favourite band to drop a surprise album, some unpredictability is involved. Clear skies, solar activity, and a bit of luck all play a part.

So, if you're planning a trip to Tromso, pack your patience and thermal underwear. Check the aurora forecasts, watch the weather, and get ready to be wowed when those lights decide to grace you with their presence. It's not just tourist bait; it's a thrilling adventure with the sky's most dazzling performer! The chase's anticipation and thrill make the experience all the more exciting.

Do the Northern Lights have the power to lift your spirits or make you feel moody?

Absolutely! Think of them as the universe's ultimate mood ring, but way more spectacular.

Picture this: you're standing under a vast, starry sky, and suddenly, the Northern Lights start their celestial dance. Swirling greens, vibrant pinks, and occasional purples light up the night, and it's like the universe just threw you a surprise party. It's hard not to feel your spirits soar when witnessing such a magical display.

But could the Northern Lights also make you feel moody? If you're anything like me, the only moodiness might come from staying up all night chasing those elusive lights! The excitement of seeing them can make the wait worth it, but you might feel a tad frustrated on those cloudy nights when they decide to play hide-and-seek.

Can astronauts get a front-row seat in Aurora from space?

Indeed, astronauts have a unique vantage point, floating high above the Earth, and witnessing a celestial spectacle that's beyond our imagination. It's like having a front-row seat at the universe's most exclusive light show, a privilege that fills us with awe and wonder.

In the International Space Station, astronauts have the best view in the house. They see the auroras from above, where they look even more like cosmic jellyfish pulsating with colourful light. It's as if the universe decided to throw a rave, and the astronauts are the lucky ones with the best vantage point.

But, let's be real—while they're floating around, snapping jaw-dropping photos of the auroras, they're probably also dealing with floating snacks and zero-gravity bedhead. Space life isn't all glam, but those views? Worth it!

So yes, astronauts get a front-row seat to the auroras, and it's a show. Meanwhile, back on Earth, we'll keep craning our necks and hoping for clear skies. One day, we'll join them up there and share the popcorn.

Can you catch the Northern Lights show on a flight?

Buckle up because the answer is a high-flying "yes"! Picture this: you're cruising at 35,000 feet, munching on your complimentary pretzels, when suddenly, the in-flight entertainment takes a celestial turn.

If you're on a nighttime flight over the Arctic Circle during aurora season, you might get treated to the Northern Lights' magical dance outside your window. The universe gave you a first-class upgrade minus the extra legroom.

But here's the thing—remember to keep your excitement in check while trying to get that perfect Instagram shot of the auroras. Your seatmate might be asleep, blissfully unaware of the cosmic spectacle you're witnessing. You wouldn't want to accidentally elbow them in the face while fumbling for your phone, right?

So, next time you book a flight, opt for a window seat (the side of the plane can vary based on the flight) on those northern routes. You never know when you might get a front-row ticket to the most incredible light show on (and above) Earth. Don't forget to look up from your in-flight movie—you wouldn't want to miss the real blockbuster outside!

Do the Northern Lights still shine if it's cloudy, or do they take a rain check?

The Northern Lights are not the ones to cancel their show just because of a few clouds! They're still up there, shimmering and dancing away, even if the clouds are being total party poopers and blocking your view.

Think of it like this: the auroras are throwing a spectacular celestial rave, but those pesky clouds are the bouncers keeping you from seeing the action. The lights don't take a rain check—they're still grooving up a storm behind the cloud curtain. Unfortunately for us ground-dwellers, it's like being invited to the most incredible concert in town but having a giant curtain dropped right in front of the stage.

Sun just threw a solar flare. Should we grab our popcorn for tonight's Aurora?

A solar flare by itself doesn't cause those dazzling auroras. Solar flares can sometimes launch massive clouds of solar plasma, known as coronal mass ejections (CMEs). These CMEs pack the punch to trigger auroras when they smack into Earth. But here's the catch—not every solar flare sends out a CME. Most don't! Even if we get a big, flashy solar flare, it must come from a sunspot near the centre of the Earth-facing side of the Sun. The CME might fly past Earth like a cosmic drive-by if it's off to the side. While the light from a solar flare reaches us in just 8 minutes, CMEs are a bit more laid-back travellers. The speediest CMEs can make the journey in about a day, but usually, they take their sweet time, arriving in two to four days.

So, while a solar flare might excite us, we're waiting for CMEs. Keep an eye on those space weather reports, and get your popcorn ready for when the real show begins!

Do Coronal Holes make a comeback every 27 days like a cosmic boomerang?

Coronal holes are like windows on the Sun's surface, where the magnetic field lines open up and let solar wind escape into space. These holes look dark in images because they're less dense and more relaxed than the surrounding areas. Imagine them as the Sun's way of letting off steam!

Every 27 days, the Sun completes a full rotation. If you were to mark a spot on the Sun and wait, that spot would come back into view. This regularity in the Sun's rhythm, the predictable return of coronal holes, makes us feel connected to the cosmic dance of the universe.

If a coronal hole is stable and doesn't change much, it will rotate with the Sun and come back into view like clockwork every 27 days. So, watch out—these cosmic boomerangs love to make a return appearance!

CHASING NORTHERN LIGHTS

Can the Northern Lights mess with your beauty sleep?

Well, if you're an aurora chaser, they sure can! Imagine this: you're all snuggled up in bed, but you hear there's a chance of seeing the Northern Lights. Suddenly, your cozy pillow doesn't seem as exciting as the glowing sky outside.

You hop out of bed, throw on warm clothes, and rush outside. You spend hours staring at the sky, waiting for the magic to happen. When the lights finally appear, you're wide awake, amazed, and forgetting about sleep.

So yes, chasing the Northern Lights can mess with your beauty sleep. It's worth having a few extra yawns for a spectacular show the next day!

Do the Northern Lights make a nightly appearance?

Well, not exactly! The Northern Lights are like the world's most unpredictable rock stars. Sometimes, they show up and put on the most fantastic show; other times, they decide to skip town and leave you staring at a boring, dark sky.

These dazzling lights depend on solar activity, clear skies, and luck. So, while some nights might be filled with magical, dancing colours, others could be a total no-show. It's like trying to catch a glimpse of a shooting star—worth it when it happens, but there are no guarantees.

Do sunspot regions get a brand-new I.D. when they return to face Earth?

Yes, they do! When sunspot regions return to the Earth-facing side of the Sun, they get a brand-new number. They've returned from vacation with a fresh new identity, ready to be tracked and studied again. So, every time they swing back around, it's like meeting them for the first time—new number, same old sunspots, always keeping things interesting!

Do sunspots on the Sun's far side get their I.D. numbers, or are they left in the dark?

Once they spin around to face Earth, they get their special I.D.s.

It's like they're in witness protection, keeping a low profile until they're ready for the spotlight. Once they come into view, they get their official number and all the attention they deserve. So, until then, those far-side sunspots are just biding their time, waiting for their moment to shine!

Do sunspots have any say in the Northern Lights' spectacular shows?

Oh, absolutely! Think of sunspots as the party planners for the Northern Lights. These dark spots can send out solar flares and coronal mass ejections (CMEs) when they get active. These solar bursts are like VIP invitations for the auroras to light up the sky.

So, whenever you see a sunspot, know it might be cooking something special for the Northern Lights. Without sunspots, the sky's light show would be much less exciting.

Do the Northern Lights have a secret soundtrack, or is that just folklore?

Well, it's a bit of both! Picture this: you're standing under a sky ablaze with auroras, and you hear a faint, magical hum. It sounds like Mother Nature decided to add a soundtrack to her celestial light show. Some claim they've heard soft crackles, whooshes, or even a gentle whispering while watching the Northern Lights.

Scientists still need to figure out this one. While there's no solid proof that the auroras make sounds, there are some theories. One idea is that these sounds are caused by electrical charges in the atmosphere, which can create faint noises. Another theory is that the sounds come from the listener's imagination, inspired by the awe-inspiring visuals.

So, is it folklore or reality? The jury's still out. But next time you're out aurora-hunting, keep your ears open. Whether it's the wind, atmospheric electricity, or just your mind playing tricks, a night with the Northern Lights is always a symphony for the senses!

Does it have to be COLD to see the northern lights?

Surprisingly, no! The Northern Lights aren't picky about the temperature. They're all about solar activity and clear, dark skies.

Sure, the best spots to see the auroras—like Alaska, Norway, and

Canada—are often chilly. That's because winter nights are longer, giving you more time to catch the show. But the lights themselves don't need it to be cold.

So, why do we always picture people freezing their tails off while watching the Northern Lights? This is mainly because the places with the best views are in colder regions. But with the right timing and some luck, you might catch the auroras without needing a parka.

Does moonlight dim the Northern Lights' brilliance, or do they shine just as bright?

Well, it's a bit of both! Picture this: the Northern Lights are like the ultimate headliner at a cosmic concert, and the moon is the bright, chatty friend who sometimes steals a bit of the spotlight.

When the moon is full and shining brightly, it can make the auroras appear less intense, like trying to see fireflies under a streetlamp. The Northern Lights will still be there, doing their dazzling dance, but the moon's glow can make it harder to see.

However, the auroras can shine when the moon is just a sliver or nowhere in sight, giving you a spectacular, unobstructed view of their magical performance.

So, while moonlight can dim their brilliance a bit, the Northern Lights still put on a fantastic show. Just think of it as a duet between the moon and the auroras, with the Northern Lights always ready to steal the show when the moonlight fades!

How do sneaky protons from far-off eruptions manage to reach Earth sometimes?

Imagine the Sun as a giant cosmic smoothie blender. When it whips up a storm on the far side, those energetic protons still find a way to reach us. These sneaky protons travel along the Sun's magnetic field lines, which twist and turn through space like a crazy roller coaster, allowing them to zip around and reach Earth even if the flare happens on the Sun's far side. So, next time you see the Northern Lights, you can thank those protons for taking the wild ride to get here!

CHASING NORTHERN LIGHTS

How long does the Aurora's dazzling display last?

It's like asking how long a great party lasts—it can vary! Sometimes, the Northern Lights put on a quick but stunning show, like a brilliant flash of fireworks. Other times, they're the life of the cosmic party, dancing across the sky for hours.

The duration of an aurora display depends on solar activity and how it interacts with Earth's magnetic field. You might catch a brief, breathtaking glimpse or be treated to an all-night spectacle.

So, when you're out chasing auroras, be prepared for anything. Bring some snacks, a cozy blanket, and maybe a thermos of hot cocoa. Whether it's a short and sweet performance or a marathon of mesmerising lights, you're in for a treat!

How long should you plan to catch the Northern Lights without going bonkers?

Well, it's all about balancing patience and adventure!

Aim for a trip of at least 3 to 7 days to increase your chances without losing your mind. This gives you an excellent window to catch clear skies and solar activity. Think of it as your Northern Lights "fishing trip"—you need time to reel in the big catch.

While you wait, explore the local sights, try some fun activities, and enjoy the chilly charm of the northern destinations. Go dog sledding, taste local cuisine, or relax in a cozy cabin. Keeping busy helps you avoid the "Will they show up tonight?" jitters.

So, pack your sense of adventure and a bit of patience. A week should be enough to give you a great shot at witnessing the magical light show without driving yourself up the wall!

How often do the Northern Lights grace us with their presence?

In places close to the Arctic Circle, like Norway, Alaska, and Canada, you might catch them dancing in the sky almost every clear night during the winter.

But just like rockstars, the Northern Lights don't perform on demand. Their appearances depend on solar activity, clear skies, and a bit of luck. Sometimes, they'll put on a breathtaking show, and other times, they might decide to take the night off.

What's the perfect attire for a night of Aurora hunting?

Ready to chase the Northern Lights? Fantastic! But before you dash out the door, let's discuss your outfit. Because let's face it: the Northern Lights might be stunning, but they won't keep you warm! Here's a fun guide to dressing for success (and warmth) on your aurora adventure.

Layers, Layers, Layers!

Base Layer: Start with a moisture-wicking base layer. Think of it as your cozy, second skin. Long underwear, thermal tops, and bottoms are your best friends here. Avoid cotton, as it loves to soak up sweat and make you chilly.

Middle Layer: Add an insulating layer to trap your body heat. Fleece jackets, down vests, or wool sweaters are perfect. This layer is like the warm hug you need while you wait for the lights.

Outer Layer: Top it off with a waterproof and windproof outer layer. A good jacket and pants prevent the icy wind and any unexpected snowflakes. This layer is your shield against the elements.

Hats and Gloves

Hat: Remember your head! A warm beanie or a thermal hat is essential. Your body loses much heat through your noggin, so keep it covered.

Gloves: Your fingers need love, too. Wear insulated gloves or mittens. If you plan to take photos, consider glove liners that let you use your touchscreen without exposing your fingers to the cold.

Footwear

Boots: Sturdy, insulated, waterproof boots are a must. Think of them as your tyre chains for icy conditions. Make sure they have good traction for those slippery spots. You can get crampons to attach to your boots for better grip. A crampon is a traction device that is attached to footwear to improve mobility on snow and ice during ice climbing, mountaineering, and hiking on glaciers. Crampons have metal spikes or teeth that dig into the ice or hard-packed snow, providing stability and grip in otherwise slippery conditions.

Socks: Thick wool socks will keep your toes toasty. Avoid cotton socks—they leave you with cold, damp feet.

Accessories

Scarf or Neck Gaiter: Protect your neck and face from the biting wind with a scarf or neck gaiter. They can make a huge difference.

Hand Warmers: Toss some hand warmers in your pockets for extra heat when needed. They're like mini radiators for your hands.

Extras for Comfort

Blanket: Bring a warm blanket or two. Not only will it add an extra layer of warmth, but it also makes sitting on cold surfaces much more comfortable.

Thermos: Fill a thermos with your favourite hot drink. Sipping hot cocoa or tea while watching the Northern Lights is a cozy experience that can't be beaten.

Camera Gear

Remember your camera gear if you remember to capture the magic. But remember, cold weather can drain batteries quickly, so bring spares and keep them warm in your pockets.

Eastern Limb, Western Limb—Sun talk sounds like a geography class! Can you explain?

We're diving into some solar lingo that might sound like your high school geography class, but I promise it's way more fun. So, let's talk about the Eastern and Western Limbs of the Sun and why they matter.

What's a "Limb" Anyway?

First, when astronomers say "limb," they're talking about the edge of the Sun as seen from Earth. Imagine the Sun as a giant pizza (yum!), and the limbs are the crust—those far edges we see in the sky. Simple, right?

Eastern Limb: The Rising Star

The Eastern Limb of the Sun is the left-hand edge as you look at it from Earth. Think of it as the Sun's version of stage left. This is where new sunspots and other solar activities appear as the Sun rotates. It's like the grand entrance for solar phenomena.

So, when you hear about something happening on the Eastern Limb, it's like getting a sneak peek at the new solar features making their debut. Exciting, right?

Western Limb: The Sun's Exit Ramp

Now, let's head over to the Western Limb, the right-hand edge of the Sun. This is where sunspots and other features make their dramatic exit as the Sun continues its rotation. If the Eastern Limb is the grand entrance, the Western Limb is the exit ramp.

When solar features head over to the Western Limb, they're on their way to disappearing from our view. Think of it like waving goodbye to a friend taking the last train out of town. But don't worry—they'll be back!

Is it easier to spot the Northern or Southern Lights (is there even a difference)?
First, let's clear up any confusion: the Northern and Southern Lights are the same phenomenon. Both are auroras created when charged particles from the Sun collide with Earth's magnetic field, lighting up the sky with dazzling colours.

The difference? Location, location, location!

Northern Lights (Aurora Borealis): These occur in the Northern Hemisphere and are primarily seen in Norway, Alaska, Canada, and Finland.

Southern Lights (Aurora Australis): These occur in the Southern Hemisphere and are mainly visible from Antarctica, southern New Zealand, and Tasmania.

Which is Easier to Spot?

Northern Lights win this round!

Here's why:

Accessibility: There are more accessible viewing spots for the Northern Lights. Think about it: places like Norway, Alaska, and Canada have towns and cities where you can base yourself while chasing the auroras. In contrast, Antarctica is the best place to see the Southern Lights, which isn't a quick weekend getaway.

Population Density: More people live in the Northern Hemisphere, which means there are more chances and more reports of sightings. Plus, with more tourists heading north, there's more infrastructure to support aurora hunting.

Tourism Industry: The Northern Lights have a booming tourism industry. There are tons of tours, guides, and apps to help you find the best viewing spots. Southern Lights tours exist, too, but they're less prevalent.

Chasing the Southern Lights

While it might be more challenging, spotting the Southern Lights is possible. Keep your eyes peeled if you find yourself in southern New Zealand or Tasmania during the right season. The experience is just as magical, and you'll have significant bragging rights!

Is the Sun heading for a long nap, like during the Maunder Minimum?

First, let's travel back to the late 1600s. Picture this: powdered wigs, elaborate gowns, and a Sun that seemed to hit the snooze button. The Maunder Minimum was a period from about 1645 to 1715 when sunspots were scarce. This 70-year-long siesta coincided with the "Little Ice Age," when Earth's temperatures dropped and winters were extra frosty.

Signs of Another Solar Snooze?

Scientists monitor the Sun's activity throughout its 11-year solar cycle, including high and low sunspot activity periods. The Sun is bustling with sunspots and solar storms during the peak or solar maximum. During the low or solar minimum, things calm down a bit.

Solar Cycles: We're in Solar Cycle 25, which started in December 2019. Predictions suggest this cycle will be average, with neither too many nor too few sunspots. Nothing too wild or sleepy.

Sunspot Numbers: While the Sun has shown periods of low activity, sunspots haven't disappeared entirely. We still see those lovely dark spots popping up, keeping things interesting.

Research: Solar scientists use advanced models and data to predict solar behaviour. So far, no solid evidence suggests we're heading into a long-term minimum like the Maunder Minimum.

Why should we care if the Sun takes a nap? Well, solar activity affects everything from satellite operations to climate patterns. Less solar activity can mean cooler temperatures on Earth, but it's not a one-to-one ratio. The Maunder Minimum was part of a complex climate system.

While it's fun to speculate, the current data suggests that the Sun isn't gearing up for another extended nap.

During the Maunder Minimum, astronomers like Galileo still observed the Sun and noted its lack of sunspots. It's a great reminder that even when things seem quiet, the Sun is still full of surprises.

Does wildlife get affected by the Northern Lights, or do they enjoy the view?

Have they ever wondered what animals think of the Northern Lights? Do they marvel at the shimmering sky like we do, or do they even notice? Let's dive into the wild world of auroras and animals.

Do Animals Even Notice the Northern Lights?

Picture this: you're a moose, munching on some tasty leaves, when suddenly the sky lights up in a dazzling display of green and purple. Do you stop and stare or keep munching? While humans rush outside with cameras and hot cocoa, animals react uniquely to the Northern Lights.

Wildlife and the Northern Lights

Moose and Reindeer: These majestic creatures probably notice the lights but focus more on finding their next meal. They might glance up and think, "Huh, nice lights," before returning to their tasty foliage.

Birds: Migratory birds may be more tuned in. They navigate using the Earth's magnetic field, which can be affected by solar activity. During intense auroras, birds might get off track. Imagine them having a "Wait, weren't we heading south?" moment.

Nocturnal Animals: Nighttime dwellers like owls and bats might find the extra light confusing. Owls might hoot in surprise, and bats might zigzag more than usual. But generally, they adapt quickly and get back to their nighttime activities.

Do Animals Enjoy the View?

While we'd love to think animals enjoy a good light show, they're more likely indifferent. For them, the Northern Lights are just another quirky feature of their environment. They're too busy surviving and thriving to stop and stargaze.

Some indigenous cultures believe animals have unique connections to the Northern Lights. For example, some Inuit legends say the lights are the spirits of animals playing in the sky. It's a beautiful thought, blending nature and mythology.

An Aurora forecast for the weekend—does that mean we're in for a marathon show?

When you hear that the Northern Lights are forecasted for the entire weekend, it's tempting to think of a continuous, dazzling light show. But here's the real deal:

On-and-Off Extravaganza: The Northern Lights are more like a series of surprise pop-up concerts than a single, endless performance. They'll dazzle you, take a break (maybe grab a cosmic coffee), and then return for an encore. It's Mother Nature's way of keeping you on your toes!

Solar Activity Shenanigans: The forecast means that conditions are ripe for auroras due to some severe solar activity. Imagine the Sun sending us VIP tickets to its light show. But, just like any weather forecast, things can be unpredictable. Sometimes, the Sun's plans change, and we must roll with it.

Nighttime Only: Remember, the Northern Lights need the dark to shine. So, they'll rest backstage during the day, prepping for the next night's performance.

What to Do

To make the most of your aurora-filled weekend, here's a game plan:

Stay Vigilant: Check real-time Aurora alerts and apps. They'll tell you when the lights are likely to appear.

Be Patient: The auroras love to keep us guessing. They might show up early, or they might make you wait. Consider it part of the excitement!

Comfort is Key: Bundle up, bring some hot cocoa, and ensure you're comfortable. Whether it's a quick show or a more extended display, you'll be glad you're cozy.

What are all the crazy shapes the Aurora can take?

The Northern Lights are like the universe's ultimate artist, painting the night sky with various shapes and patterns. Let's explore the different forms these dazzling lights can take and have some fun along the way!

1. The Classic Curtain

Imagine the sky hanging up its finest drapes. The classic aurora curtain is the most common shape, resembling waves of light flowing across the horizon. These curtains can ripple and fold, looking like the sky's preparing for a grand theatrical performance.

2. The Flaming Arc

Think of this one as the sky's fiery eyebrow. It's a smooth, glowing arc that stretches across the heavens. Sometimes, it stays still, and other times, it dances, transforming into other shapes. It's like the Aurora's warm-up routine before the big show.

3. The Spiraling Vortex

When the Aurora gets playful, you might see spirals twisting and turning like a cosmic whirlpool. These can be mesmerising and make you feel like you're being sucked into a celestial rollercoaster. Hold onto your hats!

4. The Pulsating Blob

Every so often, Aurora decides to go for a more laid-back vibe. Pulsating blobs of light appear and disappear, like the sky's having a gentle, glowing heartbeat. It's a more relaxed, but no less beautiful, display.

5. The Exploding Corona

For the grand finale, we have the corona, which looks like a giant explosion of light radiating from a single point. Picture standing directly under a firework that fills the sky with shimmering beams. It's like the Northern Lights shouting, "Look at me!"

6. The Mysterious Rays

Sometimes, the Aurora forms into tall, vertical rays shooting up the sky. They look like nature's laser light show, and you half-expect seeing a spaceship emerge behind them. The Aurora might Glow.

What's the deal with G1, G2, and G3—are they like Aurora VIP passes?

G1, G2, and G3 are like space weather grades for geomagnetic storms, letting us know just how intense these cosmic events are. Think of them as your VIP passes to the Northern Lights show!

G1 – Minor Storm: The Warm-Up Act

A G1 storm is like a light sprinkle of excitement. A minor geomagnetic storm might cause some beautiful auroras at higher latitudes. Picture it as the opening act of a concert, with flickering lights setting the mood. These storms can cause minor blips in power grids and satellite operations, but nothing too wild.

G2 – Moderate Storm: The Main Event

Now we're getting into the good stuff! A G2 storm is a moderate geomagnetic storm. This one cranks up the intensity, and the auroras can be seen further from the poles. Imagine the sky lighting up with vibrant colours and dynamic movements, like a thrilling movie night. It's more intense, more exciting, and worth watching.

G3 – Strong Storm: The Blockbuster

A G3 storm is when things get seriously exciting. It's a solid geomagnetic storm that can create stunning auroras visible much further from the poles, sometimes even in places you wouldn't expect. Think of it as the blockbuster hit of the geomagnetic world, with dazzling lights filling the sky. These storms can cause disruptions to power systems and satellite operations, making it a real space-weather adventure!

What are Geomagnetic Substorm and Growth/Expansion/Recovery Phases?

A geomagnetic substorm is like a surprise fireworks show in space! An intense burst of activity in the Earth's magnetosphere causes the auroras to light up spectacularly.

Let's break down the three phases of this cosmic event:

Growth Phase

Picture this: it's like the warm-up act before the main concert. During the growth phase, the Sun's charged particles build energy in the Earth's magnetic field. The auroras might glow softly, like the stage lights dimming before the big performance. This phase can last for about 30 to 60 minutes.

Expansion Phase

Now, the real show begins! The expansion phase is when things get exciting. The built-up energy is suddenly released, causing the auroras to burst into bright, dancing lights. The sky can go from a gentle glow to a vibrant, swirling spectacle. This phase is like the crescendo of a symphony, where everything is at its peak. It usually lasts 10 to 30 minutes, but it's the most thrilling part of the substorm.

Recovery Phase

After the grand finale, the lights start to calm down. The recovery phase is like the gentle encore after the main event. The auroras gradually fade to a softer glow as the magnetic field settles. This phase can take several hours, giving you a lingering sense of the magical show you've just witnessed.

Are there any downsides to the Northern Lights, or are they all good vibes?

First, let's bask in the glow of the good vibes. The Northern Lights are stunning. They light up the sky with brilliant greens, purples, and reds, making you feel like you're in a dream. Plus, they're a perfect excuse to travel to some of the most beautiful places on Earth, like Norway, Iceland, and Alaska.

But hold on. Before you pack your bags and head north, let's examine some potential downsides.

Freezing Your Tush Off Chasing the Northern Lights often means braving the cold. We're talking bone-chilling, face-numbing, wish-you-had-another-layer cold. So, while you're gazing up at the sky, your toes might be thinking, "Why didn't we stay by the fire?"

Sleep Deprivation: The best time to see the auroras is usually late at night or early in the morning. That means many late nights and early mornings, which can turn you into a sleep-deprived zombie. Who needs sleep when you've got nature's most epic light show, right?

Unpredictability: The Northern Lights are notoriously

unpredictable. You might spend hours (or days!) waiting for them to appear, only for the sky to stay stubbornly dark. It's like waiting for your favourite band to come on stage only to realise they're not even in town.

Light Pollution: Finding a spot away from city lights is crucial for a good aurora experience. So, if you're in a big city, you'll need to trek out to the countryside, which is a hassle. But think of it as part of the adventure!

Geomagnetic Storms: On a more serious note, intense auroras are caused by geomagnetic storms, which can sometimes mess with satellites, GPS systems, and even power grids. It's like the Northern Lights saying, "Look at me!" while causing some trouble on the side.

What are the Sun's features, and how do they jazz up the Auroras?

The Sun, our dynamic and fiery star, is the ultimate showrunner behind the breathtaking auroras we see on Earth. Let's take a fun tour of our favourite star to understand how different parts of the Sun contribute to these magical light shows.

The Sun's Main Attractions:

Core: This is the powerhouse of the Sun where nuclear fusion happens, creating enormous amounts of energy. Think of it as the Sun's engine room.

Radiative Zone: Surrounding the core, this layer transports energy outward through radiation. It's like the Sun's central heating system.

Convective Zone: Energy moves through convection currents, bringing heat to the surface. Imagine a cosmic lava lamp!

Photosphere: The visible surface of the Sun that is observable from Earth, where phenomena such as sunspots and solar flares occur.

Chromosphere: A layer above the photosphere, visible during solar eclipses as a reddish glow. It's the Sun's atmospheric blush.

Corona: The outermost layer of the Sun's atmosphere extends millions of kilometres into space and is visible during a total solar eclipse. It is the Sun's majestic crown.

How These Features Create Auroras:

Sunspots: The Cool Kids

Sunspots are dark patches on the Sun's surface where intense magnetic activity is brewing. These spots are like cosmic hotspots where solar flares and coronal mass ejections (CMEs) often kick-off, sending charged particles zooming toward Earth to light up our skies with auroras. You can think of sunspots as the ultimate party planners, setting the stage for the solar system's most dazzling light show!

Solar Flares: The Fireworks

Solar flares are sudden, intense bursts of radiation from the Sun's surface near sunspots. When directed toward Earth, these flares can release charged particles into space, enhancing auroras. It's like the Sun's saying, "Let's get this party started!"

Coronal Mass Ejections (CMEs): The Big Boom

CMEs are enormous bursts of solar wind and magnetic fields that rise above the solar corona or are released into space. When directed toward Earth, these CMEs interact with our magnetic field, causing spectacular auroras. You can think of CMEs as the grand finale of a fireworks display, lighting the sky with vibrant colours.

What causes Aurora to diffuse all over us?

A diffuse aurora is like the Northern Lights' mellow cousin. Instead of the intense, dancing streaks of colour, you get a more spread-out, faint glow. It's like the sky switched from a rock concert to a gentle lullaby. Here's why this happens:

Low Energy Particle Precipitation

Diffuse auroras occur when lower-energy particles from the solar wind interact with Earth's magnetic field. These particles aren't as energetic as those causing the bright, vibrant auroras, so they create a more subdued light show. It's like the difference between a sparkler and a fireworks finale.

Quiet Solar Activity

When the Sun is relatively quiet, the auroras can become diffuse. During periods of low solar activity, there aren't as many solar flares or coronal mass ejections (CMEs) to send high-energy particles our way. It's like the Sun is napping, and the auroras are just gently humming along.

Magnetospheric Conditions

Conditions in Earth's magnetosphere can also affect the appearance of auroras. When the magnetosphere is stable, the auroras tend to be more diffuse. Imagine the magnetosphere as a giant shield around Earth. When it's calm, the auroras are soft and spread out. When it's all riled up, you get bright, dynamic displays.

Latitude Matters

Diffuse auroras are commonly seen at lower latitudes, where the geomagnetic activity is less intense. So, if you're farther from the poles, you're more likely to see this gentle glow than the dramatic curtains of light. It's like getting a soft, ambient nightlight instead of a strobe light.

While diffuse auroras might not have the wow factor of their more intense counterparts, they still have their serene beauty. They paint the sky with a soft, ethereal glow that can be just as mesmerising. Plus, they allow you to appreciate the subtle side of Aurora's personality.

What happens if you whistle at the Northern Lights—will they whistle back?

In many cultures, especially among the Indigenous peoples of the Arctic regions, there's a myth that whistling at the Northern Lights can provoke a response. Some believe that the auroras are spirits or celestial beings, and whistling at them can make them come closer or even communicate with you. It's a fun and spooky thought: imagine the sky responding to your whistles!

Now, let's bring in a dash of science. Unfortunately (or maybe fortunately, depending on how you feel about ghostly lights), the

Northern Lights are not sentient beings capable of whistling back. Auroras are caused by charged particles from the Sun colliding with Earth's atmosphere, creating beautiful light displays. These particles don't have ears to hear whistles or mouths to whistle back.

While the Northern Lights don't whistle, there have been reports of people hearing sounds during intense auroral displays. These sounds are faint crackles, hisses, or even distant applause. Scientists are still debating the cause of these sounds. Some theories suggest that electrical charges in the atmosphere could cause them, while others think they might be psychological effects of the mesmerising lights.

What on Earth is a white-light solar flare?

A white-light solar flare is a type of solar flare that's so intense that it's visible in white light—the same kind of light we see with our eyes. Imagine looking at the Sun (through proper protective gear) and seeing a sudden, bright flash. That's a white-light solar flare!

White-light solar flares are unique because they are much rarer than other flares. Most solar flares are only visible in specific wavelengths like ultraviolet or X-rays, which require special instruments to detect. On the other hand, white-light flares are powerful enough to be seen in the visible spectrum, making them a spectacular (and scientifically intriguing) event.

These flares occur when an exceptionally high amount of energy is released from the Sun's magnetic fields. The energy is so intense that it heats the photosphere—the Sun's visible surface—to the point where it emits a brilliant flash of white light. Think of it as the Sun turning up the brightness dial to eleven!

English astronomer Richard Carrington observed one of the most famous white-light solar flares in 1859. This event, known as the Carrington Event, caused widespread auroras and even disrupted telegraph systems on Earth. It was a dramatic reminder of the Sun's power and impact on our planet.

What's an Earth-directed Aurora?

An Earth-directed aurora happens when a solar storm or burst of solar wind from the Sun is aimed directly at Earth. Think of it as the Sun throwing a fastball right at our planet. This usually occurs during events like coronal mass ejections (CMEs) or solar flares, which send streams of charged particles hurtling through space.

When these charged particles are Earth-directed, they travel along the solar wind and reach our planet's magnetic field. Here's the fun part: Earth's magnetic field channels these particles towards the polar regions, where they interact with gases in the atmosphere (mainly oxygen and nitrogen), creating mesmerising auroras.

An Earth-directed aurora means the conditions are just right for a spectacular light show. Because the particles are aimed directly at us, the chances of seeing intense and widespread auroras increase. This can make auroras visible much further from the poles than usual, lighting up the night sky in unexpected places.

What's BLACK AURORA?

A Black Aurora isn't a scene from a sci-fi movie. Instead, it's a lesser-known and intriguing phenomenon related to the more familiar colourful auroras. Unlike the vibrant greens, pinks, and purples of the Northern and Southern Lights, Black Auroras are areas of the sky that appear darker than their surroundings. It's like the Aurora has decided to take a break and left a patch of the sky in shadow.

Black Auroras occur in the same regions as their colourful counterparts—high up in the polar skies. They are formed by the same interactions between the solar wind and Earth's magnetic field. However, instead of producing light, certain conditions cause areas where the auroral activity is significantly reduced, resulting in dark patches.

Electron Vacuums: Black Auroras happen when there are regions in the sky where fewer electrons precipitate into the atmosphere. Think of this as an auroral "dead zone" with fewer light-emitting collisions.

Contrast Effect: These dark patches are often more noticeable because they contrast sharply with the bright surrounding auroras. It's like having a few burnt-out bulbs in a dazzling Christmas light display.

Black auroras interest scientists as they offer insight into the complex interactions between solar wind, Earth's magnetic field, and the upper atmosphere. Understanding them helps researchers learn about space weather and its effects on our planet.

Spotting a Black Aurora isn't as straightforward as watching a traditional aurora. They tend to be less dramatic and are often overshadowed by the more vibrant auroras. But if you're an aurora enthusiast or a dedicated sky-watcher, knowing about Black Auroras adds more intrigue to your stargazing experience.

Who or what is STEVE in the Aurora world?

Meet STEVE, the new star in the aurora world! No, STEVE isn't a person, and he's not your average Aurora. Let's dive into STEVE's fascinating and fun world and discover what makes this phenomenon unique.

STEVE stands for "Strong Thermal Emission Velocity Enhancement." Catchy, right? This charming acronym represents a unique atmospheric phenomenon discovered by aurora chasers and scientists. Unlike the typical green auroras, STEVE is usually seen as a narrow ribbon of purplish light, often accompanied by a green picket fence structure below it.

STEVE was discovered thanks to the keen eyes of citizen scientists—yes, regular folks like you and me who love watching the skies. Aurora enthusiasts started noticing this unusual light show and brought it to the attention of researchers. Initially thought to be a type of Aurora, STEVE turned out to be something entirely different.

What Makes STEVE Special?

Unique Appearance: STEVE's main feature is a thin, purplish arc stretching across the sky, sometimes with green vertical stripes resembling a picket fence. This makes STEVE a striking and easily distinguishable sight.

Different Cause: Unlike traditional auroras, which are caused by charged particles from the solar wind colliding with Earth's atmosphere, STEVE is linked to a different process. It's associated with hot, fast-moving streams of particles in Earth's ionosphere, making STEVE a unique player in the sky's light shows.

Science in Action: STEVE's discovery and ongoing study highlight the power of citizen science. Enthusiastic skywatchers teamed up with researchers to unveil the mysteries of this phenomenon, showcasing how collaboration can lead to exciting discoveries.

Can You See STEVE?

Yes, you can! STEVE is most observed in the same regions where you'd look for the Northern Lights, typically at higher latitudes. The best time to spot STEVE is during geomagnetic activity, similar to when you'd look for auroras. Look for that distinctive purplish ribbon and the green picket fence below it.

What's the rarest colour of the Northern Lights?

Among the spectrum of aurora colours, pure red is considered the rarest. This striking hue is typically seen during powerful solar storms and is created by high-altitude oxygen interactions occurring more than 200 miles above the Earth's surface. When you see pure red auroras, the sky puts on a unique, once-in-a-lifetime performance just for you.

Why is Red So Rare?

High Energy Requirement: The conditions to produce pure red auroras are specific and require significant energy. This only happens during the most intense solar activity.

Altitude Factor: Pure red auroras occur at high altitudes, where oxygen atoms can be excited to the right energy state. Charged particles from the Sun less frequently reach these heights.

Geomagnetic Storm Intensity: A powerful geomagnetic storm is needed to produce the conditions for pure red auroras. These storms are less common, making the red auroras a rare treat.

To increase your chances of seeing this rare colour, keep an eye on space weather forecasts for predictions of intense geomagnetic storms. Head to a location with minimal light pollution and clear skies. And remember, patience is vital—catching the rare red auroras is all about being in the right place at the right time.

How do the Northern Lights look to the naked eye—Instagram perfect or just a faint glow?

You've seen the stunning Northern Lights photos on Instagram, with vibrant colours and dramatic swirls lighting up the night sky. But how do these celestial wonders look to the naked eye? Are they really that Instagram-perfect, or is it just a faint glow? Let's dive into the reality of Aurora watching with a fun and engaging twist!

The Instagram Illusion

Those jaw-dropping Instagram shots of the Northern Lights are often taken with high-quality cameras, long exposure times, and some post-processing magic. Cameras can capture more light than our eyes, making the colours pop and the auroras look even more dramatic. So, while the photos are real, they might be enhanced.

The Naked Eye Experience

When you see the Northern Lights with your own eyes, the experience is slightly different—but still magical! Here's what to expect:

Subtle Colours: The colours of the auroras can be more subdued to the naked eye. You might see green as the dominant colour, with hints of pink, red, or purple. The colours are usually not as intense as in photos, but they're still beautiful.

Movement and Dance: One of the most mesmerising aspects of the Northern Lights is their movement. They dance and swirl across the sky, creating changing and shifting patterns. This dynamic display is something cameras can't fully capture, and it's a highlight of seeing the auroras in person.

Brightness Variations: The brightness of the auroras can vary. Sometimes, they appear as a faint glow on the horizon and other times, they're bright enough to light up the landscape. Your location, the level of geomagnetic activity, and the sky's darkness all play a role.

Managing Expectations

It's essential to manage your expectations. The Northern Lights might not always look like the neon light show you see on Instagram, but that doesn't mean they're any less spectacular. The subtle beauty, the gentle glow, and the serene dance of the lights are enchanting in their own right.

If the Carrington Event happened today, would we be toast?

First, a quick recap: The Carrington Event was a massive solar storm that hit Earth in 1859. Named after British astronomer Richard Carrington observed the solar flare, this event caused spectacular auroras and knocked out telegraph systems worldwide. Back then, it was more of an electrifying curiosity than a catastrophe.

Fast forward to our tech-savvy, interconnected world. If the Carrington Event happened today, things would get interesting.

Power Grids: Flickering Lights and More

Our modern power grids would be the first to feel the burn. High-energy particles from the solar storm could induce electric currents in power lines, potentially causing transformers to overheat and fail. Imagine your neighbourhood's power grid getting an unexpected jolt and going dark. Candles, anyone?

Satellites: Space Junkyard?

Next up, our satellites. The solar storm's intense radiation could fry these high-tech space gadgets. GPS, weather forecasts, satellite T.V.—poof, gone instantly. It'd be like the ultimate "you've lost signal" message, only everywhere.

Communications: Back to the 1800s

With satellites down, our communication systems would take a significant hit. Internet, mobile networks, and even radio communications could go haywire. We'd return to using smoke signals and carrier pigeons—or maybe just shouting.

Transportation: Grounded Flights and Lost Ships

The aviation and shipping industries rely heavily on GPS for navigation. A massive solar storm could disrupt these systems, grounding flights and leaving ships wandering the seas like confused ducks. Airports and seaports would be chaos, with travellers wishing they'd packed an extra book.

The Bright Side: Epic Auroras!

On the bright side—literally—we'd be treated to some of the most spectacular auroras ever seen. The Northern and Southern Lights would be visible much further from the poles, painting the skies with brilliant colours. It'd be a light show to remember, assuming you can look up from your now-useless smartphone.

So, would we be toast if the Carrington Event happened today? Not quite, but we'd be in for a rough ride. While it wouldn't end the world, it would cause significant disruptions and force us to appreciate life's simpler pleasures—like board games by candlelight and talking to our neighbours.

What would happen if you tried to touch the Northern Lights?

First things first—while the Northern Lights look close enough to touch, they're far away. The auroras occur about 60 to 200 miles above the Earth's surface. So touching them is out of reach unless you're a superhero with some flying severe abilities. But let's pretend for a moment that you could.

You'd be in for a surprise because there's nothing there to touch! The Northern Lights aren't solid objects you can hold—they're like nature's light show, created when charged particles from the Sun slam into gases in Earth's atmosphere. This cosmic collision releases energy as dazzling light, painting the sky with stunning auroras. So, trying to touch them is like catching a rainbow or a beam of sunlight—there's no physical substance to hold onto, just pure magic in the air!

But, for fun, you could interact with these charged particles. Would it be shocking? Electrifying? Surprisingly, not really. The particles that create auroras are primarily electrons and protons, and while they're energetic, they're not concentrated enough to zap you like an electric fence. So, no superhero powers for you!

What's a CH HSS?

A CH HSS, or Coronal Hole High-Speed Stream, is like the Sun blowing us a high-speed kiss! Imagine the Sun with areas on its surface called coronal holes. The Sun's magnetic field opens up in these regions, allowing solar wind to escape. Think of them as the Sun's "windows" letting out gusts of charged particles.

These solar wind streams shoot out at super-fast speeds, zooming through space. When one of these high-speed streams heads toward Earth, it interacts with our planet's magnetic field. When a CH HSS hits Earth's magnetic field, it stirs things up and can create beautiful auroras. It's like the Sun sending a burst of energy our way, making the night sky sparkle with colourful lights.

CH HSS events aren't as dramatic as the more intense Coronal Mass Ejections (CMEs) but happen more frequently. While they usually cause only minor geomagnetic storms, they still significantly create those stunning auroras we love to see.

What's the biggest rookie mistake when chasing Auroras?

Let's set the scene: you're all pumped for a night of aurora hunting. You've got your gear ready, your cozy clothes on, and your camera primed. But then you think, "Hey, why not have a nice, leisurely dinner first? The Aurora will wait, right?" One of the most common rookie mistakes.

Auroras show up unannounced, hang around for a bit, and then poof—they're gone, leaving only whispers and Instagram posts behind. Deciding to head out after dinner could mean missing the main event entirely. You finish your meal, maybe linger over dessert, and finally head out, only to find that while you savoured that last bite, the Aurora put on a spectacular show and vanished. Timing is everything with auroras. They don't run on your schedule; you've got to be ready to drop everything and head out when the conditions are right. The urgency of the moment, the need to be prepared and quick, adds a thrilling element to the aurora chase.

What are the pitfalls of the Kp or K index?

First, a quick refresher: the Kp index is a scale from 0 to 9 that measures geomagnetic activity. The higher the number, the better your chances of seeing the auroras. Sounds simple. Well, only sometimes!

Pitfall #1: The "Overly Optimistic" Kp

You see a high Kp index, say 6 or 7, and you're ready to pack your bags and head out. But wait! Just because the high Kp index doesn't guarantee a spectacular show. Geomagnetic activity can be unpredictable, and a high Kp doesn't always translate to bright auroras right above you. It's like seeing a movie trailer and expecting a blockbuster, only to find out it's a rom-com.

Pitfall #2: The "Local Conditions" Conundrum

The Kp index gives a global measure of geomagnetic activity, but local conditions are crucial. Even with a high Kp, cloudy skies, light pollution, or your location can spoil the fun. Imagine being all set for a barbecue, but it starts raining. Check the local weather and find a dark, clear spot for the best viewing experience.

Pitfall #3: The "Timing" Trap

The Kp index doesn't tell you exactly when the auroras will appear. You might see a promising Kp index, but the auroras could arrive at 2 AM while fast asleep. It's like waiting for a surprise party that doesn't have a set start time. Monitor real-time aurora alerts to catch the lights at their peak.

Pitfall #4: The "Geographic Variability" Vexation

A high Kp index means auroras could be visible at lower latitudes, but this isn't guaranteed. The further you are from the poles, the fainter the auroras might be, even with a good Kp reading. It's like expecting a front-row seat and ending up in the nosebleeds. Manage your expectations based on your location.

Pitfall #5: The "Magnetic Latitude" Mix-Up

Your magnetic latitude, different from your geographic latitude, also affects aurora visibility. You might be at a high latitude geographically but lower magnetically, affecting your aurora odds. It's like thinking you're at the correct address but realising you're on the wrong street. Use aurora apps that factor in magnetic latitude for more accurate forecasts.

What's a Magnetometer?

A magnetometer is like a supercharged compass on steroids! This nifty gadget doesn't just point north—it's a magnetic field detective, sniffing out the strength and direction of magnetic forces, whether they're coming from our Earth, the blazing Sun, or some other cosmic mystery. It's the ultimate tool for anyone who wants to track down magnetic vibes in style!

Magnetometers come in various shapes and sizes, but they all work on the same principle: detecting changes in magnetic fields. Here's a simple way to understand it:

Sensing Magnetic Fields: Like a compass needle aligns with Earth's magnetic field, a magnetometer's sensor responds to magnetic fields around it.

Measuring Strength and Direction: It measures the strength (how strong the magnetic field is) and the direction (where the magnetic field is coming from).

Providing Data: This information is then converted into readable data, which can be used for various applications.

There are several types of magnetometers, but here are the most common ones:

Scalar Magnetometers: Measure the total strength of the magnetic field.

Vector Magnetometers: Measure the strength and direction of the magnetic field in three dimensions.

Magnetometers are used in various applications, from everyday gadgets to cutting-edge scientific research. Here's why they're so important:

Navigation: They're used in smartphones, GPS devices, and ships to help navigation by detecting magnetic north.

Geological Surveys: Scientists use them to study the Earth's magnetic field, which can help find mineral deposits or track tectonic movements.

Space Exploration: Magnetometers on spacecraft measure the magnetic fields of other planets and the solar wind, helping us understand more about our universe.

Aurora Forecasting: They play a crucial role in predicting the Northern Lights by detecting changes in Earth's magnetic field caused by solar activity.

What's a Substorm?

A substorm is like Aurora's surprise party. When you think the show is over, the sky bursts into an intense display of lights, swirling and dancing more energetically than before. It's a temporary but dramatic disturbance in Earth's magnetosphere that amps up the auroral activity.

Please think of the magnetosphere as Earth's protective bubble, shielding us from the Sun's charged particles. When these particles build up enough energy, they can trigger a substorm. Here's a playful breakdown of the process:

Buildup Phase (The Anticipation): The Sun sends out streams of charged particles, which get caught in Earth's magnetosphere. It's like the buildup of excitement before a big party. The energy accumulates, and everyone's waiting for the main event.

Expansion Phase (The Big Reveal): Suddenly, the stored energy is released, and the sky lights up in a burst of colours. This is the party's peak, where everything goes wild. Auroras brighten, move faster, and spread out, creating a spectacular display.

Recovery Phase (The Cool Down): After the intense activity, the energy settles down. The auroras return to their usual calm state, and the sky breathes. It's like the party winding down, with everyone catching their breath.

Why Are Substorms Special?

Substorms are unique because they add extra excitement to Aurora watching. When you think you've seen it all, a substorm can turn a beautiful display into unforgettable. They can happen several times during a single night, keeping sky watchers on their toes.

Did you know that substorms were first described by a scientist named Kristian Birkeland in the early 1900s? He was so passionate about studying auroras that he even set up camps in the Arctic to get a closer look. Talk about dedication!

What's Hemispheric Power, and why does it sound so dramatic?

Hemispheric Power measures the total energy hitting the upper atmosphere from the solar wind in either the northern or southern hemisphere. Imagine it as the amount of juice the Sun is sending our way to power those dazzling auroras. The higher the Hemispheric Power, the more likely you will see a spectacular light show.

The term "Hemispheric Power" might sound like a superhero's name, but there's a reason it sounds so grand. It captures the immense scale and energy involved in these space weather events. Let's dive into why it's so epic:

Massive Energy: Hemispheric Power represents vast amounts of energy being dumped into our atmosphere, sparking auroras. It's like the Sun saying, "Here, have some of my cosmic energy!"

Global Impact: This energy affects entire hemispheres, not just small regions. People can see the Northern or Southern Lights when hemisphere power is high. It's a show for everyone under the sky.

Dynamic Displays: High Hemispheric Power means more intense and vibrant auroras. Imagine the difference between a small campfire and a fireworks display. When the power is high, the auroras put on a fireworks show.

Scientists use satellites to measure the energy flowing into the polar regions. These measurements help them predict the intensity of auroras. When the Hemispheric Power values are high, it's time to grab your coat and head outside!

Long-Duration vs. Impulsive Solar Flares—what's the buzz about?

Solar flares are powerful bursts of radiation caused by the Sun's magnetic energy. They can affect everything from satellite communications to auroras. However, not all solar flares are created equal. They come in two primary flavours: Long-Duration and Impulsive.

Long-Duration Solar Flares: The Slow Burn

Think of Long-Duration Solar Flares as the slow-burn romance in a movie. They take their time, building up the tension and drama before delivering a powerful climax. Here's the scoop:

Extended Show: These flares can last for hours, slowly releasing energy. It's like watching a sunset that keeps getting better and better.

Coronal Mass Ejections (CMEs): Long-duration flares often include CMEs, massive clouds of solar plasma that can cause geomagnetic storms when they hit Earth. These are the big plot twists that keep things exciting!

Impact: Because of their extended nature, they can cause longer-lasting disruptions to communications and create spectacular auroras. It's the gift that keeps on giving.

Impulsive Solar Flares: The Quick Flash

Now, Impulsive Solar Flares are the action-packed, blink-and-you-miss-it kind of flares. They're the solar equivalent of a firecracker. Here's what you need to know:

Short and Sweet: These flares release energy quickly, usually in minutes. It's like a thrilling car chase scene—fast, intense, and over before you know it.

No CMEs: Impulsive flares typically don't come with CMEs, so their effects are usually limited to brief disruptions. They're the quick bursts of excitement without the lingering drama.

Impact: While they can still cause radio blackouts and affect satellites, their effects are usually shorter-lived. It's a quick shock and then back to normal.

Understanding the difference between Long-Duration and Impulsive Solar Flares is essential for predicting space weather and preparing for its effects. Here's why people are buzzing about it:

Space Weather Forecasts: Knowing which type of flare is coming helps scientists predict potential impacts on Earth, like satellite disruptions and auroras.

Aurora Chasing: For those who love watching the Northern Lights, Long-Duration flares can signal a better chance of seeing a spectacular show.

Tech Protection: Satellite operators and power grid managers must be aware of what's coming to protect their equipment from solar storm damage.

IMF North vs. IMF South—what's the difference in Aurora lingo?

Regarding auroras, the term "IMF" often pops up, and it's not talking about the International Monetary Fund. In Aurora lingo, IMF stands for Interplanetary Magnetic Field. Understanding the difference between IMF North and IMF South is critical to predicting when those magical lights will dance across the sky. Let's break it down in a fun and engaging way!

What is the Interplanetary Magnetic Field (IMF)?

The IMF is the magnetic field carried with the solar wind from the Sun through space. It's like the Sun's way of extending its magnetic influence far beyond its surface. When the solar wind reaches Earth, the IMF interacts with Earth's magnetic field, significantly creating auroras.

IMF North: The Calm Before the Storm

Orientation: When we say the IMF is "north," the magnetic field lines are oriented northward.

Effects on Auroras: An IMF North situation is like the calm before the storm. It stabilises Earth's magnetic field and usually results in less auroral activity. Think of it as the auroras taking a peaceful nap.

Why It Matters: If you hope to see the Northern Lights, IMF North means you have to wait longer. The conditions could be better for sparking those bright, colourful displays.

IMF South: The Aurora Party Starter

Orientation: When the IMF is "south," the magnetic field lines are oriented southward.

Effects on Auroras: IMF South is the party starter for Auroras. It creates a more favourable interaction with Earth's magnetic field, leading to geomagnetic activity. This means more vibrant and active auroras lighting up the night sky. It's like the cosmic D.J. just turned up the volume!

Why It Matters: For aurora chasers, IMF South is what you're looking for. It signals that the conditions are ripe for a spectacular light show, so get your camera ready and head outside.

Understanding the difference between IMF North and IMF South helps predict auroral activity. Here's why it's important:

Aurora Forecasts: Scientists use the IMF's orientation to forecast auroras. Knowing whether the IMF is north or south helps determine the likelihood and intensity of auroras.

Preparation: If the IMF is predicted to be south, you should plan your aurora-hunting adventure at that time. If it's north, hold off on those late-night excursions.

Kp5 vs G1—what's the deal?

Kp and G1 are scales used to measure geomagnetic activity, which is a fancy way of saying how likely you are to see the Northern Lights. Think of them as your aurora weather forecast.

Scale: The G scale ranges from G1 (minor storm) to G5 (extreme storm).

G1: A G1 storm is the mildest on the G scale but still packs a punch. It's equivalent to a Kp index of 5. So, when you hear G1, think "party time," but with a bit more cosmic flair. This level of storm can cause minor disruptions to power grids and satellite operations, but nothing too dramatic.

Kp5 and G1 are the Same: Kp5 and G1 indicate the same level of geomagnetic activity. They're just different ways of describing it. Think of Kp5 as the numerical score and G1 as the label for that score.

Different Uses, Same Excitement: The Kp index is straightforward to understand. The G scale adds more context, especially for those interested in the impacts of geomagnetic storms on technology and infrastructure.

What's the minimum Kp index to see the Northern Lights in Alaska?

Let's explore what Kp index you need to see the magical lights in some of Alaska's top cities.

Fairbanks

Minimum Kp Index: 1 to 2
Why: Fairbanks is one of the best places in the world to see the Northern Lights. It's located under the auroral oval, where geomagnetic activity is naturally higher. Even a low Kp index can result in stunning auroras.

Anchorage

Minimum Kp Index: 4 to 5
Why: Anchorage is further south than Fairbanks, requiring more geomagnetic activity to see the lights. A Kp index of 4 or higher

increases your chances of catching the auroras.

Juneau

Minimum Kp Index: 5 to 6
Why: Juneau is much further south, so you'll need a stronger geomagnetic storm to see the Northern Lights. A Kp index of 5 or 6 is usually necessary to spot auroras from this city.

Nome

Minimum Kp Index: 3 to 4
Why: Nome, located in Western Alaska, has good aurora visibility with a moderate Kp index. When the Kp hits 3 or 4, you've got a decent chance of seeing the lights.

What's the minimum Kp index to catch the Northern Lights in Canada?

Canada is a fantastic place to chase the Northern Lights, with several cities offering prime viewing opportunities.

Here's a breakdown of the minimum Kp index you need to see the auroras in some of Canada's top cities.

Whitehorse, Yukon

Minimum Kp Index: 1 to 2
Why: Whitehorse is located in the auroral zone, making it an excellent spot for Aurora watching. Even a low Kp index can light up the sky with stunning auroras.

Yellowknife, Northwest Territories

Minimum Kp Index: 1 to 2
Why: Yellowknife, like Whitehorse, is located under the auroral oval, making it one of the best places in the world to witness the Northern Lights. The displays are frequent, even at a low Kp index.

Churchill, Manitoba

Minimum Kp Index: 3 to 4
Why: Churchill is further south than Whitehorse and Yellowknife

but still offers excellent aurora views. A Kp index of 3 or higher usually ensures a good chance of seeing the lights.

Edmonton, Alberta

Minimum Kp Index: 4 to 5
Why: Edmonton requires more geomagnetic activity to see the Northern Lights. A Kp index of 4 or higher is generally needed for aurora visibility in this city.

Calgary, Alberta

Minimum Kp Index: 5 to 6
Why: Being further south, Calgary needs stronger geomagnetic activity for aurora sightings. Aim for a Kp index of 5 or higher to catch the lights.

Toronto, Ontario

Minimum Kp Index: 7 to 8
Why: Toronto is much further south, so seeing the Northern Lights here is rare and requires a strong geomagnetic storm. A Kp index of 7 or higher is necessary for aurora visibility in this bustling city.

What's the minimum Kp index for a Northern Lights show in Finland?

Finland is a prime destination for Northern Lights enthusiasts. With its location under the auroral oval, several cities in Finland offer fantastic opportunities to catch the auroras. Here's a breakdown of the minimum Kp index you need to see the Northern Lights in some of Finland's top cities.

Rovaniemi

Minimum Kp Index: 2 to 3
Why: Located just south of the Arctic Circle, Rovaniemi is an excellent spot for Aurora watching. A Kp index of 2 to 3 can often bring the Northern Lights into view.

Ivalo

Minimum Kp Index: 1 to 2

Why: Ivalo, situated further north, is well within the auroral zone. This makes it possible to see the Northern Lights with a relatively low Kp index of 1 to 2.

Inari

Minimum Kp Index: 1 to 2

Why: Like Ivalo, Inari is located in the auroral zone, which provides frequent Aurora displays even with a low Kp index.

Kemi

Minimum Kp Index: 4 to 5

Why: Kemi, located further south on the coast, requires more geomagnetic activity to see the Northern Lights. A Kp index of 4 or higher is generally needed.

Helsinki

Minimum Kp Index: 6 to 7

Why: As Finland's southern capital, Helsinki needs a significantly higher Kp index to witness auroras. Aim for a Kp index of 6 or higher, ideally closer to 7, to see the lights.

What's the minimum Kp index to see the Northern Lights in Greenland?

Here's a breakdown of the minimum Kp index for the auroras in some of Greenland's top cities.

Nuuk

Minimum Kp Index: 4 to 5

Why: Nuuk, the capital of Greenland, is located further south than some other prime aurora spots. A Kp index of 4 to 5 is generally needed to see the Northern Lights here.

Ilulissat

Minimum Kp Index: 2 to 3

Why: Ilulissat, located further north, near the Arctic Circle, offers excellent aurora viewing opportunities. A Kp index of 2 to 3 can often produce a beautiful light show.

Sisimiut

Minimum Kp Index: 3 to 4
Why: One of Greenland's largest towns, Sisimiut, is a good location for aurora sightings. A Kp index of 3 to 4 is typically required to see the Northern Lights.

Kangerlussuaq

Minimum Kp Index: 2 to 3
Why: Kangerlussuaq is a prime spot for Northern Lights chasers because of its clear skies and excellent aurora visibility. A Kp index of 2 to 3 is often sufficient to witness the auroras.

Qaanaaq

Minimum Kp Index: 1 to 2
Why: Qaanaaq, located in northern Greenland, is well within the auroral oval. A low Kp index of 1 to 2 can often bring spectacular aurora displays.

What's the minimum Kp index to spot the Northern Lights in Iceland?

Here's a breakdown of the minimum Kp index you need to see the auroras in some of Iceland's top cities.

Reykjavik
Minimum Kp Index: 4 to 5
Why: Reykjavik, the capital and located in the southwest, requires more geomagnetic activity due to its southern position in Iceland. A Kp index of 4 to 5 is generally needed to see the Northern Lights here.

Akureyri

Minimum Kp Index: 3 to 4
Why: Akureyri offers better chances for aurora sightings in northern Iceland than Reykjavik. A Kp index of 3 to 4 can often result in visible Northern Lights.

Ísafjörður

Minimum Kp Index: 3 to 4
Why: Ísafjörður, situated in the Westfjords, provides suitable conditions for aurora viewing. A Kp index of 3 to 4 is usually required to see the lights.

Egilsstaðir

Minimum Kp Index: 3 to 4
Why: As a town in eastern Iceland, Egilsstaðir also benefits from its higher latitude. A Kp index of 3 to 4 is typically enough for aurora sightings.

Vik

Minimum Kp Index: 4 to 5
Why: Vik, located in southern Iceland, requires a higher Kp index similar to Reykjavik due to its more southern position. Aim for a Kp index of 4 to 5 to catch the Northern Lights.

What's the minimum Kp index to view the Northern Lights in Norway?

Thanks to its location within the auroral oval, Norway is a dream destination for Northern Lights chasers. Here's a breakdown of the minimum Kp index you need to see the auroras in some of Norway's top cities.

Tromsø
Minimum Kp Index: 1 to 2
Why: Tromsø is situated well within the auroral oval, making it one of the best places in the world to see the Northern Lights. Even a low Kp index of 1 to 2 can result in stunning displays.

Alta

Minimum Kp Index: 1 to 2
Why: Like Tromsø, Alta is in northern Norway and provides excellent aurora viewing opportunities. A Kp index of 1 to 2 is often sufficient to see the lights.

Bodø

Minimum Kp Index: 3 to 4
Why: Bodø is further south than Tromsø and Alta, requiring more geomagnetic activity. A Kp index of 3 to 4 is generally needed to see the Northern Lights here.

Lofoten Islands

Minimum Kp Index: 3 to 4
Why: The Lofoten Islands are another fantastic spot for Aurora. In this scenic region, a Kp index of 3 to 4 can often bring the Northern Lights into view.

Oslo

Minimum Kp Index: 6 to 7

Why: Being much further south, Oslo needs significantly higher geomagnetic activity for aurora sightings. A Kp index of 6 to 7 is necessary to catch the Northern Lights in the capital city.

What's the minimum Kp index for Northern Lights in Russia?

With its vast northern territories, Russia offers fantastic opportunities to witness the Northern Lights. Here's a breakdown of the minimum Kp index you need to see the auroras in some of Russia's top cities.

Murmansk

Minimum Kp Index: 2 to 3
Why: Located above the Arctic Circle, Murmansk is a prime spot for aurora viewing. A Kp index of 2 to 3 can often result in visible Northern Lights.

Arkhangelsk

Minimum Kp Index: 4 to 5
Why: Arkhangelsk, further south than Murmansk, requires more

geomagnetic activity. A Kp index of 4 to 5 is generally needed to see the Northern Lights here.

Norilsk

Minimum Kp Index: 1 to 2
Why: Situated in northern Siberia, Norilsk offers excellent conditions for aurora viewing. Even a low Kp index of 1 to 2 can produce stunning displays.

St. Petersburg

Minimum Kp Index: 6 to 7
Why: Being much further south, St. Petersburg needs significantly higher geomagnetic activity to see the Northern Lights. Aim for a Kp index of 6 to 7 to witness the auroras.

Yakutsk

Minimum Kp Index: 3 to 4
Why: Yakutsk, located in eastern Siberia, is in a good position for Aurora viewing. A Kp index of 3 to 4 is typically required to see the Northern Lights.

What's the minimum Kp index to see the Northern Lights in Svalbard?

Svalbard, an archipelago located far north of the Arctic Circle, is one of the prime locations on Earth for observing the Northern Lights. Here's the essential information about the minimum Kp index needed to view the auroras in Svalbard.
Minimum Kp Index: 0 to 1
Why: Svalbard is located well within the auroral oval, making it ideal for viewing Aurora. Even a low Kp index of 0 to 1 can result in visible Northern Lights. The location's high latitude means that geomagnetic activity frequently lights up the sky with beautiful displays.

What's the minimum Kp index for Northern Lights in Sweden?

Let's discuss the Northern Lights, nature's most amazing light show! Imagine the sky getting all dressed up for a dazzling night out. But what does it take for this party to be visible from fabulous Swedish cities?

Kiruna

Kiruna, the superstar of Northern Lights sightings! This city is so far north that the Northern Lights practically live there. All you need is a Kp index of about 2. It's like the lights need a whisper to show up.

Luleå

Luleå, a little further south, needs a bit more persuasion. A Kp index of around 4 should do the trick. Think of it as the Northern Lights needing a formal invitation, but they're still happy to attend.

Umeå

Umeå, now we're getting into the "I need a solid reason to get off my couch" territory for the lights. Here, a Kp index of 5 to 6 is necessary. The lights need a pretty good reason to come down.

Stockholm

Ah, Stockholm, our beautiful capital. The Northern Lights are a diva here and need a grand gesture. With a Kp index of 7 to 8, they need fireworks and a marching band even to consider appearing.

Malmö

Malmö, way down south, is a tough crowd. For the Northern Lights to show up here, you need a Kp index of 8 to 9. Imagine trying to convince a celebrity to attend a small-town event. Yeah, it's kind of like that.

So, if you're chasing the Northern Lights in Sweden, head north for the best chances. And remember, the higher the Kp index, the more likely you'll see the sky put on a show.

What's the minimum Kp index for the Northern Lights in the U.K.?

Here's the lowdown on the minimum Kp index needed for a

glimpse of this natural wonder, city by city:

Shetland Islands

Minimum Kp Index: 4
Why: The Shetland Islands are the northernmost part of the U.K., making them prime real estate for spotting the Northern Lights. The Earth's magnetic field is relatively strong here, so even moderate geomagnetic activity can bring out the lights.

Edinburgh

Minimum Kp Index: 6
Why: Edinburgh is further south, so you'll need more geomagnetic activity to see the lights. A Kp index of 6 means the Northern Lights need to be more enthusiastic to make an appearance.

Belfast

Minimum Kp Index: 6-7
Why: In Belfast, the Kp index is 6 to 7. This means the geomagnetic storm needs to be vital to push the lights down to this latitude.

Newcastle

Minimum Kp Index: 6-7
Why: Newcastle is at a similar latitude to Belfast, so you need a Kp index of around 6 to 7 to have a good chance of seeing the lights. The lights need to be active to shine this far south.

Manchester

Minimum Kp Index: 7-8
Why: In Manchester, the Northern Lights are a rare treat. A Kp index of 7 to 8 is needed. The geomagnetic activity has to be strong enough to make the journey this far south.

London

Minimum Kp Index: 8-9
Why: London is quite far south, so seeing the Northern Lights here

is a real rarity. It would help if you had a Kp index of 8 to 9, which means the geomagnetic storm must be mighty for the lights to reach this far.

What's the minimum Kp index for Northern Lights in the USA except Alaska?

Here's what you need to know about the minimum Kp index for spotting these incredible lights in various cities:

Minneapolis, Minnesota

Minimum Kp Index: 5
Why: Minneapolis is far north, making it one of the best spots in the contiguous USA to see the Northern Lights. The Earth's magnetic field is reasonably strong here, so the lights don't need to be super active to be visible.

Milwaukee, Wisconsin

Minimum Kp Index: 6
Why: Milwaukee is slightly further south than Minneapolis, so more geomagnetic activity is needed. A Kp index 6 means the Northern Lights must ramp up their energy to shine here.

Detroit, Michigan

Minimum Kp Index: 6
Why: Detroit is on par with Milwaukee in terms of latitude. So, for the lights to be visible, Detroit also needs a Kp index of 6. The geomagnetic activity needs to be moderate to strong.

Chicago, Illinois

Minimum Kp Index: 7
Why: Chicago is further south, requiring a stronger geomagnetic storm. A Kp index of 7 means the lights need to be active to travel this far.

Boston, Massachusetts

Minimum Kp Index: 7

Why: Boston is at a similar latitude to Chicago. A Kp index of 7 is necessary for the Northern Lights to appear, requiring relatively geomagnetic solid activity.

New York City, New York

Minimum Kp Index: 7-8

Why: NYC is quite a bit south, so the lights need a solid push to reach here. A Kp index of 7 to 8 is needed, indicating a powerful geomagnetic storm.

Denver, Colorado

Minimum Kp Index: 7-8

Why: Despite its elevation, Denver is further south and needs a Kp index of 7 to 8. The Northern Lights need to be very active to be visible here.

Seattle, Washington

Minimum Kp Index: 5-6

Why: Seattle is far north, giving it a better chance than many other U.S. cities. Thanks to its higher latitude, a Kp index of 5 to 6 is often enough to see the lights.

Portland, Oregon

Minimum Kp Index: 6

Why: Portland is just a bit further south than Seattle, so it needs a Kp index 6. The lights need moderate geomagnetic activity to be visible.

San Francisco, California

Minimum Kp Index: 8-9

Why: San Francisco is quite far south, so seeing the Northern Lights here is rare. A Kp index of 8 to 9 means you need a strong geomagnetic storm.

Washington, D.C.

Minimum Kp Index: 8-9

Why: Washington, D.C., like San Francisco, needs a Kp index of 8 to 9 for the Northern Lights to be visible. Geomagnetic activity must be vital for the lights to reach this far south.

What's the minimum Kp index to see the Northern Lights in Ireland?

Minimum Kp Index: 7

Ireland's latitude, ranging from approximately 51.5° to 55.5° N, places it farther south than the typical auroral zone. As a result, stronger geomagnetic activity, corresponding to a Kp index of 7 or higher, is required to see the Northern Lights in this region. At this level, the aurora can extend far enough south to be visible in Ireland, particularly in areas with minimal light pollution and clear skies.

What's the minimum Kp index for the Northern Lights in the Faroe Islands?

Minimum Kp Index: 4

Why: The Faroe Islands are situated at a high latitude, approximately 62° N, within the auroral zone. Because of this, the Northern Lights can often be seen with a relatively low Kp index of 4 or higher. This lower threshold reflects the proximity to the geomagnetic pole, where auroras are more frequent and visible even with moderate geomagnetic activity.

Why do you need a camera to appreciate the Northern Lights fully?

Here's why you should always bring a camera along for the Northern Lights show:

Colour Capture

The Northern Lights love to play hide-and-seek with their colours. To our naked eyes, they might look like faint green or white streaks. But snap a photo and bam! You've got a kaleidoscope of vibrant greens, purples, and reds. Your camera says, "You thought I was just here for selfies? Think again!"

Long Exposure Magic

Cameras have this superpower called prolonged exposure. They keep their eyes open longer, soaking in all the light and detail we might miss. It's like the camera is saying, "Hold my lens cap and watch this!" The result? Stunning, crystal-clear images of the Northern Lights in all their glory.

Sharing the Spectacle

Only some people get to see the Northern Lights in person. With your camera, you can share the beauty with others. It's like being the ambassador of the auroras, spreading joy and wonder one photo at a time. You'll be the hero of your social media feed!

Seeing Beyond Sight

Our eyes adjust to darkness, but not like a camera can. Cameras can pull in details from the dimmest scenes, revealing the true brilliance of the Northern Lights. It's like having night vision goggles that transform the sky into a masterpiece.

Fun with Filters

Once you've captured the Northern Lights, you can have a blast editing your photos. Add filters, play with contrasts, and create your artistic interpretations. It's like being a painter with the universe as your canvas.

Inspiring Others

Your photos can inspire others to chase their own Northern Lights dreams. When they see your amazing shots, they think, "I want to experience that!" You're not just capturing the lights but sparking dreams and adventures.

What makes Tromso the perfect spot for Aurora viewing?

Let's discuss why Tromsø is the Northern Lights' favourite hangout spot. Imagine it as the ultimate nightclub where the auroras love to show off their best moves. Here's why Tromsø is the perfect spot for Aurora viewing:

CHASING NORTHERN LIGHTS

1. Prime Location

Tromsø is nestled way up in Northern Norway in the middle of the auroral oval. It's like the Northern Lights' living room. They feel so at home here that they pop by to dance almost every night. It's prime real estate for Aurora viewing!

2. Clear Skies Club

Tromsø has relatively clear skies during the aurora season. Sure, it gets chilly, but that's just nature's saying, "Get cozy and look up!" The more precise the skies, the better the light shows. It's like Mother Nature pulls back the curtains just for you.

3. Long Aurora Season

From September to April, Tromsø is the place to be. That's seven whole months of prime Aurora action. The Northern Lights calendar is packed, so you'll likely catch a show whenever you visit. It's like having a VIP pass to an extended festival.

4. City Lights vs. Northern Lights

Tromsø is a city, but it's not too bright to drown out the Northern Lights. You get the best of both worlds – a comfy city vibe with easy access to dark spots for the ultimate aurora viewing. It's like living in a city that never sleeps but always makes time for the Northern Lights.

5. Aurora Tourism Pros

The folks in Tromsø know their auroras. Many guided tours, aurora camps, and even aurora chasers are ready to help you get the best view. It's like having a team of Northern Lights enthusiasts on your side, ensuring you don't miss a thing.

6. Scenic Backdrop

The landscape around Tromsø is stunning. Imagine the Northern Lights dancing over fjords, mountains, and snowy landscapes. It's like the lights have their stage set with the most dramatic and beautiful scenery. Even the backdrop deserves applause.

7. Northern Lights Festivals

Tromsø takes its auroras seriously – so seriously that festivals are dedicated to them! During these festivals, the whole town celebrates with music, food, and aurora viewing. It's like a giant party with the Northern Lights as the guest of honour.

8. Friendly Folks

The locals in Tromsø are super friendly and always excited to share their love of the Northern Lights. They'll give you tips, tell you the best spots, and might even share a cup of hot cocoa while you wait for the show. It's like having your own Aurora fan club.

9. Cool Science

Tromsø is also home to the Northern Lights Observatory, where scientists study the auroras. The city is on the cutting edge of Aurora research, making it even more remarkable (pun intended). You can learn all about the science behind the magic.

10. Unforgettable Memories

Seeing the Northern Lights in Tromsø isn't just a visual treat; it's a whole experience. The cold, crisp air, the excitement of spotting the first glimmers, and the awe as the sky lights up are something you'll remember forever. It's like catching the best concert ever but in the sky.

Why is it so tricky to figure out the magnetic arrangement of sunspots near the Sun's edges?

1. The Slanted View Problem

When we look at sunspots near the Sun's edges, it's like trying to watch a movie from the side seat of a cinema. Everything's at a weird angle, making it hard to see the whole picture. The magnetic fields look all squished and distorted, making it tricky to understand their proper arrangement.

2. The Wobbly Sun Mirage

The Sun's edges are like a wobbly funhouse mirror at a carnival. The Sun's surface is churning and bubbling with hot plasma, creating a lot of turbulence. This turbulence messes with the light, making the magnetic fields appear more like a mirage than a clear image.

3. The Disappearing Act

Sunspots are shy performers who get stage fright near the Sun's edges. They tend to look smaller and fainter as they approach the limb (the edge of the Sun). This vanishing act makes it challenging for scientists to understand what's happening with their magnetic fields.

4. The Twisting Light Trick

Light from the Sunspots near the edge has to travel through more of the Sun's atmosphere before reaching us. This extra journey twists and bends the light, like how a straw looks bent in a glass of water. This light-bending trick makes it harder to figure out the exact magnetic layout.

5. The Magnetic Field Fuzziness

Magnetic fields are already invisible and tricky to detect. Near the edges of the Sun, they get even fuzzier. It's like trying to read a map through a foggy window. Scientists use special tools to measure these fields, but the foggy edges make the data less transparent and more challenging to interpret.

6. The Solar Salsa Dance

The Sun is constantly rotating and dancing, and sunspots move with it. Near the edges, this movement appears more pronounced and chaotic, making it harder to track the magnetic fields accurately. It's like trying to follow a dancer's every move while they're spinning wildly.

7. The Resolution Riddle

Telescopes have more difficulty capturing high-resolution images at the Sun's edges. The further you go from the centre, the less sharp the images become. It's like trying to take a clear photo of a moving car from the side window – it's all a bit blurry and challenging to pin down the details.

8. The Depth Deception

Sunspots have depth, and near the edges, we see them at an angle that mixes up their proper structure. It's like looking at a mountain range from the side and trying to guess the height of each peak. The perspective makes everything look squished together.

Will the Aurora completely vanish during solar minimum or take a break?

Imagine the Aurora as a spectacular DJ at the hottest celestial nightclub. When the solar minimum hits, does this DJ pack up, vanish, or take a coffee break? Here's the scoop:

Our Sun—usually a wild party host—decides to chill out during a solar minimum. It's like the Sun is saying, "I need a break from all this solar flaring and sunspot shenanigans." This period of calm means fewer solar eruptions and charged particles that create our beloved Northern Lights.

But don't worry! The Aurora doesn't completely disappear. Think of it as the DJ turning down the volume instead of leaving the building. The lights might not be as frequent or intense, but they still appear. It's like the sky plays a soothing, mellow tune instead of a high-energy dance track.

Even during solar minimum, the Sun can surprise us with a burst of activity. It's like the DJ suddenly deciding to play a hit song to keep the crowd on their toes. These surprise solar flares can still send charged particles our way, sparking beautiful auroras. You might still catch an unexpected light show!

Will there be an Aurora tonight?

Nobody can predict exactly when an aurora will light up your sky, whether by eye or on camera. But don't worry; there are excellent sources for up-to-date forecasts! The NOAA Space Weather

Prediction Center offers an Aurora Dashboard, which includes maps and animations showing expected aurora visibility and intensity for the next 30 minutes and the night ahead. For a deeper dive, the Geophysical Institute provides forecasts based on the Kp index, which measures geomagnetic activity influencing aurora visibility. This can give you a good idea of how lively the auroras might be over the next few nights.

What is solar wind, and how is it measured?

The solar wind is like the Sun's way of sending a little cosmic breeze our way—only instead of a gentle breeze, it's a stream of charged particles zooming through space. This solar wind is constantly switching things up, changing speed, density, and temperature like it's got a mind of its own. The real action happens when the solar wind escapes from a coronal hole or during a coronal mass ejection (CME). Think of coronal holes as the Sun's steady exhale, sending out a fast, consistent stream of particles, while CMEs are more like the Sun sneezing out a massive, fast-moving cloud of solar plasma.

When these solar gusts reach Earth, they don't just blow past us—they crash into our magnetic field, especially around the poles, where they put on a spectacular light show known as auroras.

Now, the speed of the solar wind is a big deal. Faster winds pack a punch, shaking up Earth's magnetic field and sometimes triggering geomagnetic storms. On a typical day, solar wind speeds cruise around 300 km/sec, but during a CME, they can ramp up to 500 km/sec or more, like the Sun hitting turbo boost!

The density of the solar wind is another key player. The more particles in the wind, the better the chances of seeing those dazzling auroras—though it's a bit of a team effort, with speed and magnetic conditions needing to align just right.

To monitor all this solar activity, we've got some high-tech space sentinels like the Deep Space Climate Observatory (DSCOVR) and the Advanced Composition Explorer (ACE) hanging out between the Sun and Earth. These satellites give us a heads-up before the solar wind arrives, letting us know when to expect a solar show—or maybe just some cosmic turbulence.

What is a coronal hole?

When we peek at solar images from NASA's Solar Dynamics Observatory in extreme ultraviolet light, we get a front-row seat to the Sun's outer atmosphere, known as the corona. It's like looking at the Sun's high-energy halo, where the magnetic field plays a starring role. The bright spots in these images are superheated, dense gas that the Sun's magnetic field has captured. But then there are the dark patches—mysterious coronal holes. They aren't actual holes but look like them because they're more relaxed and less dense.

Coronal holes are where the Sun's magnetic field lines decide to detour into space instead of looping back to the surface. This open-door policy lets hot gas escape, creating high-speed solar winds that can stir things up here on Earth. When these coronal holes face Earth, they can send gusts of solar wind our way, sparking geomagnetic disturbances and sometimes treating us to stunning auroras. The bigger the coronal hole, the faster the solar wind and the more intense the auroras!

These coronal holes are like cosmic shape-shifters, appearing anywhere on the Sun, sticking around for weeks or months, and constantly changing their size and shape. The most steady coronal holes hang near the Sun's poles, especially during solar minimum. Still, they usually keep to themselves unless they stretch down towards lower latitudes, where they might give Earth a little extra solar wind.

How do we know if a CME is Earth-directed and when it will arrive?

First, we've got our eyes on the Sun 24/7, thanks to some space-age paparazzi like NASA's Solar Dynamics Observatory (SDO) and the Solar and Heliospheric Observatory (SOHO). These satellites snap glam shots of the Sun from different angles, capturing any significant solar eruptions. When a CME blows, scientists analyze these images to see which direction it's heading. Things get exciting if it looks like it's coming straight for Earth.

To really determine if it's Earth-directed, we use a "coronagraph," a special camera that blocks out the bright light from the Sun, making it easier to see the CME as it moves through space. If the CME appears to expand evenly around the Sun in the coronagraph images, like a halo, it's likely heading our way. Think of it as a cosmic bullseye!

Once we know a CME is Earth-bound, the next big question is, "When will it get here?" CMEs don't all travel at the same speed—some are slowpokes, while others are in a cosmic hurry. Scientists measure the speed of the CME using those satellite images and then do some fancy math (don't worry, they've got it covered) to predict its arrival time. Typically, it takes anywhere from one to three days for a CME to reach Earth.

What is a Solar filament?

Imagine the Sun as a giant ball of fiery spaghetti, with each noodle representing a twisting, writhing line of magnetic energy. Now, picture one of those noodles stretching out from the Sun's surface like it's trying to grab a piece of space pizza. That's a solar filament!

A solar filament is a vast, elongated cloud of hot, charged gas (plasma) suspended above the Sun's surface by magnetic forces. These filaments can be thousands of miles long and can last days or even weeks. When seen against the bright background of the Sun, they look like dark, thread-like structures, but if they're viewed from the side, they appear as bright arcs known as prominences.

Sometimes, these filaments get too ambitious and break away, hurling all that energy into space. If the Earth is in the way, we might see an aurora or, in extreme cases, experience some effects on our satellites and communication systems.

25
SPACE WEATHER GLOSSARY

Acronyms and abbreviations in space weather reports can be a bit of a puzzle, leaving some people feeling in the dark. But don't worry – we're here to shed some light! In this section, you'll find an informative list of common terms. Let's start decoding together and become space weather experts!

ADF (Active Dark Filament)

Picture a long, dark, and twisty noodle hanging out on the Sun's surface. That's the Active Dark Filament (ADF) for you! It's like a solar spaghetti strand, chilling in the Sun's atmosphere, planning its next move. Sometimes it stays put, and other times it breaks free and zooms into space like it's late for a cosmic party.

AIA (Atmospheric Imaging Assembly)

Think of the AIA as the Sun's personal paparazzi. This high-tech gadget captures high-definition photos of the Sun's atmosphere. It's like the Sun has its own Instagram account, but instead of brunch pics, it's snapping shots of solar flares and sunspots. Say cheese, Sun!

AR (Active Region)

An Active Region on the Sun is like a bustling city centre. It's where the Sun gets really energetic and flexes its magnetic muscles. This area is full of sunspots, solar flares, and other exciting stuff. Imagine the Sun doing an intense workout routine, and you've got an Active Region.

APR (Active Prominence Region)

Imagine the Sun growing a fancy handlebar moustache. That's sort of what an Active Prominence Region looks like. These are huge, looping structures of hot gas extending from the Sun's surface. They can look like arches, loops, or giant moustaches. Fancy!

ASR (Active Surge Region)

An Active Surge Region is like the Sun's version of a geyser. It's where solar material shoots up from the surface like water from Old Faithful. This hot gas zooms into the solar atmosphere and then falls back down, making it look like the Sun is having a dramatic moment.

BBSO (Big Bear Solar Observatory)

Bears don't run the Big Bear Solar Observatory, but it's just as fantastic. This observatory is located near Big Bear Lake in California and has some of the best solar telescopes. Scientists use it to observe the Sun and study its crazy antics.

BSD (Bright Surge on the Disk)

Think of a Bright Surge on the Disk as the Sun's version of fireworks. These sudden, bright bursts of light appear on the Sun's surface.

BSL (Bright Surge on the Limb)

Similar to BSD, a Bright Surge on the Limb happens on the edge of the Sun. Imagine the Sun putting on a light show right on its horizon.

CH (Coronal Hole)

Imagine the Sun got lazy and forgot to cover part of its surface. That's a Coronal Hole for you! These are cooler, darker areas where the Sun's magnetic field lets out a breeze of charged particles. It's like the Sun is venting out some steam.

CIR (Corotating Interaction Region)

Picture two streams of solar wind racing around the Sun. When they collide, it creates a Corotating Interaction Region. It's like the Sun is having a bumper car party with streams of hot gas crashing into each other. Whee!

CME (Coronal Mass Ejection)

A Coronal Mass Ejection is the Sun's version of a sneeze but way more intense. It blasts out vast amounts of plasma and magnetic field into space.

CMP (Central Meridian Passage)

This is the Sun's way of crossing the finish line. When a solar feature moves across the Sun's central line, it is called the Central Meridian Passage. Think of it as the Sun's magnetic marathon.

CRN (Coronal Rain)

Coronal Rain is the Sun's version of a rain shower. But instead of water, it's raining superhot plasma. Imagine molten lava raindrops falling back to the Sun's surface. Talk about a fiery forecast!

CTM (Continuum Storm)

A Continuum Storm is like a solar thunderstorm without Rain. It's a burst of energy that travels across the Sun's surface, lighting up in intense brightness.

DSD (Dark Surge on the Disk)

Imagine a dark, shadowy wave sweeping across the Sun's surface. That's a Dark Surge on the Disk. It's like the Sun is suddenly feeling moody and casting dark ripples.

DSF (Disappearing Solar Filament)

A Disappearing Solar Filament is like a magic trick on the Sun. One moment, there's a dark filament, and poof, it's gone!

DSCOVR (Deep Space Climate Observatory)

DSCOVR is the ultimate space weatherman. It's a satellite that monitors space weather from an excellent spot between the Earth and the Sun. It tells us when solar storms are coming so we know when to grab our cosmic umbrellas.

Dst (Disturbance Storm Time)

Disturbance Storm Time measures how grumpy Earth's magnetic field is. When the Sun sends us a blast of energy, Dst lets us know how much our magnetic field is disturbed.

EIT (Extreme Ultraviolet Imaging Telescope)

EIT is like the Sun's X-ray machine. It takes pictures of the Sun in extreme ultraviolet light, revealing all its wild and hidden details—like seeing the Sun's secret tattoos.

EPAM (Electron, Proton, and Alpha Monitor)

EPAM is the Sun's particle detector. It monitors electrons, protons, and alpha particles zooming around. Think of it as a cosmic traffic cop, keeping tabs on all the charged particles speeding by.

ESD (Electrostatic Discharge)

Have you ever felt a tiny zap when touching a doorknob? That's an electrostatic discharge. It's like a giant static shock on the Sun, but way more powerful. It's the Sun's way of saying, "Zap! Gotcha!"

ESA (European Space Agency)

ESA is Europe's ticket to the stars. They send out satellites, rovers, and all kinds of space gadgets to explore the universe. It's like Europe's very own cosmic adventure club.

EUV (Extreme Ultraviolet)

Extreme Ultraviolet is like the Sun's special light show, beyond what our eyes can see. It's like having a superhero vision that can see the Sun's most energetic and exciting moments.

EVE (Extreme Ultraviolet Variability Experiment)

EVE is a super-sensitive gadget that measures the Sun's extreme ultraviolet light. It's like the Sun's personal DJ, tracking all the changes in its energetic beats.

GFZ (German Research Centre for Geosciences)

GFZ is Germany's hub for studying Earth and space. Its scientists investigate everything from earthquakes to solar storms. It's like Germany's brainy space squad, always on a mission to understand our planet and beyond.

GIC (Geomagnetically Induced Current)

GIC occurs when the Sun messes with Earth's magnetic field and creates electric currents in power lines. It's like the Sun playing a prank on our electrical grid, causing some serious mischief.

GOES (Geostationary Operational Environmental Satellite)

Imagine a satellite chilling in space, always hovering over the same spot on Earth like it's on a cosmic hammock. That's GOES for you! It monitors the weather and helps us know if we need to bring an umbrella or sunscreen.

HMI (Helioseismic and Magnetic Imager)

HMI is like the Sun's stethoscope. It listens to the Sun's internal vibrations and checks its magnetic field. It's like a solar doctor ensuring the Sun is healthy and happy.

HPI (Hemispherical Power Input)

HPI measures the amount of power going into the Earth's magnetic field from the Sun. It's like tracking how much juice the Sun is giving our planet. It's Earth's very own energy monitor.

HSC (Heliospheric Science Center)

The HSC is like the Sun's fan club. Scientists here study everything about the Sun and its influence on the solar system. They're like the ultimate solar groupies, always keeping tabs on their favourite star.

HSS (High-Speed Stream)

Think of HSS as a speedy solar wind. It's a stream of fast-moving particles that the Sun blows out into space. Imagine the Sun releasing a powerful gust of wind, making space slightly breezier.

IMF (Interplanetary Magnetic Field)

IMF is like an invisible magnetic highway that runs through space. The Sun's magnetic field extends out and influences everything in the solar system.

IRIS (Interface Region Imaging Spectrograph)

IRIS is the Sun's close-up photographer. It takes super-detailed images of the Sun's lower atmosphere, like a super-zoom camera that can capture all the Sun's secret details.

L1 (Lagrange Point 1)

L1 is a sweet spot in space where the gravitational forces of the Earth and Sun balance out. It's like a cosmic chill zone where satellites can hang out without drifting away. Perfect for space parties!

LASCO (Large Angle and Spectrometric Coronagraph)

LASCO is like a pair of solar sunglasses. It blocks out the bright light from the Sun's surface so we can see the corona, the outermost part of the Sun's atmosphere. It's like getting to see the Sun's fabulous halo.

LMSAL (Lockheed Martin Solar and Astrophysics Laboratory)

LMSAL is where scientists and engineers cook cool gadgets to study the Sun. It's like a high-tech workshop where solar magic happens. They build all the nifty tools that let us peek at the Sun's secrets.

MDI (Michelson Doppler Imager)

MDI is like a motion detector for the Sun. It measures the movements and flows on the Sun's surface. It's like keeping an eye on the Sun's dance moves.

MLSO (Mauna Loa Solar Observatory)

MLSO is a solar observatory located on a Hawaiian volcano. It's like having the best seat in the house to watch the Sun. Scientists here get a front-row view of all the solar action.

NASA (National Aeronautics and Space Administration)

NASA is like the ultimate space adventure company. They send people and robots into space to explore and discover new things. It's like having a ticket to the most incredible show on Earth.

NOAA (National Oceanic and Atmospheric Administration)

NOAA is like Earth's weather wizard. They study everything from the ocean's depths to the heights of space weather.

nT (nanotesla)

A nanotesla is a tiny unit of magnetic field strength. Think of it as a minuscule magnetometer measuring the faint whispers of the Earth's magnetic field. It's small but mighty!

PFU (Proton Flux Unit)

PFU measures the number of energetic protons hitting a particular area. It's like counting the number of energetic popcorn kernels popping out in space. The more PFUs, the more space popcorn!

PlasMag (Plasma and Magnetometer Instrument)

PlasMag is the gadget that measures plasma (hot, charged gas) and magnetic fields in space. It's like having a thermometer and compass rolled into one for space weather.

PROBA2 (Project for On-Board Autonomy 2)

PROBA2 is a super-intelligent satellite that takes care of itself while studying the Sun. It's like a space robot with a mind of its own, cruising through space and sending back solar selfies.

SAA (South Atlantic Anomaly)

SAA is a quirky region where Earth's magnetic field weakens a bit. It's like a magnetic Bermuda Triangle, causing satellites passing through to experience some chaos. Watch out, space travellers!

SC (Sudden Commencement)

Sudden Commencement is like Earth's magnetic field, which gets a jolt of energy from the Sun. It's like getting an unexpected high-five that makes the magnetic field shake slightly.

SDO (Solar Dynamics Observatory)

SDO is like the Sun's personal TV station. It continuously watches the Sun and broadcasts all the solar drama to Earth. It's like having 24/7 Sun TV with all the latest solar news.

SIDC (Solar Influences Data Analysis Center)

SIDC is where scientists analyze all the Sun's data. It's like the Sun's data detectives figuring out what all the solar activity means for us. They decode the Sun's messages for us.

SI (Sudden Impulse)

An Impulse is a quick burst of magnetic activity from the Sun. It's like the Sun giving Earth a little magnetic nudge—just a quick tap to say hello.

SIR (Stream Interaction Region)

SIR is where different streams of solar wind collide. It's like a busy intersection in space where solar winds meet and mix. It can get a bit bumpy!

SOHO (Solar and Heliospheric Observatory)

SOHO is a space telescope that watches the Sun constantly. It's like the Sun's paparazzi, always ready to capture the latest solar flares and

SWPC (Space Weather Prediction Center)

SWPC is like the weather channel for space. They predict solar storms and other space weather events. It's like tuning in to find out if we need to brace for a solar wind or enjoy calm cosmic weather.

TEC (Total Electron Content)

TEC measures the number of electrons in a column of the atmosphere. It's like counting all the cosmic sprinkles in a vertical slice of the sky. The more electrons, the more sprinkles!

UTC (Coordinated Universal Time)

UTC is the time standard used worldwide. It's like the cosmic clock that everyone agrees on, ensuring we're all on the same page, whether on Earth or out in space.

VHF (Very High Frequency)

VHF is like the Sun's radio station broadcasting at high frequencies. It's used for communication signals and other transmissions. Tune in for some cosmic tunes and space chatter!

VLF (Very Low Frequency)

VLF is the Sun's low-frequency channel. It's like the deep bass of space communication, sending out signals that travel far and wide—perfect for long-distance cosmic calls.

XRS (X-ray Sensor)

XRS is like the Sun's X-ray vision. It detects X-rays from the Sun, revealing the hottest and most energetic parts.

Å (Angstrom)

An Ångstrom is a tiny unit of length used to measure things like wavelengths of light. It's like using a magnifying glass to see the teeniest details, perfect for the Sun's intricate patterns.

ABOUT THE AUTHOR

Arun Chandran, a dedicated explorer and community enthusiast, resides in Melbourne with his wife. Hailing from India, he has embraced Australia as his home for over 12 years, demonstrating his commitment to the community wherever he goes.

Arun has successfully pursued the Aurora in both hemispheres. His adventures have taken him to 59 countries, each providing a unique chance to connect with diverse cultures and expand his horizons.

During the week, Arun is a committed tech professional, but come the weekend, he transforms into an event organizer, creating unforgettable experiences. His passion for bringing people together inspired him to start the Explore Melbourne Meetup group in September 2016. Today, with an impressive 38,000 members, Australia's largest meetup group is a true reflection of Arun's dedication to community and adventure.

This is Arun's second book, which is focused on chasing the Aurora. His first book, published in June 2024, was dedicated to pursuing the Aurora Australis.

In October 2023, Arun organized a unique event for Aurora enthusiasts. The event offered a rare opportunity to chase the Northern Lights across Norway, Svalbard, and Iceland, guided by Arun's expertise and passion for exploration.

Arun aims to make chasing the Northern Lights accessible to more people through this book. He also offers custom travel itineraries specifically tailored for Northern Lights chasers.

You can reach Arun at chasingnorthernlights@outlook.com or visit his website at ChasingNorthernLights.com

www.ingramcontent.com/pod-product-compliance
Lightning Source LLC
Chambersburg PA
CBHW030547080526
44585CB00012B/290

coronal mass ejections.

SPE (Solar Proton Event)

SPE is when the Sun spits out a bunch of high-energy protons. It's like a solar spitball fight with protons zooming through space. Watch out for those energetic protons!

SSBC (Solar System Boundary Crossing)

Imagine a cosmic road trip where you cross the border of our solar system. That's SSBC! It's like the ultimate space adventure, zooming past the planets and heading into interstellar territory.

SSC (Storm Sudden Commencement)

SSC is like when the Sun decides to throw a surprise party for Earth's magnetic field. Suddenly, everything gets a jolt of energy.

SSN (Sunspot Number)

Think of SSN as the Sun's daily spot count. Sunspots are cooler, darker areas on the Sun's surface, and counting them is like tallying up freckles. Some days, the Sun is extra freckly; others, not so much.

STA (Solar Terrestrial Activity)

STA is the cosmic dance between the Sun and Earth. It's all about how solar activity affects our planet. Picture the Sun and Earth doing a tango, with flares and storms as their dramatic moves.

STB (Solar Terrestrial Relations Observatory B)

STB is a satellite that watches the Sun from a unique angle. It's like having a backstage pass to the Sun's concerts, seeing all the solar action hidden from Earth's view.

SUVI (Solar Ultraviolet Imager)

SUVI is like the Sun's UV camera. It captures images in ultraviolet light, revealing the Sun's wild and energetic side.